新编美国文学经典作品选读

程朝翔·总主编
叶春莉·主编

Selected Readings of
Classical American
Literary Works

北京大学出版社
PEKING UNIVERSITY PRESS

图书在版编目（CIP）数据

新编美国文学经典作品选读 / 程朝翔总主编；叶春莉主编. —北京：北京大学出版社，2023.9
ISBN 978-7-301-34515-3

Ⅰ.①新… Ⅱ.①程… ②叶… Ⅲ.①英语–阅读教学–高等学校–教材 ②文学–作品–介绍–美国 Ⅳ.① H319.37

中国国家版本馆 CIP 数据核字 (2023) 第 187391 号

书　　名	新编美国文学经典作品选读
	XINBIAN MEIGUO WENXUE JINGDIAN ZUOPIN XUANDU
著作责任者	程朝翔　总主编　叶春莉　主编
责任编辑	吴宇森
标准书号	ISBN 978-7-301-34515-3
出版发行	北京大学出版社
地　　址	北京市海淀区成府路 205 号　100871
网　　址	http://www.pup.cn　　新浪微博：@ 北京大学出版社
电子邮箱	编辑部 pupwaiwen@pup.cn　　总编室 zpup@pup.cn
电　　话	邮购部 010-62752015　发行部 010-62750672　编辑部 010-62759634
印 刷 者	北京溢漾印刷有限公司
经 销 者	新华书店
	720 毫米 ×1020 毫米　16 开本　14 印张　330 千字
	2023 年 9 月第 1 版　2023 年 9 月第 1 次印刷
定　　价	58.00 元

未经许可，不得以任何方式复制或抄袭本书之部分或全部内容。
版权所有，侵权必究
举报电话：010-62752024　电子邮箱：fd@pup.cn
图书如有印装质量问题，请与出版部联系，电话：010-62756370

前　言

　　《新编英国文学经典作品选读》和《新编美国文学经典作品选读》是北京大学与石河子大学的又一次缘分。

　　2002年年初，中东部重点高校对口支援西部高校的序幕拉开，教育部指定北京大学对口支援石河子大学。是年3月，北京大学外国语学院的程朝翔教授作为第一批支援者，不远千里来到石河子大学为英语专业大三的学生讲授英国文学。程师的拿手好戏是莎翁作品研究，当时教室里并无多媒体设备，他便用粉笔在黑板上满屏书写，生怕落下一个知识点。莎翁之外，程师还重点讲解了乔伊斯的著名短篇《阿拉比》（"Araby"）。继程师而来者为王继辉教授，王师所讲为其专长之乔叟与中古文学。王师或西装革履，或着白衬衫一丝不苟，上课时仅手持几张小卡片而知识源源而至，倾倒一片。之后便是何卫老师来讲授语言学，何师风格与王师迥然相异。何师常着T恤衫与牛仔裤，授课如邻家大哥亲切自然。2004—2005年间，北大外院胡壮麟教授来校举办功能语言学讲座，姜望琪教授为专业学生讲授语用学等课程。2006年，早已年过花甲的刘意青教授来石大做讲座，刘师融自身经历于学理讲授，而常怀忧国忧民之襟抱，为学生所崇仰。刘师风格极为亲和，被学生和年轻老师戏称为"刘姥姥"，但她毫不介怀。2008年，年近古稀的刘师欣然挂职石河子大学外国语学院的援疆院长。她不仅亲自为学生授课，还组织年轻教师做读书会，为他们讲解文学难点。她得知当时学院缺乏合适的文学选读教材，便组织骨干教师自主编纂选读材料。刘师亲自选定篇目和选段，之后由参与者作篇内注释。内容确定之后，交由复印店打印成册，作为教学的自主编纂教材，这便是读者面前这两部经典作品选读的前身。自2009年起，该自主编纂教材便在石大外院英语专业本科课程及部分大学英语选修课程中使用，屈指算来，已有14年之久。

　　2008年年底，刘师听说部分年轻教师在职称评定时经常铩羽而归，原因是缺乏有分量的著作和教材，她便主动提出在选读中选出若干短篇小说，以专题的形式分为若干章节，每章依术语阐释、正文、注释、赏析的体例编排，并附上若干短篇作为附录。书稿编成之后，刘师即联系北京大学出版社，得到出版社张冰主任的热情支持，并委任素养超强的李娜老师作为责任编辑。该教材很快于2010年8月出版，题名《英语短篇小说选读》，署名方岩主编，刘意青审定，叶春莉、欧光安等参编。实际上，刘师不仅校对了全部的文字，不少篇章的赏析文字亦出自其手。2015年，在一次学术会议上，编者与刘师和张冰主任等同席讨论，得隙向张冰主任提议对《英语短篇小说选读》进行修订，张冰主任欣然同意，而刘师亦当即同意继续承担审定工作。2018年6月，该书第二版成功推出。2021年，该书荣获石河子大学首届优秀教材奖一等奖。① 而同在2010年，在一个寒风凛冽的冬日，刘师在由办公室回住处的路上摔倒在薄冰覆盖的路面，骨裂而伤，无奈只好由石返京，而她对石大外院的关注却从未停止过。

除2002年集中为石大学生授课外，自2002年迄今，程朝翔老师不时来石大外院，或讲学，或交流，其中最重要的活动之一是在2012年组织北京大学、淡江大学和石河子大学联合举办外国文学研讨会，一时影响甚广。2018年，程朝翔老师更是来石大外院任援疆院长②，从各方面提携年轻教师，其中一项便是为了推动外院翻译专业建设，组织臧红宝等老师翻译《韦氏英汉双解扩词手册》，该词典同样由北京大学出版社出版（2021年10月初版）。2021年，编者提议将英美文学经典作品选读进一步调整体例出版，程师当即表示赞同并立即联系北京大学出版社，同样得到张冰主任的大力支持，此次则由李娜老师和吴宇森老师担任责任编辑，这可说是刘意青先生、程朝翔院长对石大外院倾力支持的前后赓续。

钱锺书先生曾考证近代第一首译为汉语的英诗乃朗费罗之《人生颂》（"A Psalm of Life"），其汉译时间约为19世纪60年代。与诗歌相比，小说的读者接受群应该更广，在我国近代英文小说被译介为汉语的时间也应该不会太晚，林纾在19世纪末、20世纪初"翻译"的那些西文小说更是影响深远。不过在中国学生中使用英文原文教材的情况，可能在20世纪10年代之后才较为常见。钱锺

---

① 一等奖为最高，只有两部教材获此殊荣，另一部教材为石大传统强势学科农学类教材。
② 继刘意青先生担任石大外院援疆领导的还有北大外院凌建侯教授（常务副院长，2011—2012年度），他曾在北大连招三名石大外院教师为博士。

书先生的老师吴宓，20 世纪 10 年代就读清华学校时，就读过不少原文小说[①]。留学归来后，吴宓一度将萨克雷的名著《钮康氏家传》（The Newcomes）和《名利场》（Vanity Fair）的前几章以文言译出，刊登于《学衡》杂志，成为中国现代文学史上的独特风景。20 世纪 30 年代，吴宓回到母校清华任教，同样提倡阅读文学作品的原文，并曾为清华外籍教师吴可读（A. L. Pollard-Urquhart）编著的英文著作 Great European Novels and Novelists 题写书名《西洋小说发达史略》，该著作即吴可读教授学生时所用教材[②]。吴宓常被视为文化保守主义者，其人主张"昌明国粹，融化新知"，实际上并非反对引入和译介西洋文学，而是希望有一种比较的视野和方法。百年后回顾之，其观念仍自有价值。因此，我们在编排中一方面注重原文阅读和注释，同时在提问等环节以比较的视野来实践文明互鉴的宗旨，也是试图在同类的文学选读著作中"走一点不一样的路"。钱锺书在清华就读时，曾因年轻气盛和好玩调皮，常与同学一道嘲笑有时过于迂腐的老师吴宓，而一生坚持随事随记的吴宓将这些记入了日记中。近半个世纪后，曾经的学生钱锺书在读到老师的日记时，为自己曾经的鲁莽"愧生颜变，无地自容"，并为老师的宽容而更感愧疚，希望自己这个"头白门生倘得免乎削籍而标于头墙之外"。[③] 我们也希望自己所做的这两本小册子，能够抵得上北大外院诸位教师教诲之一毫，而不被逐出门墙之外。

本套经典文学作品选读分英国卷和美国卷，由程朝翔教授任总主编，英国卷由欧光安任主编，编者为张娟、刘小姣、阿依努尔；美国卷由叶春莉任主编，编者为邹晓惠、卞赛赛、马艺文。目前任教于石大的外籍教师 Ralph Leong 校对了全部英文，在此表示感谢。

编者
2023 年 6 月

---

① 无独有偶，吴宓在清华读书时喜爱朗费罗的长诗 Evangeline，并将前几节改译为《沧桑艳传奇》。小说方面，他喜读华盛顿·欧文的《见闻杂记》（The Sketch Book），而"最爱其中'The Wife'一篇"（吴宓：《吴宓自编年谱》，吴学昭整理，北京：生活·读书·新知三联书店，1995 年，第 122 页）。

② 据吴心海考证，吴可读在中国期间至少出过五部编著，其中除《西洋小说发达史略》之外，还被用作教材的尚有《英国散文选》（Selections of English Prose: From Chaucer to Thomas Hardy，商务印书馆 1931 年 11 月初版）。见吴心海：《吴宓珍视的一本书及其作者》，载 2013 年 8 月 18 日《东方早报》。

③ 钱锺书：《吴宓日记序》，载吴宓：《吴宓日记》（第一册），吴学昭整理注释，北京：生活·读书·新知三联书店，1998 年，序言第 2 页。

目 录

Part One   The Colonial Period

1. Benjamin Franklin ··· 1
   Autobiography ·· 2
2. Anne Bradstreet ··· 6
   To My Dear and Loving Husband ·· 7
3. Philip Freneau ·· 9
   The Wild Honey Suckle ·· 10
4. Hector St. John de Crèvecoeur ··· 13
   Letters from an American Farmer ··· 14
5. Thomas Jefferson ··· 19
   Declaration of Independence ··· 20

Part Two   The Romantic Period

6. Washington Irving ·· 23
   Rip Van Winkle ··· 24
7. Nathaniel Hawthorne ··· 37
   Young Goodman Brown ··· 38
8. Walt Whitman ·· 55
   Song of Myself ··· 56
   O Captain! My Captain! ·· 58
9. Emily Dickinson ·· 61
   I Heard a Fly Buzz — When I Died — ·· 62
   Because I Could Not Stop for Death — ··· 62
   Wild Nights — Wild Nights! ·· 63

A Bird, Came down the Walk — 64
This Is My Letter to the World 65
I Know That He Exists. 65

10. Edgar Allan Poe 67
Annabel Lee 68

11. Henry Wadsworth Longfellow 71
The Tide Rises, the Tide Falls 72
The Arrow and the Song 74

Part Three American Realism

12. Mark Twain 76
Running for Governor 77

13. Bret Harte 84
The Luck of Roaring Camp 85

14. Kate Chopin 97
The Story of an Hour 98

15. Theodore Dreiser 102
Sister Carrie 104

16. Jack London 114
Love of Life 116

17. Edwin Arlington Robinson 138
Richard Cory 139
Miniver Cheevy 141

Part Four Modern American Literature

18. Ezra Pound 145
In a Station of the Metro 146

19. Robert Frost 148
The Road Not Taken 149

20. William Carlos Williams ········152
    The Red Wheelbarrow ········153
    This Is Just to Say ········154

21. Carl Sandburg ········156
    Fog ········157

22. Wallace Stevens ········159
    Anecdote of the Jar ········160

23. Edward Estlin Cummings ········162
    (Me up at does) ········164

24. Francis Scott Fitzgerald ········165
    The Great Gatsby ········166

25. Ernest Hemingway ········173
    Cat in the Rain ········175

26. William Faulkner ········179
    A Rose for Emily ········181

27. Langston Hughes ········192
    The Negro Speaks of Rivers ········194
    As I Grew Older ········195
    I, Too, Sing America ········197
    Ballad of the Landlord ········197

28. Sherwood Anderson ········200
    The Egg ········202

Part One

The Colonial Period

1. Benjamin Franklin

Benjamin Franklin, also called Ben Franklin, pseudonym Richard Saunders (born January 17, 1706, Boston, Massachusetts, died April 17, 1790, Philadelphia, Pennsylvania), is the only Founding Father to have signed all four of the key documents establishing the U.S.: the *Declaration of Independence* (1776), the *Treaty of Alliance with France* (1778), the *Treaty of Paris Establishing Peace with Great Britain* (1783) and the U.S. *Constitution* (1787). Besides being a printer and publisher, author, inventor, scientist and diplomat, he was the first postmaster of the United States, an important figure and scientist of the American enlightenment.

Benjamin Franklin was a second-generation immigrant to America, his father being a Puritan[1]. Franklin's life illustrates the impact of the Enlightenment[2] on a gifted individual after his family's move from England to Boston in 1683. Self-educated but well-read in Enlightenment writers, Franklin learned to apply rational thinking to his life and to break with the old-fashioned Puritan tradition. While young, Franklin read widely, practiced writing constantly and even taught himself several languages.

By the time he was twenty-four, he had become the sole owner of a printing shop, and established a club for exchanging ideas. In Philadelphia, he founded America's first circulating library. Later he founded the college that was to become the University of Pennsylvania. In addition, Benjamin Franklin's scientific achievements were quite notable. His many inventions won him acclaims throughout the world: the lightning rod, the stove, bifocal glasses, and others. Moreover, Franklin served his nation with distinction. As one of the foremost of the Founding Fathers, Franklin helped Jefferson draft the *Declaration of Independence* and was one of its signers. He represented the United States in France during the American Revolution, and was a delegate to the Constitutional Convention.

Franklin wrote not just to express and advise, but also to help others. He tried to help other ordinary people achieve success by sharing his experience and thoughts. This is where the quintessential American writing genre — the self-help book originated. His *Poor Richard's Almanack* which was first published in 1732 and continued for quite a number of years, won him much acclaim all throughout the colonies. His most excellent writing — his own *Autobiography*, which includes the famous thirteen virtues, has become one of the most influential models of an autobiography ever written so far. He started it in 1771, and in it, he recorded his early life. In part, Franklin's *Autobiography* is another self-help book. It is written in the first-person point of view, not only to tell about his life but to tell the readers what life was like in the 18th century, what he did to improve himself and make his life better. Initially, intending to advise his son, Franklin sought to cultivate his character by a plan of 13 virtues: temperance, silence, order, resolution, frugality, industry, sincerity, justice, moderation, cleanliness, tranquility, chastity, and humility. This has become the most famous section of his writings.

Autobiography

Part One (excerpt)[3]

From a child I was fond of reading, and all the little money that came into my hands was ever laid out in books. Pleased with the *Pilgrim's Progress*, my first Collection was of John Bunyan's[4] Works, in separate little Volumes. I afterwards sold them to enable me to buy R. Burton's *Historical Collections*; they were small chapmen's books and cheap, 40 or 50 in all. My father's little library consisted chiefly of books in polemic divinity, most of which I read, and have since often regretted that, at a time when I had such a thirst for knowledge, more proper books had not fallen in my way, since it was now resolved I should not be a clergyman. Plutarch's *Lives* there was, in which I read abundantly, and I still think that time spent to great advantage.

There was also a book of Defoe's[5], called an *Essay on Projects*, and another of Dr. Mather's[6], called *Essays to do Good*, which perhaps gave me a Turn of Thinking that had an influence on some of the principal[7] future events of my life.

This Bookish Inclination at length determined my father to make me a printer, tho' he had already one son, (James) of that Profession. In 1717 my Brother James returned from England with a press and letters[8] to set up his Business in Boston. I liked it much better than that of my Father, but still had a Hankering to prevent the apprehended effect of such an Inclination, my Father was impatient to have me bound to my brother. I stood out some time, but at last was persuaded and signed the indentures[9], when I was yet but 12 years old. I was to serve as an apprentice till I was 21 years of age, only I was to be allowed Journeyman's Wages during the last Year. In a little time I made great proficiency in the Business, and became a useful hand to my brother. I now had access to better books. An acquaintance with the apprentices of booksellers enabled me sometimes to borrow a small one, which I was careful to return soon and clean. Often I sat up in my room reading the greatest part of the night, when the book was borrowed in the evening and to be returned early in the morning, lest it should be missed or wanted...

There was another bookish lad[10] in the town, John Collins by name, with whom I was intimately acquainted. We sometimes disputed, and very fond we were of argument, and very desirous of confuting one another, which disputatious turn, by the way, is apt to become a very bad habit, making people often extremely disagreeable in company by the contradiction that is necessary to bring it into practice[11]; and thence, besides souring and spoiling the conversation, is productive of disgusts and perhaps enmities[12] where you may have occasion for friendship. I had caught it by reading my father's books of dispute about religion. Persons of good sense, I have since observed, seldom fall into it, except lawyers, university men, and men of all sorts that have been bred at Edinburgh[13].

A question was once, somehow or other, started between Collins and me, of propriety[14] of educating the female sex in learning, and their abilities for study. He was of opinion that it was improper, and that they were naturally unequal to it. I took the contrary side, perhaps a little for dispute's sake. He was naturally more eloquent[15], had a ready plenty of words, and sometimes, as I thought, bore me down more by his fluency than by the strength of his reasons. As we parted without settling the point, and were not to see one another again for some time, I sat down to put my arguments in writing, which I copied fair and sent to him. He answered, and I replied. Three or four letters of a side had passed, when my father happened to find my papers and read them. Without entering into the discussion, he took occasion to talk to me about the manner of my writing; observed that, though I had the advantage of my antagonist in correct spelling and pointing (which I owed to the printing-house), I fell far short in elegance of expression, in method, and in perspicuity[16], of which he convinced me by several instances. I saw the justice of his remarks, and thence grew more attentive to the manner in writing, and determined to endeavor at improvement.

Notes

1. Puritans (Puritanism is part of the Protestant Movement) believed in God instead of the institution of the state Church. They valued self-discipline and introspection, and held the view that the *Bible* was the final authority on matters of faith and life.

2. Enlightenment: The American Enlightenment is a period of intellectual ferment in the thirteen American colonies in the period 1714–1818, which led to the American Revolution.

3. *Autobiography* — Part One: Benjamin Franklin began writing Part One of his *Autobiography* in 1771 at the age of 65 while on a country vacation in England in the town of Twyford. In the opening pages, he addresses his son William, then the Royal Governor of New Jersey, telling him that he, Benjamin, has always taken pleasure in hearing stories about his family members, and suggesting that William might enjoy hearing the story of his father's life. It is the perfect time for him to set his life to paper because he was in a period of leisure.

4. John Bunyan: John Bunyan (1628–1688) published *The Pilgrim's Progress* in 1678; his works were enormously popular and were available in cheap one-shilling editions.

5. Defoe: Known as Daniel Defoe (1660–1731), English novelist, pamphleteer, and journalist, author of *Robinson Crusoe* (1719–1722) and *Moll Flanders* (1722).

6. another of Dr. Mather's: "Dr. Mather" refers to Cotton Mather. He published *Bonifacius*, or *Essays to Do Good* in 1710.

7. principal: most important.

8. letter: type.

9. indenture: a formal contract, especially in the past, between an apprentice and his master, or the act of arranging this.

10. lad: (old-fashioned or informal) a boy or a young man.

11. by the way, is apt to become a very bad habit, making people often extremely disagreeable in company by the contradiction that is necessary to bring it into practice: Getting used to dispute is a bad thing sometimes — especially it may bring about outrage when dispute is needed.

12. enmity: a state of deep-seated ill-will.

13. Edinburgh: (in Scottish Gaelic: Dùn Èideann) capital city of Scotland, located in southeastern Scotland with its center near the southern shore of the Firth of Forth, an arm of the North Sea that thrusts westward into the Scottish Lowlands.

14. propriety: correctness of social or moral behavior.

15. eloquent: expressing oneself readily, clearly, effectively.

16. perspicuity: plain to the understanding especially because of clarity and precision of presentation.

Questions for Discussion

(1) Benjamin Franklin's *Autobiography* contains the insights of life-long struggle and success, as well as the moral essence of all kinds of goodness and beauty. It is recognized as an American spiritual reader that has changed the fate of countless people. What are Benjamin Franklin's writing features? What kind of world did Benjamin Franklin describe in his writing?

(2) What elements of Benjamin Franklin's family tradition and upbringing help partially to explain the man's later versatility and achievement?

Suggested Reading

● 富兰克林（Benjamin Franklin）：《富兰克林自传》，北京：外语教学与研究出版社，2010年。

● 高斯达（Edwin S. Gaustad）：《本杰明·富兰克林：创造美国》，北京：外语教学与研究出版社，2007年。

2. Anne Bradstreet

Anne Bradstreet was born in 1612, in England. She is considered to be one of the most intelligent and accomplished poets of the New World, not solely due to being the very first woman to publish an American book, but also of her diverse writing techniques and themes despite not having received any formal education at all.

Anne Bradstreet was the daughter of an earl's estate manager. She emigrated with her family when she was 18 in 1630. Her future Simon Bradstreet helped her father manage his estate in Sempringham. While having to devote much of her time and energy to managing the home with her husband away on business, Anne Bradstreet nonetheless wrote poetry which expressed her commitment to the craft of writing. Her tortuous childhood, sickness, burdensome married life (taking care of eight children and her family) made it understandable that images of the human body, illness and mortality are dominant in her writing. And as she joined her father and her husband to embark on a Puritan mission, she joined a church at Boston, which made herself ambivalent about the subjects in religion, i.e. redemption, for most of her life.

In addition, her work reflects the religious and emotional conflicts she experienced as a female writer and a Puritan. Throughout her life, Bradstreet had been concerned with sin and redemption, physical and emotional fragility, death and immortality. Most of her work shows that it is difficult for her to resolve the conflict between the fun of sensory and family experience and the promise of heaven. As a Puritan, she tried to restrain her attachment to the world; but as a woman, she sometimes felt more connected with her husband, children and community than with God.

Her first published work, *The Tenth Muse*[1] *Lately Sprung up in America*, received considerable favorable attention when it was first published in London in 1650, and brought her reputation and recognition. The book shows the influence of Edmund Spencer, Philip Sidney and other poets, including "To My Dear and Loving Husband", "The Author to Her Book", "The Flesh and the Spirit", "Upon the Burning of Our House", etc. She often uses well-designed concepts or extended metaphors in her writing, intertwined with themes of daily life, warmth and love. In the poem "To My Dear and Loving Husband", Bradstreet praised her husband with clear, plain and humble words, regarding him as her own supplement that made her complete. For her, his love is more valuable than all the wealth of the East and all the gold in the world. Her love for him will never dry up.

To My Dear and Loving Husband[2]

If ever two were one, then surely we.
If ever man were lov'd by wife, then thee;
If ever wife was happy in a man,
Compare with me ye women if you can.
I prize[3] thy love more than whole Mines of gold,
Or all the riches that the East[4] doth hold.
My love is such that Rivers cannot quench,
Nor ought[5] but love from thee, give recompence[6].
Thy love is such I can no way repay,
The heavens[7] reward thee manifold[8] I pray.
Then while we live, in love let's so persever[9],
That when we live no more, we may live ever.[10]

Notes

1. Muse: In Greek mythology the Muses were nine daughters of Zeus. Each was the patron of a particular art, such as poetry, dance and music.

2. "To My Dear and Loving Husband": The poem is autobiographical and describes the passionate love between the narrator and her husband. The narrator

describes that love as pure and redemptive. The poem thus implicitly argues against some religious poets who describe love as a sinful or unholy act. "To My Dear and Loving Husband" reflects the life of Puritans in North America from another aspect, that is, its human side.

3. prize: value.

4. the East: East Indies, southeast Asia, including India; the English East India Company began in 1600. Here the poet is not referring to a direction, but rather to a culture (or a set of cultures) distant from her own. For people living in colonial America in the 17th century, the East was an exotic and opulent place, full of sensual and material riches. It symbolizes, for the narrator, all of the pleasures and wealth available in this world. It is thus also implicitly a sinful place full of earthly delights — just the opposite of the simplicity and piousness that Puritans like Bradstreet prized.

5. ought: anything.

6. recompence: equals recompense, to give someone a payment for trouble or losses that you have caused them or a reward for their efforts to help you.

7. heavens: Literally, the "heavens" include everything that hangs over the earth: stars, moon, sun, clouds, atmosphere, etc. But the narrator of "To My Dear and Loving Husband" is not asking the stars or the clouds to reward her husband for his love. She is hoping that her husband's devotion to her will help him earn salvation in this life and a place in heaven in the next.

8. manifold: in abundance.

9. persever: both to continue steadfastly, and in the theological sense to remain in a state of grace. An earlier spelling of the word is persevere.

10. That when we live no more, we may live ever: That when we die, our souls will live eternally.

Questions for Discussion

(1) Though a pious Puritan, Anne Bradstreet's poem to her "Dear and Loving Husband" is a passionate plea for true and everlasting romantic love. How might the ideas she expresses here be considered contrary to the prevailing sentiments of her

time and place?

(2) Bradstreet equates her love to "riches", which she prizes "more than whole Mines of gold", though the Puritans considered themselves above such capitalistic goals. Why, then, would Bradstreet make such a comparison? What other metaphors does she use in her poem? What do words like "recompence", "repay" and "reward" have to do with her argument?

(3) Try to find all the metaphors used in the poem. Explain their meanings.

Suggested Reading

- Anne Bradstreet. *The Works of Anne Bradstreet*. Jeannine Hensley, ed. Cambridge, MA: Harvard University Press, 1967.
- Anne Bradstreet. *The Works of Anne Bradstreet*. Jeannine Hensley, ed. Cambridge, MA: The Belknap Press of Harvard University Press, 2010.

3. Philip Freneau

Philip Freneau is perhaps the most outstanding writer of the post-Revolutionary period. His dual role as a poet and political journalist in the traditional revolutionary era is consistent with the contradictions of his poetry. Freneau's training and taste are neoclassical, but romantic in essence.

Philip Freneau was born on January 2, 1752, in New York. After Freneau graduated from the College of New Jersey (Princeton University today) in 1771 and had an unsatisfactory teaching experience, he made his first success in New York as a satirist of the British. In 1776, He made a voyage to West Indies and produced many fine poems such as "The House of Night". He was captured and imprisoned by the British for his satirical writings. He suffered both physically and mentally during the six-week imprisonment. Thus, he poured his bitterness into his political writing and much of his voluminous poetry of the early 1780s. "The British Prison Ship", particularly, reveals the brutality of his captivity and was considered to be a good piece of invective.

Freneau became an author and edited a newspaper in New York City. At the start of the George Washington administration, Philip Freneau was persuaded by his old college friend, James Madison to work for Thomas Jefferson. Encouraged by James Madison and Thomas Jefferson, Freneau established a newspaper, the *National Gazette*, in Philadelphia, which promoted Jefferson's principles. By the early 1800s, Freneau had retired to his farm to write essays and poetry.

Even with his many political pieces and various life experiences, Freneau remained a poet first. Freneau was quite prolific, actually. It is most appropriate that Philip Freneau be titled "Father of American Poetry". He had the spirit of a poet, and he had begun to write as early as he was in college. Although his life was full of ups and downs, he never gave up writing. Influenced by the traditional English poets, his poems are obviously imitated in theme and form, but he is the first to apply the traditional English poetry mode to eulogize the unique native people and natural scenery of North America. Therefore, his poetry is very American and in his fresh and natural style, readers can appreciate the poet's sincere affection for nature. Among Freneau's many wonderful works on nature, "The Wild Honey Suckle" is the most representative one. The comparatively short poem has only four six-line stanzas of iambic tetrameter arranged in the quite traditional rhyme scheme ababcc. The narrator in Freneau's "The Wild Honey Suckle" addresses a lovely honeysuckle flower, marveling in its beauty and the surroundings in which he finds the flowers, and how its living situation changes with the seasons, growing and dying in the wild unnoticed and unseen.

The Wild Honey Suckle[1]

Fair[2] flower, that dost so comely[3] grow,
Hid in this silent, dull retreat,
Untouched thy honeyed blossoms blow,
Unseen thy little branches greet:[4]
No roving foot shall crush thee here,
No busy hand provoke a tear.

By Nature's self in white arrayed[5],
She bade[6] thee shun[7] the vulgar[8] eye,
And planted here the guardian shade,
And sent soft waters murmuring by;[9]
Thus quietly thy summer goes,
Thy days declining to repose[10].

Smit[11] with those charms, that must decay,
I grieve to see your future doom[12];
They died — nor were those flowers more gay[13],
The flowers that did in Eden[14] bloom;
Unpitying frosts, and Autumn's power
Shall leave no vestige[15] of this flower.

From morning suns and evening dews
At first thy little being came:
If nothing once, you nothing lose,
For when you die your are the same;
The space between, is but an hour,
The frail duration[16] of a flower.

Notes

1. wild honey suckle: then the popular name for a familiar shrub, sometimes called "swamp honeysuckle" — a climbing plant with nice-smelling yellow or pink flowers. The poem was written in 1786. Freneau was inspired by the beauty of the wild honey suckle while he was taking a walk in Charleston, South Carolina.

2. fair: beautiful.

3. comely: beautiful.

4. Fair flower... greet: the disadvantage of being in clusters of grass and flowers is without appreciation. The two lines that follow are the opposite advantage.

5. arrayed: dressed.

6. bid: to try to do, get or achieve sth.

7. shun: to avoid someone or something to another place.

8. vulgar: dealing with or talking in a way people consider disgusting and not socially acceptable.

9. By Nature's... murmuring by: In late summer and autumn, the good times don't last long.

10. repose: rest.

11. smit: attracted.

12. doom: bad fortune.

13. gay: happy.

14. Eden: the Garden of Eden. In Abrahamic religions, the Garden of Eden or Garden of God, also called the Terrestrial Paradise, is the biblical paradise.

15. vestige: a small part or amount of something that still remains when most of it does not exist anymore.

16. duration: the length of time that something continues.

Questions for Discussion

(1) Philip Freneau is famous for his beautiful lyric poetry. The poem "The Wild Honey Suckle" describes a flower that grows in a secluded bush and retains its unique beauty even though no one cares about it. The poem depicts a full picture of the Wild Honey Suckle's life. Do you think the flower in the poem has a symbolic meaning, considering the historical background of the time Philip Freneau lived in?

(2) This poem depicts the beauty of nature with lyrical tone, and reveals the beauty of the flower, as well as the fragility of the honeysuckle. Do you think there are any deeper themes the poet is trying to illustrate in "The Wild Honey Suckle"?

Suggested Reading

- Philip Morin Freneau. *Poems Written Between the Years 1768 & 1794.* Charleston, SC: Nabu Press, 2011.

- Philip Morin Freneau. *The American Village: A Poem.* South Yarra: Leopold Classic Library, 2017.

4. Hector St. John de Crèvecoeur

J. Hector St. John de Crèvecoeur is an important figure in the history of American literature for his 1782 work — *Letters from an American Farmer* with its changed title as "What Is an American?", which is often cited by American history and literature professors for its definition of American identity at the time the new nation was born.

Hector St. John de Crèvecoeur was born in a family of minor nobility in Normandy, France, on December 31, 1735. In 1755, he moved to New France in North America. There, he worked as a cartographer for the French colonial militia in the French Indian War. After Britain defeated the French army in 1759, he moved to New York and obtained US citizenship, and changed his name to John Hector St. John. In 1770, he married an American woman. She was the daughter of a New York businessman, named Mehitable Tippet. He bought a fairly large farm called "Pine Hill" in Orange County, New York, where he succeeded as a farmer. He also traveled extensively as a surveyor. He began to write about the life of American colonies and the emergence of American society.

In 1780, Crèvecoeur returned to France. In 1782, *Letters from an American Farmer* was published and was widely praised. This book soon became the first literary achievement of American writers in Europe, and made Crèvecoeur a famous figure. He was the first writer to use many American English words to describe American frontier to Europeans and explore the concept of the American dream. He described American society as being characterized by the principles of equal opportunity and self-determination. His works provided useful information and understanding about the "New World", and helped Europeans establish an American identity in their minds by describing a completely new country rather than another regional colony. A year later, he returned to Pine Hill in New York only to find his house burned down and his wife dead.

His book *Letters from an American Farmer* was selectively edited by later scholars from a large number of various manuscripts of the author. Each letter highlights a different aspect of life in the British Colonies and the complete set covers a range of genres and sociological observations. It is made up of two parts: the first part consists of twelve letters from a farmer in the American continent; and the second part, American 18th century notes, also comprises 12 chapters. This is a record of the author's real life recording his real feelings and his ideological understanding of the new world with simple feelings and concise language. Having experienced two peak periods of social change during the formation of the nation, the author's point of view also changed greatly, from the high evaluation and praise of the New World to the chattering criticism of the society. Being the earliest European to develop a considered view of America and the new American character, Crèvecoeur's writing gave Europeans a general idea of opportunities for peace, wealth and pride in America. Moreover, he is considered to be the first to exploit the "melting pot" image of America.

Letters from an American Farmer

"What Is an American?"[1]

He is arrived on a new continent; a modern society offers itself to his contemplation, different from what he had hitherto seen. It is not composed, as in Europe, of great lords who possess everything and of a herd of people who have nothing. Here are no aristocratical[2] families, no courts, no kings, no bishops, no ecclesiastical dominion[3], no invisible power giving to a few a very visible one; no great manufacturers employing thousands, no great refinements of luxury. The rich and the poor are not so far removed from each other as they are in Europe...

Some few towns excepted, we are all tillers of the earth, from Nova Scotia[4] to West Florida[5]. We are a people of cultivators, scattered over an immense territory, communicating with each other by means of good roads and navigable rivers, united by the silken bands of mild government, all respecting the laws without dreading their power, because they are equitable.[6] We are all animated with the spirit of an industry which is unfettered and unrestrained[7] because each person works for himself. If he travels through our rural districts, he views not the hostile castle and the haughty[8] mansion, contrasted with the clay-built hut and miserable cabin where cattle and men help to keep each other warm and dwell in meanness, smoke, and indigence[9]. A pleasing uniformity of decent competence appears throughout our habitations. The meanest of our log-houses is a dry and comfortable habitation. Lawyer or merchant are the fairest titles our towns afford — that of a farmer is the only appellation of the rural inhabitants of our country.[10] It must take some time ere[11] he can reconcile himself to our dictionary, which is but short in words of dignity and names of honor. There, on a Sunday, he sees a congregation of respectable farmers and their wives, all clad in neat homespun, well mounted[12] or riding in their own humble wagons. There is not among them an esquire, saving the unlettered magistrate.[13] There he sees a parson[14] as simple as his flock, a farmer who does not riot[15] on the labor of others. We have no princes for whom we toil, starve, and bleed. We are the most perfect society now existing in the world. Here man is free as he ought to be; nor is this pleasing equality so transitory as many others are. Many ages will not see the shores of our great lakes replenished with inland nations, nor the unknown bounds of North America entirely peopled. Who can tell how far it extends? Who can tell the millions of men whom it will feed and contain? For no European foot has as yet travelled half the extent of this mighty continent!

    The next wish of this traveller will be to know whence came all these people? They are a mixture of English, Scotch, Irish, French, Dutch, Germans, and Swedes[16]. From this promiscuous breed[17], that race now called Americans have arisen. The eastern provinces[18] must indeed be excepted, as being the unmixed descendants of Englishmen. I have heard many wish that they had been more intermixed also: for my part, I am no wisher, and think it much better as it has happened. They exhibit a most conspicuous figure in this great and variegated picture; they too enter for a great share in the pleasing perspective displayed in these thirteen provinces. I know it is fashionable to reflect on them[19], but I respect them for what they have done — for the accuracy and wisdom with which they have settled their territory; for the decency of their manners; for their early love of letters[20]; their ancient college, the first in this hemisphere[21]; for their industry[22], which to me, who am but a farmer, is the criterion of everything. There never was a people, situated as they are, who with so ungrateful a soil have done more in so short a time. Do you think that the monarchical ingredients which are more prevalent in other governments have purged them from all foul stains? Their histories assert the contrary.

What then is the American, this new man? He is either an European, or the descendant of an European, hence that strange mixture of blood, which you will find in no other country. I could point out to you a family whose grandfather was an Englishman, whose wife was Dutch, whose son married a French woman, and whose present four sons have now four wives of different nations. He is an American, who, leaving behind him all his ancient prejudices and manners, receives new ones from the new mode of life he has embraced, the new rank he holds. He becomes an American by being received in the broad lap of our great Alma Mater[23].

Here individuals of all nations are melted into a new race of men, whose labours and posterity[24] will one day cause great changes in the world... The Americans were once scattered all over Europe; here they are incorporated into one of the finest systems of population which has ever appeared, and which will hereafter become distinct by the power of the different climates they inhabit. The American ought therefore to love this country much better than the wherein either he or his forefathers were born. Here the rewards of his industry follow with equal steps the progress of his labour; ... Wives and children, who before in vain demanded of him a morsel of bread, now, fat and frolicsome[25], gladly help their father to clear those fields whence exuberant[26] crops are to arise to feed and to clothe them all; without any part being claimed, either by a despotic prince[27], a rich abbot[28], or a mighty lord... The American is a new man, who acts upon new principles; he must therefore entertain new ideas, and form new opinions. From involuntary idleness, servile[29] dependence, penury[30], and useless labour, he has passed to toils of a very different nature, rewarded by ample subsistence. — This is an American.

Notes

1. It's a letter, the third letter-part of a series of letters called *Letters from an American Farmer* by J. Hector St. John de Crèvecoeur, written in 1782.

2. aristocratical: privileged.

3. ecclesiastical dominion: religious control.

4. Nova Scotia: one of the thirteen provinces and territories of Canada. It is one of the three maritime provinces and one of the four Atlantic provinces. Nova Scotia is

Latin for "New Scotland". Most of the population are native English-speakers.

5. West Florida: a region on the northern coast of the Gulf of Mexico that underwent several boundary and sovereignty changes during its history. As its name suggests, it was formed out of the western part of former Spanish Florida, along with lands taken from French Louisiana; Pensacola became West Florida's capital. The colony included about two thirds of what is now the Florida Panhandle, as well as parts of the modern U.S. states of Louisiana, Mississippi, and Alabama.

6. We are a people of cultivators... because they are equitable: It answers the question "Who are we".

7. unfettered and unrestrained: not restricted or limited.

8. haughty: having or showing arrogant superiority to and disdain of those viewed as unworthy.

9. indigence: state of extreme poverty and need.

10. that of... our country: i.e., with no European titles of nobility such as lord, duke, etc.

11. ere: before.

12. mount: it refers to getting on a horse.

13. There is not among them an esquire, saving the unlettered magistrate: i.e., there is no titled and privileged "gentleman", the rank designated with "esquire" in England (and in the American colonies); "saving the unlettered magistrate", i.e., except for a relatively uneducated judge or local judicial official.

14. parson: a person authorized to conduct religious worship.

15. riot: live in excess.

16. mixture of English, Scotch, Irish, French, Dutch, Germans, and Swedes: Crèvecoeur believed that American was "mixture of English, Scotch, Irish, French, Dutch, Germans, and Swedes". The "new man" abandoned his ancient biases and adapted a new lifestyle, traditions, and etiquette through education. He put into account the perspective of the America as a melting-pot.

17. promiscuous breed: i.e., made up of a mixture of people brought together by happenstance, not by plan; not referring to sexual promiscuity.

18. province: colony.

19. I know it is fashionable to reflect on them: i.e., comment disparagingly on

them.

20. letters: learning.

21. the first in this hemisphere: Harvard College, founded in Boston in 1636.

22. for their industry: i.e., industriousness.

23. Alma Mater: literally, nourishing mother; often used to refer to one's college or university [Latin].

24. posterity: future generation.

25. frolicsome: enthusiastic and liking to play.

26. exuberant:(especially of people and their behavior) very energetic.

27. despotic prince: of or typical of a despot; tyrannical.

28. abbot: religious leader.

29. servile: inferior.

30. penury: the state of being very poor.

Questions for Discussion

(1) *Letters from an American Farmer* is a landmark in the history of American literature and thought, and the new concept "new American" has become an eternal theme in the development of American literature. Where does the concept of the "new American" originate from? What makes the "new American" different from individuals, families and groups of European society?

(2) What does Crèvecoeur mean by "The rich and the poor are not so far removed from each other as they are in Europe"?

Suggested Reading

● Andrew Moore. "The American Farmer as French Diplomat: J. Hector St. John de Crèvecoeur in New York after 1783," *Journal of the Western Society of French History*, Vol. 39, 2011.

● Tina Hannappel. *Susanna Moodie and Hector St. Jean de Crèvecoeur — Two Models of Success*. Munich: Grin Verlag, 2009.

5. Thomas Jefferson

Jefferson was an American stateman, diplomat, lawyer, architect, musician, philosopher, and Founding Father who served as the third president of the United Stated from 1801 to 1809. He is best known as the principal author of the *Declaration of Independence* in 1776, decades before he was elected as president.

Jefferson was born into a family living on a Virginia farm of 5,000 acres in 1743. Coming from a privileged background, he entered the prestigious College of William and Mary at the age of 17. He was very interested in scientific subjects and the study of law and philosophy. After his focus shifted from law to political movement, he abandoned being a lawyer. His first political work that gained broad acclaim was a 1774 draft of directions for Virginia's delegations to the First Continental Congress. But soon Jefferson left Congress in 1776, and returned to Virginia to serve in the legislature. He drafted the *Declaration of Independence* together with John Adams, Benjamin Franklin, Roger Sherman, and Robert R. Livingston in the same year. He had been drawn into public service since 1770s. He served as Vice President from 1797 to 1801 under President John Adams. In 1801, he became the third president of America and served a second term till 1809. The Louisiana Purchase of 1803 was considered Jefferson's greatest accomplishment as president. Effectively doubling the territory of the United States, the Louisiana Purchase is viewed to have been a very shrewd move, and cemented Jefferson's reputation as a skilled negotiator and visionary leader.

Like Benjamin Franklin, Thomas Jefferson was well read and proficient in many fields of knowledge, including law, philosophy, and government. The *Declaration of Independence* drafted in June 1776 is not only a symbol of national freedom, but also Jefferson's a crowning achievement as a politician and statesman. The purpose of the declaration was to free the colonists from the shackles of King George. The document has become the cornerstone of the United States and is one of the most important documents in American history.

In lofty eloquence and unforgettable phrasing, the document expressed the convictions of the American people. In order to be easily understood by the public, the language of the *Declaration of Independence* had to be brief and directly to the point. The text falls into five sections: the introduction — the preamble, the indictment of King George III, the denunciation of the British people, and the conclusion. The very famous line "We hold these truths to be self-evident, that all men are created equal" is from the introduction.

Declaration of Independence

THE UNANIMOUS DECLARATION OF THE THIRTEEN UNITED STATES OF AMERAICA (IN CONGRESS, JULY 4, 1776)

When in the course of human events, it becomes necessary for one people to dissolve[1] the political bands[2] which have connected them with another, and to assume among the powers of the earth, the separate and equal station to which the laws Nature and Nature's God entitle them, a decent respect to the opinions of mankind requires that they should declare the causes which impel them to the separation.[3]

We hold these truths to be self-evident, that all men are created equal, that they are endowed by their Creator[4] with certain unalienable rights, that among these are life, liberty and the pursuit of happiness.[5] That to secure these rights, governments are instituted among them, deriving their just power from the consent[6] of the governed. That whenever any form of government becomes destructive of these ends, it is the right of the people to alter or to abolish it, and to institute new government, laying its foundation on such principles and organizing its powers in such form, as to them shall seem most likely to effect their safety and happiness. Prudence[7], indeed, will dictate[8] that governments long established should not be changed for light and transient causes[9]; and accordingly all experience hath shown that mankind are more disposed to[10] suffer, while evils are sufferable, than to right themselves by abolishing the forms to which they are accustomed. But when a long train of abuses and usurpations[11], pursuing invariably the same object evinces[12] a design to reduce them under absolute despotism[13], it is their right, it is their duty, to throw off such government, and to provide new guards for their future security. Such has been the patient sufferance[14] of these Colonies; and such is now the necessity, which constrains[15] them to alter their former systems of government. The history of the present King of Great Britain[16] is usurpations, all having in direct object tyranny over these States. To prove this, let facts be submitted to a candid world[17]...

Notes

1. dissolve: remove.

2. political band: political constraint.

3. When in the course... to the separation: i.e., when in the process of human activities, it is necessary for a nation to dissolve the political groups associated with another nation and assume the independent and equal status given to them by the laws of nature and the God of nature in the power of the earth. In order to respect the opinions of mankind, it is necessary to announce the reasons for their separation.

4. their Creator: God.

5. ... among these are life, liberty and the pursuit of happiness: John Locke defined man's natural rights in his "Second Treatise on Government" to "Life, Liberty and property".

6. consent: permission.

7. prudence: discretion in practical affairs.

8. dictate: issue commands or orders for.

9. light and transient causes: Governments sometimes violate rights. The opposite of "light and transient causes" is the more ordinary violations of rights by government. Such has been the patient sufferance of these colonies; and such is now the necessity which constrains them to alter their former systems of government.

10. be more disposed to: be willing to do something.

11. abuse and usurpation: In the *Bible*, usurper means to seize or exercise authority or possession wrongfully. Usurpation is the exercise of powers by an agent which have not been delegated to him by the principal. Besides usurpations, there is a larger class of abuses which include corruption and violations of constitutional statutes.

12. evince: give expression to.

13. absolute despotism: refers to the actions of a government that are failing to protect the rights of citizens. This type of government is extremely controlling and does not consider the rights/needs of the individual.

14. patient sufferance: Sufferance is a type of patience, especially the patience

to endure pain and suffering. Sufferance is a quality possessed by people who endure such pains patiently without complaining.

15. constrain: force under the circumstance of being abused without other alternatives.

16. the present King of Great Britain: George III, king from 1760 to 1820, was the responsible engineer of those policies of his government which evoked rebellion.

17. To prove this... candid world: note the archaic use of "candid", which in this case means "unbiased". To what does "this" refer? To the preceding lines: "The history of the present King of Great Britain is usurpations, all having in direct object tyranny over these States." Stephen E. Lucas points out that "this sentence is so innocuous one can easily overlook its artistry and importance."

Questions for Discussion

(1) In the second paragraph, the declaration writes: "We hold these truths to be self-evident, that all men are created equal, that they are endowed by their Creator with certain unalienable rights." According to the declaration, what are the unalienable rights of men?

(2) In literary writing, writers may apply certain writing techniques to achieve some goals. For example, many paralleled structures are used in the declaration. What effects can be achieved by using these paralleled structures?

(3) The *Declaration of Independence* officially declared the independence of the United States from Britain to the world. This marked a new stage in the North American War of Independence. What are the causes and influences of the American Revolutionary War?

Suggested Reading

● 杰弗逊：《杰弗逊政治著作选》，Joyce Appleby，Terence Ball编，北京：中国政法大学出版社，2003年。

● 斯蒂芬·康威：《美国独立战争简史》，邓海平译，北京：化学工业出版社，2018年。

● 托马斯·杰斐逊：《杰斐逊选集》，强梅梅导读，北京：中国人民大学出版社，2013年。

Part Two

The Romantic Period

6. Washington Irving

Washington Irving (1783–1859) was born in New York City. He was called the Father of American literature, the Father of the American short stories, the "first American man of letters" and regarded as an early Romantic writer in the American literary history. His father William was a Scottish-American merchant, and his mother, Sarah Sanders was the daughter of an English clergyman. At the time of his birth, the American Revolution was just ending. According to Irving's biographer Mary Weatherspoon Bowden, "Irving maintained close ties with his family his entire life." Washington Irving liked reading very much when he was a boy, reading works like *Robinson Crusoe, Sinbad the Sailor*, and *The World Displayed*. After a series of accidental events, he was driven to be a professional writer because of his talents. With the help of friends, he was able to publish a collection of essays and short stories — *The Sketch Book of Geoffrey Crayon, Gent.* (commonly referred to as *The Sketch Book*) (1819–1820) in England and America and got copyrights and payment in both countries. Washington Irving married Matilda Hoffmann, the daughter of a prominent local family who died at a very young age. Irving never became engaged or married anyone after her death. This loss indeed had a big effect on the rest of his life.

His major works include *A History of New York, The Sketch Book, Bracebridge Hall, Tales of a Traveler* and so on. Irving created his unique writing style which is fresh, natural, musical and humorous, absorbing the essence of European culture and literature. His works with popular but elegant style have given great enjoyment to the readers.

Rip Van Winkle[1]

Anyone who has made a voyage up the Hudson River surely remembers the Kaatskill mountains. They are part of the great family of mountains in the Eastern section of our country, called the Appalachians, though the Kaatskills are separate from the other members of the Appalachian group. The Kaatskill mountains rise on the west of the Hudson River, high above the surrounding country.

Every change of season, every change of weather, indeed, every hour of the day, produces some change in the colors and shapes of these mountains. By looking at the Kaatskills from time to time, the people of the area can guess what the weather is going to be. When the weather is fair and fine, the mountains are a deep blue, and the tops of the mountains can be clearly seen against the evening sky. But sometimes, when there are no clouds anywhere else, the mountains seem to wear a loose gray cap, which glows like a crown of glory in the light of the setting sun.

Just below these strange mountains, the traveler may have observed the thin smoke rising up from a village among the trees. It is a little village many years old; the Dutch settled there in the early years of the colony. Until recently, some of the houses of the old settlers were still there, built in the Dutch fashion, and with materials brought from Holland.

In the same village, and in one of those houses, Rip Van Winkle lived. He lived there many years ago, while our country still belonged to England. Rip Van Winkle was a simple, good-natured[2] fellow, whose ancestors had fought bravely in the days of the Dutch governor, Peter Stuyvesant. Rip, however, had little of his ancestors' warlike character. I have said that he was a simple, good-natured man. He was, in addition, a kind neighbor, and a husband who obeyed his wife. Being firmly controlled by his wife at home, he seemed to have formed the habit of being easy-going to all. As a result, he was thought highly of by everyone except his wife.

Certainly he was a great favorite among all the good wives of the village. Whenever they discussed the Van Winkle family's quarrels, they always decided that Dame Van Winkle was wrong. The children of the village, too, always shouted with joy when Rip Van Winkle came. He watched them at their sports, made playthings for them, taught them how to play various games, and told them long stories of the most exciting kind. Wherever he went, he was usually surrounded by a crowd of children; and no dog in the village ever barked at him.

Rip Van Winkle had one great fault; he disliked — indeed, he hated — any kind of profitable labor. It is hard to understand just why he did not like to work, for he had plenty of patience and the ability to continue one form of activity for a long time. Often, for example, he sat on a wet rock, with a heavy fishing pole, and fished all day without a word, even though he might not succeed in catching a single fish. He was willing to carry a hunting gun on his shoulder, hour after hour, up and down hills, just to shoot a few rabbits and birds. He never refused to help a neighbor, even with the roughest sort of work, such as helping people build stone walls. The women of the village, too, often used him to carry messages for them, or to do small jobs that their husbands were not willing to do. In other words, Rip was ready to take care of anybody's business except his own. As for his family duties, and for keeping his farm in order, he found such work impossible.

In fact, he declared it was no use to work on his farm: it was the worst little piece of ground in the whole country; everything about it was wrong. His fences were continually falling to pieces; his cow was always getting lost or else eating up the vegetables in the garden. Nothing ever grew well in his fields; and the rain always started just as soon as he had begun to do some work outside. As a result, although he had lost much of his family's land during years of bad management until very little remained, yet his small farm was in worse condition than any neighboring farm.

His children, too, went about looking as poor as his farm. His son Rip, who was very much like him, ran around wearing a pair of his father's old trousers, which he had to hold up with one hand in order to prevent them from falling.

Rip Van Winkle, however, was one of those fortunate people, with foolish, well-oiled natures, who take the world easy and cheerfully, eat fine food or poor, whichever can be got with least thought or trouble. If permitted, he would have sat whistling his life away in perfect contentment, but his wife kept continually reminding him about his idleness[3], his carelessness, and the ruin he was bringing on his family. Morning, noon, and night, her tongue was endlessly going. Everything he said or did was sure to produce more angry talk.

Rip had just one way of replying to his wife's talk; by frequent use it had become a habit. He merely put his head back on his shoulders, looking up toward heaven, and said nothing. This, however, always produced a fresh burst of anger from his wife. There was nothing for Rip to do then except to leave the house.

Rip's only friend in the Van Winkle home was his dog, whose name was Wolf. Wolf was often the object of Dame Van Winkle's displeasure, for she considered the two of them companions in idleness; indeed, she sometimes even blamed the dog for Rip's wandering ways. True, in the woods Wolf was very brave; but what dog is ever brave enough to stand firm against the terrors of a woman's tongue? As soon as Wolf entered the house, his head bent low, his tail lay on the ground or folded between his legs. He went around the house with a guilty look, watching Dame Van Winkle out of the corner of his eye, ready to run from the room at the slightest sign of her displeasure.

Rip Van Winkle's troubles increased as the years of his marriage passed. A hard woman never becomes soft with age, and a sharp tongue is the only edged tool that cuts better with constant use. For a long while he used to comfort himself by sitting with other idle men, when Dame Van Winkle's talk had forced him out of the house. He and these other idle persons used to sit in front of the village inn, a small hotel whose name was suggested by a picture of His Majesty George the Third[4]. Here they often sat in the shade through a long summer day, telling endless sleepy stories about nothing. Sometimes, by chance, one of the men found an old newspaper which had been left behind by some passing traveler. Then how seriously they would listen to the contents, as the newspaper was read aloud by Drick Van Bummel, the schoolteacher, a man of great learning, who was not afraid of the longest word in the dictionary. And how wisely they would discuss the public events which had occurred several months before.

The opinions of this group were completely controlled by Nicholas Vedder, the oldest man in the village, who owned the inn. He sat at the door of the inn from morning till night, moving just enough to avoid the sun and keep in the shade of a large tree. It is true that he almost never spoke, but smoked his pipe continually. His admirers, however, understood him perfectly, and knew how to get his opinions on any subject. When anything that was read or told displeased him, he smoked his pipe angrily, but when he was pleased, he smoked slowly and calmly. Sometimes, taking the pipe from his mouth, he let the smoke wind about his nose and moved his head up and down as a sign of agreement with what was being said.

But even the comforting companionship of this group was finally taken from the unlucky Rip. His wife suddenly broke in upon the pleasant discussion-club and gave its members her opinion of their worthlessness. Not even the great Nicholas Vedder himself was safe from the tongue of this daring woman who blamed him directly for much of her husband's idleness.

Poor Rip was thus made almost hopeless. His only remaining means of escape was to take his gun and walk away into the woods. Here he would sometimes seat himself at the foot of a tree with his devoted dog and fellow-sufferer[5], Wolf. "Poor Wolf," he would say. "Your life is hard and sad indeed, but never fear. While I live there will always be one friend to stand by you!" Wolf would wag his tail and look sadly into his master's face. If dogs can feel pity, I truly believe he pitied Rip with all his heart.

After a long, wandering walk of this kind on a certain autumn day, Rip found that he had climbed to one of the highest parts of the Kaatskill mountains. He was busy with his favorite sport of hunting, and the lonely stillness of the woods had often been broken by the sound of his gun. Tired and breathless, he threw himself, late in the afternoon, on a little green hill at the highest point of land. From an opening between the trees he could see all the lower country for many miles of rich woodland. He saw at a distance the Hudson River, far, far below.

On the other side he looked down into a deep valley, wild, lonely, and covered with trees. The bottom was filled with pieces of broken rock from the stony mountain side. For some time Rip lay observing this scene. Evening had almost come; the mountains began to throw their long blue shadows over the valleys; he saw that it would be dark long before he could reach the village, and he sighed deeply when he thought of Dame Van Winkle's angry face.

Just as he was about to go down the mountain, he heard a voice from the distance calling , "Rip Van Winkle! Rip Van Winkle!" He looked around, but could see nothing except a large bird winging its lonely flight across the mountain. He decided he had merely imagined the voice, and had turned again to climb down, when he heard the same crying through the quiet evening air; "Rip Van Winkle! Rip Van Winkle!" At the same time, the hairs on his dog's back stood up straight, and the dog moved to his master's side, looking fearfully into the valley. Rip now felt the same fear within him, and he looked anxiously in the same direction. There he saw a strange figure slowly climbing up the rocks, bending under the weight of something he carried on his back. Rip was surprised to see any human being in this lonely place. But supposing it was some neighbor in need of help, he hurried down to give it.

As he came more closely, he was still more surprised at the strangeness of the stranger's appearance. He was a short old fellow, built quite square with thick bushy hair and grayish beard[6]! His clothes were in the old Dutch fashion — a short cloth jacket with a belt, and several pairs of trousers. The outer trousers were wide and loose, with rows of buttons down the sides. On his shoulder he carried a wooden bucket which seemed full of wine; and he signed to Rip to come over and help him with his load.

Though not entirely trusting this strange-looking stranger, Rip advanced to aid him. They carried the bucket together up a narrow cut in the mountain side which might once have been made there by a mountain stream. As they climbed, Rip began to notice some unusual sounds. They were somewhat like the sounds of distant thunder, and they seemed to rise out of a deep and narrow valley among the high rocks toward which their rough path led.

He paused for a moment to listen, but decided there must be a passing thunderstorm not far away. Satisfied with this explanation of the noise, he went on. Passing through the cut in the mountain, they came to a small cave, like one of the theatres cut into the earth in ancient Greece. During this whole time, Rip and his companion had laboured on in silence, for though Rip wondered why anyone should carry a bucket of wine up this wild mountain, he lacked the courage to question his strange new friend.

When they entered the cave, new objects of wonder could be seen. On a flat spot in the corner, a group of strange-looking persons were playing ninepins. The players were dressed in a most unusual way. Some had knives in their belts, and most of them had long, loose trousers similar to those worn by Rip's guide. Their faces, too, were strange. The face of one seemed to be made up entirely of a nose, topped by a large white hat. They all had beards, of various shapes and colors. There was one who seemed to be the leader of the group. He was a thick-bodied old gentleman, wearing a broad belt, a tall hat with a feather, red stockings, and high-heeled shoes. The whole group reminded Rip of the figures in a certain old Dutch painting that had been brought to the village from Holland during the time of the first settlers.

Something else seemed particularly strange to Rip. Although these folk were clearly playing a game, yet their faces were serious. They played in silence and were, in fact, the saddest party of pleasure that he had ever seen. Nothing interrupted the stillness of the scene except the noise of the balls. Whenever these were rolled, the sound broke through the mountain air like thunder.

As Rip and his companion came to them, they suddenly stopped their game and stared at him with such a strange look that his heart turned within him and his knees knocked together. His companion now emptied the contents of the bucket into large metal cups, and signed to him to serve the company. He obeyed with fear and trembling[7]. They drank the wine in deepest silence, and then turned to their game.

Little by little Rip's nervous fear began to leave him. He even dared, when no one was looking, to taste the drink, and he liked it very much. He soon felt it was time to take another taste. One taste followed another, until at last his eyes refused to stay open, his head dropped upon his chest, and he fell into a deep sleep.

On waking, he found himself on the green hill where he had first seen the old man with the bucket. He rubbed his eyes, and found it was a bright, sunny morning. The birds were singing happily among the bushes, where leaves were moving with every movement of the pure mountain air.

"Surely," thought Rip, "I have not slept here all night!" He remembered all that had happened before he fell asleep. The strange men with the bucket of wine — the way they had climbed down through the rocks — the serious players at ninepins — the excellent drink in the metal cup. "Oh! That cup! That powerful cup!" thought Rip. "What excuse shall I make to Dame Van Winkle?"

He looked around for his gun, but instead of the clean, well-oiled hunting-gun, he found an ancient, rusty gun lying beside him. He now decided that the sad ninepins players of the mountain had tricked him: having put him to sleep with wine, they had then stolen his gun.

His dog Wolf, too, had disappeared. Perhaps he had wandered off to hunt a bird or a rabbit. Rip whistled for him and called his name, but all was useless. The mountains sent back his whistle and his shout, but no dog was to be seen.

Rip decided to return to the scene of the last evening's party. "If I meet any of those men," he said to himself, "I'll demand my dog and gun."

As he stood up to walk, he found that his legs seemed stiffer than usual; he felt pains in his legs and his back. "These mountain beds are not good for the health," thought Rip. "If this adventure puts me to bed sick, I shall hear nothing pleasant from Dame Van Winkle."

With some difficulty, he went down into the valley. He found the cut in the mountain through which he and his companion had climbed the evening before, but to his great surprise a mountain stream was now running down it, jumping from rock to rock and filling the valley with gentle laughs. However, he attempted to climb up its sides, pushing his way through bushes and climbing plants.

At last he reached the place where the rocks had opened up, at the entrance to the ninepins playing ground. But now no signs of such an opening remained. The rocks formed a high wall over which the mountain stream fell noisily to a pool below. Here poor Rip was forced to stop. He again called and whistled for his dog, but was answered only by a flock of birds.

What could he do? The morning was passing away and Rip's stomach sharply told him he had had no breakfast. He felt sad about the loss of his dog and his gun; he hated the thought of meeting his wife. But he did not wish to die of hunger in the mountains. He shook his head, put the rusty old gun on his shoulder; then, with a troubled and anxious heart, he turned his steps toward home.

As he went close to the village, he met several people, but he knew none of them — a fact which surprised him, for he had thought he knew everyone in the country around. Their clothes, too, were of a different fashion from the clothes of his friends and neighbors. They all stared at him with equal marks of surprise, and all who looked at him lifted their hands to touch their chins. This happened so often that Rip, without thinking, did the same. Imagine his surprise when he found that his beard was a foot longer than it had been before!

He had now reached the edge of the village. A crowd of strange children ran at his heels, shouting after him and pointing at his gray beard. The dogs, too, were all different from the dogs he knew. They barked at him in a most unfriendly way. Even the village had changed; it was larger than it had been. There were rows of houses which Rip had never seen before, and those which he remembered had disappeared. Strange names were over the doors — strange faces at the windows — everything was strange[8]. Rip was now more anxious and puzzled than before. He began to think that some evil spirit controlled both himself and the world around him. Surely this was his native village, which he had left just the day before. There stood the Kaatskill mountains — there ran the silver Hudson at a distance — there was every hill and valley exactly as it had always been. Rip was sadly troubled. "That cup last night," thought he, "has ruined my poor brain."

With some difficulty, he found the way to his own house, which he went up to with silent fear, expecting every moment, to hear the sharp voice of Dame Van Winkle. He found that the house was little more than a pile of old boards. The roof had fallen in, the windows were broken, and the doors were lying on the ground. A bony dog that looked like Wolf was standing beside the ruined house. Rip called him by name, but the dog merely showed his teeth and then walked away. This was the cruelest wound of all. "My dog, my devoted dog," sighed Rip, "even my dog has forgotten me."

He entered the ruins of the house, which, to tell the truth, Dame Van Winkle had always kept in good order. It was empty; they had all gone away. Rip's loneliness grew stronger than his fear of Dame Van Winkle's tongue. He called loudly for his wife and children. The empty rooms rang for a moment with his voice; then all again was still.

He now hurried forth, to the village inn where he had spent so many idle hours. But it, too, was gone. A large old wooden building stood in its place, with great windows, some of which were broken. Over the door there was a sign saying, "The Union Hotel, by Jonathan Doolittle." Instead of the tree that used to shelter the quiet little Dutch inn, there was now a tall pole, with a flag bearing a strange collection of stars and strips. All this was strange, impossible to understand. But Rip recognized the picture on the sign: it was the face of King George, under which he had smoked so many a peaceful pipe. But even that was strangely different from what it had been. His Majesty's red coat was changed to blue, his head wore a hat instead of a crown, and below there were the words, GENERAL WASHINGTON.

There was, as usual, a crowd of folk around the door, but Rip recognized none of them. He looked for the wise Nicholas Vedder, with his broad face and double chin and his long pipe, blowing out clouds of smoke instead of foolish speeches, but failed to find him. He looked for Van Bummel, the schoolteacher, reading aloud the contents of an ancient newspaper. In place of these, a thin, unpleasant-looking fellow was talking loudly about the rights of citizen — election — members of congress — liberty — and other words, which meant nothing to the puzzled Van Winkle.

The group of hotel politicians soon noticed Rip, with his long gray beard, his old-fashioned clothes, his rusty gun, and the curious women and children at his heels. People crowded around him, studying his appearance from head to foot. The political speaker came to him and asked, in low voices, "Oh, which side do you vote?"

Another short but busy little fellow pulled him by the arm and asked what party he belonged to. While Rip was considering what these questions might mean, an important-looking old gentleman pushed his way through the crowd and planted himself in front of Rip Van Winkle, demanding, "Why have you come to the election with a gun on your shoulder and a noisy crowd following you? Do you intend to start trouble in this village?"

"Alas, gentlemen!" cried poor Rip. "I am a poor quiet man, a native of this place, and a devoted subject of the king, God bless him!"

Hearing this, the crowd shouted in great anger, " 'God bless the king', he says! To prison with him!" The important-looking man had great difficulty calming the crowd, after which he again demanded to know why Rip had come there and whom he was seeking. Poor Rip explained to him that he meant no harm; he had merely come there to search for some of his neighbors, who used to sit in front of the hotel.

"Well, who are they? Name them?"

Rip thought for a moment, and them asked. "Where's Nicholas Vedder?"

There was silence for a little while. Then an old man replied in a thin, high voice, "Nicholas Vedder! Why he's been dead and gone for eighteen years!"

"Where's Brom Dutcher?" asked Rip.

"Oh, he went off to the army at the beginning of the war. Some say he was killed in battle at Stony point. Perhaps he was, and perhaps he wasn't. I don't know. But he never came back again."

"Where's Van Bummel, the schoolteacher?"

"He went off to the wars, too," said the old man. "He was a great general, and is now in congress."

Rip's heart was filled with sorrow when he heard of these changes in his home and friends, finding himself thus alone in the world. Every answer puzzled him, too. The answers suggested that much time had passed, and they mentioned matters which he could not understand — war — congress — Stony Point. He was afraid to ask about any more friends, but cried out hopelessly, "Does nobody here know Rip Van Winkle?"

"Oh, Rip Van Winkle," two or three of his listeners cried in surprise. "Yes, indeed! That's Rip Van Winkle over there, leaning against the tree."

Rip looked, and saw a man who looked exactly as he had looked while climbing up the mountain. Obviously this man was no more interested in work than he himself had been. Certainly his clothes were as poor.

The unfortunate Rip was now in a most pitiable state of mind. He began to wonder whether he was himself or some other man. And while he was wondering thus, someone in the crowd demanded, "Who are you? What is your name?"

"God knows!" cried Rip, hopelessly. "I'm not myself! I'm somebody else. That's me over there. No, that's somebody else who got into my shoes. I was myself last night, but I fell asleep on the mountain, and they've changed, and I'm changed, and I can't tell my name or who I am[9]!"

His listeners now began to look at each other with meaningful smiles. It was easy to see that this old man was mad. Someone whispered. "Get his gun! Who knows what the old fellow will think of doing next?"

But just at this moment a good-looking woman pushed her way through the crowd to look at the gray-bearded man. She had a child in her arms who began to cry, frightened by his appearance. "Be quiet, you little fool; the old man won't hurt you."

The name of the child, the attitude of the mother, the tone of her voice, all awakened the memories in Rip Van Winkle's mind. "What is your name, good woman?" asked he.

"Judith Gradenier," she replied.

"And your father's name?"

"Ah, poor man! Rip Van Winkle was his name, but it is twenty years since he went away from home with his gun, and no one has heard of him since. His dog came home without him; but whether he shot himself, or was carried away by the Indians, nobody can tell. I was then just a little girl."

Rip had only one more question to ask, and he asked it in a trembling voice: "Where's your mother?"

"Oh, she died, just a little while ago. She broke a blood vessel in anger at a man who came selling things at our door."

There was a bit of comfort, at least, in this news. The honest man could no longer control his feelings. He caught his daughter and her child in his arms. "I am your father!" he cried. "Young Rip Van Winkle once — old Rip Van Winkle now. Does nobody know poor Rip Van Winkle?"

All stood too surprised to speak, until an old woman, leaving the crowd, looked up into his face for a moment, and cried, "Sure enough! It is Rip Van Winkle; it is Rip himself! Welcome home again, old neighbor! But where have you been these twenty long years?"

Rip's story was soon told, for the whole twenty years had been one night to him. The neighbors stared when they heard it. Some unbelieving ones were seen to smile at each other, and put their tongues in the side of their faces. The important-looking man pulled down the corners of his mouth and shook his head, and seeing this, there was a general shaking of the head throughout the entire crowd.

It was decided, however, to accept the opinion of old Peter Vanderdonk, who was seen slowly advancing up the road. Peter was the oldest man then living in the village. He knew all about the history of the area, He remembered Rip at once, and supported his story in the most satisfactory manner. He explained to the crowd that, in truth, strange beings lived in the Kaatskill mountains. An ancestor of his had told him that the great Hendrick Hudson, the first discoverer of the river and the area, returned there every twenty years in order to guard the river. Peter said that his father had once seen him and the old Dutchmen playing at ninepins in a cave of the mountain. He added that he himself had heard, one summer afternoon, the sound of their balls, like distant thunder.

To make a long story short, the crowd broke up and returned to the more important business of the election. Rip's daughter took him home to live with her. She had a comfortable house and a cheerful farmer for a husband, whom Rip remembered as one of the children he had often carried on his back. And Rip's son, who was an exact copy of himself was employed to work on the farm, though, like his father before him — he had the habit of attending to anything else but his business.

Rip now went back to his old ways. He soon found many of his earlier companions. As they all showed the effect of age and time, he preferred making friends among the younger folk, who soon learned to love him.

Having nothing to do at home, and having arrived at the happy age when no one blames a man for being idle, he took a seat once more at the door of the village inn. There he was respected as one of the old men of the village, who could tell stories about the old times "before the war". It was a long time before he could really understand the strange events that had occurred during his twenty years of sleep. He had to learn that there had been a revolutionary war — that the country had freed itself from England — that instead of being a subject of His Majesty George the Third, he was now a free citizen of the United States. Rip, in fact, was not a politician. The changes of states and empires made little impression on him. But he well understood one kind of independence — independence from a sharp-tongued wife. Luckily he had that independence now; he could go in and out whenever he pleased. Whenever Dame Van Winkle's name was mentioned, however, he shook his head and threw his eyes toward heaven. No one knew whether this expressed acceptance of his fate or joy at his freedom.

He used to tell his story to every stranger who arrived at Doolittle's hotel. People noticed that at first he changed some of the details every time he told the story. But at last it settled down to exactly the account which I have given; and every man, woman, and child in the village knew it by heart. Some tried to say that they doubted the reality of it; but the old Dutch members of the community were sure it was true. Even to this day, whenever they heard a thunderstorm on a summer afternoon around the Kaatskill mountains, they say Hendrick Hudson and his men are playing ninepins.

And many unhappy husbands in the area sometimes wish for a quieting drink from Rip Van Winkle's cup.

Notes

1. Due to limited space, the story here is presented in a rewritten version. Rip is the protagonist in this story but he does not get to tell it. His story is told by a third person omniscient narrator who impresses us as a humorous and effective storyteller who can distance himself to offer some mildly satirical comments on Rip.

2. good-natured: kind, friendly and patient when dealing with people. This word implies that Rip was henpecked.

3. idleness: the quality of lacking substance or value.

4. His Majesty George the Third: King of England at the time of the American Revolutionary War.

5. fellow-sufferer: companion in misfortune.

6. thick bushy hair and grayish beard: Rip became old after he slept for 20 years.

7. trembling: a reflex motion caused by fear from those strange folk.

8. everything was strange: as a metaphor, it really says this: many Americans were so confused about the changes brought about by the American Revolution that they, like Rip, felt they were 20 years behind. The confusion is a true reflection of the psychological difficulty Americans at the time felt in understanding their own recent national history.

9. I can't tell my name or who I am: In this situation, Rip is both Hamlet and Adam. Like Hamlet, he wonders who he is. Like Adam, he has a dream and wakes up finding all has changed.

Questions for Discussion

(1) Is Rip Van Winkle a tragic or comic figure? Does he symbolize human being's desire to be free from responsibility? Support your answer.

(2) What could account for all this confusion is that while Rip was in his deep sleep, 20 years had passed. As a result, his wife had died. What truth does this fact reveal about the social, literary and spiritual history of American at the beginning of

the 19th century?

(3) Mrs. Winkle is the wife of the hero of Washington Irving's short story "Rip Van Winkle". From a traditional perspective, as a wife, Mrs. Winkle is portrayed as a shrew who bullies her husband. Please analyze how she is ignored and give reasons why she is ignored from the perspective of feminism.

(4) Please identify representatives of Gothic elements in this work, such as the creation of the environment atmosphere, the description of the characters, the setting of the main plot and the expression of the theme.

Suggested Reading

- Washington Irving. *The Sketch-Book*. Oxford: Oxford University Press, 2009.
- Washington Irving. *Tales of a Traveller*. North Charleston, SC: CreateSpace Independent Publishing Platform, 2018.

7. Nathaniel Hawthorne

Nathaniel Hawthorne (1804–1864), the first great American novelist, is an extremely paradoxical figure. He was one of most democratic writers in the 19th century except for Walt Whitman. Hawthorne often invested his stories and novels with poetic elements by transforming legends of the past into allegory or symbolism.

Hawthorne was a fifth-generation American of English descent, born in a wealthy seaport north of Boston that specialized in East India trade. Some of his ancestors were notorious for the persecution of the Quakers and for the Salem Witchcraft Trials of 1629. The fortune of the family declined gradually after his sea captain father died of yellow fever when he was 4. Then the family moved to Maine where his mother relied on the assistance of relatives in rearing of her four children. From his childhood, Hawthorn read extensively and formed an ambition to be a writer. He studied at Bowdoin college in Maine from 1821 to 1825. In college Hawthorne had excelled only in composition and that led him to aspire to become a writer. While in college, he befriended two very important persons, the poet Henry Longfellow and Franklin Pierce, who later became the 14th U.S. president. He wrote a nonprofessional novel, *Fanshawe*, which he published at his own expense — only to find afterward that it was beneath him and subsequently tried to destroy all copies. After graduating from college in 1825, he returned to Salem to live in his mother's house and to pursue his literary career. Hawthorne, however, soon found his own voice, style, and subjects. And within five years of his graduation, he had published such impressive and distinctive stories as "The Hollow of the Three Hills" and "An Old Woman's Tale", followed in 1832 by "My Kinsman, Major Molineux" and "Roger Malvin's Burial", two of his greatest tales — and among the finest in the language. "Young Goodman Brown", perhaps the greatest tale of witchcraft ever written, appeared in 1835.

His major works include *The Scarlet Letter, The House of the Seven Gables, The Marble Faun,* "Young Goodman Brown", *The Blithedale Romance, Twice-Told Tales, Mosses from an Old Manse, The Snow-Image and other Twice-Told Tales* and so on. Many of Hawthorne's stories are set in Puritan New England, and his greatest novel, *The Scarlet Letter* (1850), has become a classic work of Puritan America. It portrays the forbidden and passionate love affair between a religious young man, the Reverend Arthur Dimmesdale and a beautiful woman, Hester Prynne. In this story, in order to focus on the conflicts between society and individuals, Hawthorne does not simply relate a love story, nor a story of sin, but emphasizes on the moral, emotional and psychological effects of the sin on people and the main characters in particular. For that time period, *The Scarlet Letter* was a daring book. The style of the book is very gentle, with remote historical setting and soft blurred theme, which works to calm the general public. However, some experienced writers such as Ralph Waldo Emerson and Herman Melville recognized the work for its strong emotional impact.

Young Goodman Brown[1]

Young Goodman Brown came forth at sunset into the street at Salem village[2]; but put his head back, after crossing the threshold, to exchange a parting kiss[3] with his young wife. And Faith[4], as the wife was aptly[5] named, thrust her own pretty head into the street, letting the wind play with the pink ribbons[6] of her cap while she called to

Goodman Brown.

"Dearest heart," whispered she, softly and rather sadly, when her lips were close to his ear, "prithee[7] put off your journey until sunrise and sleep in your own bed tonight. A lone woman is troubled with such dreams and such thoughts[8] that she's afeard[9] of herself sometimes. Pray tarry with me this night, dear husband, of all nights in the year."

"My love and my Faith," replied young Goodman Brown, "of all nights in the year, this one night must I tarry away from thee[10]. My journey, as thou callest it, forth and back[11] again, must needs be done 'twixt now and sunrise. What, my sweet, pretty wife, dost thou[12] doubt me already, and we but three months married?"

"Then God bless you!" said Faith, with the pink ribbons; "and may you find all well when you come back."

"Amen!" cried Goodman Brown. "Say thy[13] prayers, dear Faith, and go to bed at dusk, and no harm will come to thee."

So they parted; and the young man pursued his way until, being about to turn the corner by the meeting-house, he looked back and saw the head of Faith still peeping after him with a melancholy air, in spite of her pink ribbons.

"Poor little Faith!" thought he, for his heart smote him. "What a wretch am I to leave her on such an errand! She talks of dreams, too. Methought[14] as she spoke there was trouble in her face, as if a dream had warned her what work is to be done tonight. But no, no[15]; 't would kill her to think it. Well, she's a blessed angel on earth; and after this one night I'll cling to her skirts[16] and follow her to heaven."

With this excellent resolve for the future, Goodman Brown felt himself justified in making more haste on his present evil purpose. He had taken a dreary road, darkened by all the gloomiest trees of the forest, which barely stood aside to let the narrow path creep through, and closed immediately behind. It was all as lonely as could be; and there is this peculiarity in such a solitude[17], that the traveller knows not who may be concealed by the innumerable trunks and the thick boughs overhead; so that with lonely footsteps he may yet be passing through an unseen multitude.

"There may be a devilish Indian behind every tree," said Goodman Brown to himself; and he glanced fearfully behind him as he added, "What if the devil[18] himself should be at my very elbow!"

His head being turned back, he passed a crook of the road, and, looking forward again, beheld the figure of a man, in grave and decent attire[19], seated at the foot of an old tree. He arose at Goodman Brown's approach and walked onward side by side with him.

"You are late, Goodman Brown," said he. "The clock of the Old South was striking as I came through Boston, and that is full fifteen minutes agone[20]."

"Faith kept me back a while," replied the young man, with a tremor in his voice, caused by the sudden appearance of his companion, though not wholly unexpected.

It was now deep dusk in the forest, and deepest in that part of it where these two were journeying. As nearly as could be discerned, the second traveller was about fifty years old, apparently in the same rank of life as Goodman Brown, and bearing a considerable resemblance to him, though perhaps more in expression than features. Still they might have been taken for father and son. And yet, though the elder person was as simply clad as the younger, and as simple in manner too, he had an indescribable air of one who knew the world, and who would not have felt abashed at the governor's dinner table or in King William's[21] court, were it possible that his affairs should call him thither[22]. But the only thing about him that could be fixed upon as remarkable was his staff, which bore the likeness of a great black snake, so curiously wrought that it might almost be seen to twist and wriggle itself like a living serpent[23]. This, of course, must have been an ocular deception, assisted by the uncertain light.

"Come, Goodman Brown," cried his fellow-traveller, "this is a dull pace for the beginning of a journey. Take my staff, if you are so soon weary."

"Friend," said the other, exchanging his slow pace for a full stop, "having kept covenant[24] by meeting thee here, it is my purpose now to return whence I came. I have scruples touching the matter thou wot'st of."

"Sayest thou so?" replied he of the serpent, smiling apart. "Let us walk on, nevertheless, reasoning as we go; and if I convince thee not thou shalt turn back. We are but a little way in the forest yet."

"Too far! too far!" exclaimed the goodman, unconsciously resuming his walk. "My father never went into the woods on such an errand, nor his father before him. We have been a race of honest men and good Christians since the days of the martyrs;

and shall I be the first of the name of Brown that ever took this path and kept — "

"Such company, thou wouldst say," observed the elder person, interpreting his pause. "Well said, Goodman Brown! I have been as well acquainted with your family as with ever a one among the Puritans; and that's no trifle to say. I helped your grandfather, the constable, when he lashed the Quaker woman so smartly through the streets of Salem; and it was I that brought your father a pitch-pine knot[25], kindled at my own hearth, to set fire to an Indian village, in King Philip's war. They were my good friends, both; and many a pleasant walk have we had along this path, and returned merrily after midnight. I would fain be friends with you for their sake."

"If it be as thou sayest," replied Goodman Brown, "I marvel they never spoke of these matters; or, verily, I marvel not, seeing that the least rumor of the sort would have driven them from New England. We are a people of prayer, and good works to boot, and abide no such wickedness."

"Wickedness or not," said the traveller with the twisted staff, "I have a very general acquaintance here in New England. The deacons of many a church have drunk the communion[26] wine with me; the selectmen of divers towns make me their chairman; and a majority of the Great and General Court are firm supporters of my interest. The governor and I, too — But these are state secrets."

"Can this be so?" cried Goodman Brown, with a stare of amazement at his undisturbed companion. "Howbeit, I have nothing to do with the governor and council; they have their own ways, and are no rule for a simple husbandman like me. But, were I to go on with thee, how should I meet the eye of that good old man, our minister, at Salem village? Oh, his voice would make me tremble both Sabbath day and lecture day[27]."

Thus far the elder traveller had listened with due gravity; but now burst into a fit of irrepressible mirth, shaking himself so violently that his snake-like staff actually seemed to wriggle in sympathy.

"Ha! ha! ha!" shouted he again and again; then composing himself, "Well, go on, Goodman Brown, go on; but, prithee, don't kill me with laughing."

"Well, then, to end the matter at once," said Goodman Brown, considerably nettled, "there is my wife, Faith. It would break her dear little heart; and I'd rather break my own."

"Nay, if that be the case," answered the other, "e'en go thy ways, Goodman Brown. I would not for twenty old women like the one hobbling before us that Faith should come to any harm."

As he spoke he pointed his staff at a female figure on the path, in whom Goodman Brown recognized a very pious and exemplary dame, who had taught him his catechism[28] in youth, and was still his moral and spiritual adviser, jointly with the minister and Deacon Gookin[29].

"A marvel, truly, that Goody Cloyse[30] should be so far in the wilderness at nightfall," said he. "But with your leave, friend, I shall take a cut through the woods until we have left this Christian woman behind. Being a stranger to you, she might ask whom I was consorting with and whither I was going."

"Be it so," said his fellow-traveller. "Betake you to the woods, and let me keep the path."

Accordingly the young man turned aside, but took care to watch his companion, who advanced softly along the road until he had come within a staff's length of the old dame. She, meanwhile, was making the best of her way, with singular speed for so aged a woman, and mumbling some indistinct words — a prayer, doubtless — as she went. The traveller put forth his staff and touched her withered neck with what seemed the serpent's tail.

"The devil!" screamed the pious old lady.

"Then Goody Cloyse knows her old friend?" observed the traveller, confronting her and leaning on his writhing stick.

"Ah, forsooth, and is it your worship indeed?" cried the good dame. "Yea, truly is it, and in the very image of my old gossip, Goodman Brown, the grandfather of the silly fellow that now is. But — would your worship believe it? — my broomstick hath strangely disappeared, stolen, as I suspect, by that unhanged witch, Goody Cory[31], and that, too, when I was all anointed with the juice of smallage, and cinquefoil, and wolf's bane — "

"Mingled with fine wheat and the fat of a new-born babe," said the shape of old Goodman Brown.

"Ah, your worship knows the recipe," cried the old lady, cackling aloud. "So, as I was saying, being all ready for the meeting, and no horse to ride on, I made up my mind to foot it; for they tell me there is a nice young man to be taken into communion to-night. But now your good worship will lend me your arm, and we shall be there in a twinkling[32]."

"That can hardly be," answered her friend. "I may not spare you my arm, Goody Cloyse; but here is my staff, if you will."

So saying, he threw it down at her feet, where, perhaps, it assumed life, being one of the rods which its owner had formerly lent to the Egyptian Magi. Of this fact, however, Goodman Brown could not take cognizance. He had cast up his eyes in astonishment, and, looking down again, beheld neither Goody Cloyse nor the serpentine staff, but his fellow-traveller alone, who waited for him as calmly as if nothing had happened.

"That old woman taught me my catechism," said the young man; and there was a world of meaning in this simple comment.

They continued to walk onward, while the elder traveller exhorted his companion to make good speed and persevere in the path, discoursing so aptly that his arguments seemed rather to spring up in the bosom of his auditor than to be suggested by himself. As they went, he plucked a branch of maple to serve for a walking stick, and began to strip it of the twigs and little boughs, which were wet with evening dew. The moment his fingers touched them they became strangely withered and dried up as with a week's sunshine. Thus the pair proceeded, at a good free pace, until suddenly, in a gloomy hollow of the road, Goodman Brown sat himself down on the stump of a tree and refused to go any farther.

"Friend," said he, stubbornly, "my mind is made up. Not another step will I budge on this errand. What if a wretched old woman do choose to go to the devil when I thought she was going to heaven: is that any reason why I should quit my dear Faith and go after her?"

"You will think better of this by and by," said his acquaintance, composedly. "Sit here and rest yourself a while; and when you feel like moving again, there is my staff to help you along."

Without more words, he threw his companion the maple stick, and was as speedily out of sight as if he had vanished into the deepening gloom. The young man sat a few moments by the roadside, applauding himself greatly, and thinking with how clear a conscience he should meet the minister in his morning walk, nor shrink from the eye of good old Deacon Gookin. And what calm sleep would be his that very night, which was to have been spent so wickedly, but so purely and sweetly now, in the arms of Faith! Amidst these pleasant and praiseworthy meditations, Goodman Brown heard the tramp of horses along the road, and deemed it advisable to conceal himself within the verge of the forest, conscious of the guilty purpose that had brought him thither, though now so happily turned from it.

On came the hoof tramps and the voices of the riders, two grave old voices, conversing soberly as they drew near. These mingled sounds appeared to pass along the road, within a few yards of the young man's hiding-place; but, owing doubtless to the depth of the gloom at that particular spot, neither the travellers nor their steeds were visible. Though their figures brushed the small boughs by the wayside, it could not be seen that they intercepted, even for a moment, the faint gleam from the strip of bright sky athwart which they must have passed. Goodman Brown alternately crouched and stood on tiptoe, pulling aside the branches and thrusting forth his head as far as he durst without discerning so much as a shadow. It vexed him the more, because he could have sworn, were such a thing possible, that he recognized the voices of the minister and Deacon Gookin, jogging along quietly, as they were wont to do, when bound to some ordination[33] or ecclesiastical council[34]. While yet within hearing, one of the riders stopped to pluck a switch.

"Of the two, reverend sir," said the voice like the deacon's, "I had rather miss an ordination dinner than to-night's meeting. They tell me that some of our community are to be here from Falmouth and beyond, and others from Connecticut and Rhode Island, besides several of the Indian powwows[35], who, after their fashion, know almost as much deviltry as the best of us. Moreover, there is a goodly young woman to be taken into communion."

"Mighty well, Deacon Gookin!" replied the solemn old tones of the minister. "Spur up[36], or we shall be late. Nothing can be done, you know, until I get on the ground."

The hoofs clattered again; and the voices, talking so strangely in the empty air, passed on through the forest, where no church had ever been gathered or solitary Christian prayed. Whither, then, could these holy men be journeying so deep into the heathen wilderness? Young Goodman Brown caught hold of a tree for support, being ready to sink down on the ground, faint and overburdened with the heavy sickness of his heart. He looked up to the sky, doubting whether there really was a heaven above him. Yet there was the blue arch, and the stars brightening in it.

"With heaven above and Faith below, I will yet stand firm against the devil!" cried Goodman Brown.

While he still gazed upward into the deep arch of the firmament and had lifted his hands to pray, a cloud, though no wind was stirring, hurried across the zenith and hid the brightening stars. The blue sky was still visible, except directly overhead, where this black mass of cloud was sweeping swiftly northward. Aloft in the air, as if from the depths of the cloud, came a confused and doubtful sound of voices. Once the listener fancied that he could distinguish the accents of towns-people of his own, men and women, both pious and ungodly, many of whom he had met at the communion table, and had seen others rioting at the tavern. The next moment, so indistinct were the sounds, he doubted whether he had heard aught but the murmur of the old forest, whispering without a wind. Then came a stronger swell of those familiar tones, heard daily in the sunshine at Salem village, but never until now from a cloud of night. There was one voice of a young woman, uttering lamentations, yet with an uncertain sorrow, and entreating for some favor, which, perhaps, it would grieve her to obtain; and all the unseen multitude, both saints and sinners, seemed to encourage her onward.

"Faith!" shouted Goodman Brown, in a voice of agony and desperation; and the echoes of the forest mocked him, crying, "Faith! Faith!" as if bewildered wretches were seeking her all through the wilderness.

The cry of grief, rage, and terror was yet piercing the night, when the unhappy husband held his breath for a response. There was a scream, drowned immediately in a louder murmur of voices, fading into far-off laughter, as the dark cloud swept away, leaving the clear and silent sky above Goodman Brown. But something fluttered lightly down through the air and caught on the branch of a tree. The young man seized it, and beheld a pink ribbon.

"My Faith is gone![37]" cried he, after one stupefied moment. "There is no good on earth; and sin is but a name. Come, devil; for to thee is this world given."

And, maddened with despair, so that he laughed loud and long, did Goodman Brown grasp his staff and set forth again, at such a rate that he seemed to fly along the forest path rather than to walk or run. The road grew wilder and drearier[38] and more faintly traced, and vanished at length, leaving him in the heart of the dark wilderness, still rushing onward with the instinct that guides mortal man to evil. The whole forest was peopled with frightful sounds — the creaking of the trees, the howling of wild beasts, and the yell of Indians; while sometimes the wind tolled like a distant church bell, and sometimes gave a broad roar around the traveller, as if all Nature were laughing him to scorn. But he was himself the chief horror of the scene, and shrank not from its other horrors.

"Ha! ha! ha!" roared Goodman Brown when the wind laughed at him.

"Let us hear which will laugh loudest. Think not to frighten me with your deviltry. Come witch, come wizard, come Indian powwow, come devil himself, and here comes Goodman Brown. You may as well fear him as he fear you."

In truth, all through the haunted forest there could be nothing more frightful than the figure of Goodman Brown. On he flew among the black pines, brandishing his staff with frenzied gestures, now giving vent to an inspiration of horrid blasphemy, and now shouting forth such laughter as set all the echoes of the forest laughing like demons around him. The fiend in his own shape is less hideous than when he rages in the breast of man. Thus sped the demoniac on his course, until, quivering among the trees, he saw a red light before him, as when the felled trunks and branches of a clearing have been set on fire, and throw up their lurid blaze against the sky, at the hour of midnight. He paused, in a lull of the tempest that had driven him onward, and heard the swell of what seemed a hymn, rolling solemnly from a distance with the weight of many voices. He knew the tune; it was a familiar one in the choir of the village meeting-house. The verse died heavily away, and was lengthened by a chorus, not of human voices, but of all the sounds of the benighted wilderness pealing in awful harmony together. Goodman Brown cried out, and his cry was lost to his own ear by its unison with the cry of the desert.

In the interval of silence he stole forward until the light glared full upon his eyes. At one extremity of an open space, hemmed in by the dark wall of the forest, arose a rock, bearing some rude, natural resemblance either to an alter or a pulpit, and surrounded by four blazing pines, their tops aflame, their stems untouched, like candles at an evening meeting. The mass of foliage that had overgrown the summit of the rock was all on fire, blazing high into the night and fitfully illuminating the whole field. Each pendent twig and leafy festoon was in a blaze. As the red light arose and fell, a numerous congregation[39] alternately shone forth, then disappeared in shadow, and again grew, as it were, out of the darkness, peopling the heart of the solitary woods at once.

"A grave and dark-clad company," quoth Goodman Brown.

In truth they were such. Among them, quivering to and fro between gloom and splendor, appeared faces that would be seen next day at the council board of the province, and others which, Sabbath after Sabbath, looked devoutly heavenward, and benignantly over the crowded pews, from the holiest pulpits in the land. Some affirm that the lady of the governor was there. At least there were high dames well known to her, and wives of honored husbands, and widows, a great multitude, and ancient maidens, all of excellent repute, and fair young girls, who trembled lest their mothers should espy them. Either the sudden gleams of light flashing over the obscure field bedazzled Goodman Brown, or he recognized a score of the church members of Salem village famous for their especial sanctity. Good old Deacon Gookin had arrived, and waited at the skirts of that venerable saint, his revered pastor. But, irreverently consorting with these grave, reputable, and pious people, these elders of the church, these chaste dames and dewy virgins, there were men of dissolute lives and women of spotted fame, wretches given over to all mean and filthy vice, and suspected even of horrid crimes. It was strange to see that the good shrank not from the wicked, nor were the sinners abashed by the saints. Scattered also among their pale-faced enemies were the Indian priests, or powwows, who had often scared their native forest with more hideous incantations than any known to English witchcraft.

"But where is Faith?" thought Goodman Brown; and, as hope came into his heart, he trembled.

Another verse of the hymn arose, a slow and mournful strain, such as the pious love, but joined to words which expressed all that our nature can conceive of sin, and darkly hinted at far more. Unfathomable to mere mortals is the lore of fiends. Verse after verse was sung; and still the chorus of the desert swelled between like the deepest tone of a mighty organ; and with the final peal of that dreadful anthem there came a sound, as if the roaring wind, the rushing streams, the howling beasts, and every other voice of the unconcerted wilderness were mingling and according with the voice of guilty man in homage to the prince of all. The four blazing pines threw up a loftier flame, and obscurely discovered shapes and visages of horror on the smoke wreaths above the impious assembly. At the same moment the fire on the rock shot redly forth and formed a glowing arch above its base, where now appeared a figure. With reverence be it spoken, the figure bore no slight similitude, both in garb and manner, to some grave divine of the New England churches.

"Bring forth the converts[40]!" cried a voice that echoed through the field and rolled into the forest.

At the word, Goodman Brown stepped forth from the shadow of the trees and approached the congregation, with whom he felt a loathful brotherhood by the sympathy of all that was wicked in his heart. He could have well-nigh sworn that the shape of his own dead father beckoned him to advance, looking downward from a smoke wreath, while a woman, with dim features of despair, threw out her hand to warn him back. Was it his mother? But he had no power to retreat one step, nor to resist, even in thought, when the minister and good old Deacon Gookin seized his arms and led him to the blazing rock. Thither came also the slender form of a veiled female, led between Goody Cloyse, that pious teacher of the catechism, and Martha Carrier, who had received the devil's promise to be queen of hell. A rampant hag was she. And there stood the proselytes beneath the canopy of fire.

"Welcome, my children," said the dark figure, "to the communion of your race. Ye have found thus young your nature and your destiny. My children, look behind you!"

They turned; and flashing forth, as it were, in a sheet of flame, the fiend worshippers were seen; the smile of welcome gleamed darkly on every visage.

"There," resumed the sable form, "are all whom ye have reverenced from youth. Ye deemed them holier than yourselves, and shrank from your own sin, contrasting it with their lives of righteousness and prayerful aspirations heavenward. Yet here are they all in my worshipping assembly. This night it shall be granted you to know their secret deeds: how hoary-bearded elders of the church have whispered wanton words to the young maids of their households; how many a woman, eager for widows' weeds[41], has given her husband a drink at bedtime and let him sleep his last sleep in her bosom; how beardless youths have made haste to inherit their fathers' wealth; and how fair damsels — blush not, sweet ones — have dug little graves in the garden, and bidden me, the sole guest to an infant's funeral. By the sympathy of your human hearts for sin ye shall scent out all the places — whether in church, bedchamber, street, field, or forest — where crime has been committed, and shall exult to behold the whole earth one stain of guilt, one mighty blood spot. Far more than this. It shall be yours to penetrate, in every bosom, the deep mystery of sin, the fountain of all wicked arts, and which inexhaustibly supplies more evil impulses than human power — than my power at its utmost — can make manifest in deeds. And now, my children, look upon each other."

They did so; and, by the blaze of the hell-kindled torches, the wretched man beheld his Faith, and the wife her husband, trembling before that unhallowed altar.

"Lo, there ye stand, my children," said the figure, in a deep and solemn tone, almost sad with its despairing awfulness, as if his once angelic nature could yet mourn for our miserable race. "Depending upon one another's hearts, ye had still hoped that virtue were not all a dream[42]. Now are ye undeceived. Evil is the nature of mankind. Evil must be your only happiness. Welcome again, my children, to the communion of your race."

"Welcome," repeated the fiend worshippers, in one cry of despair and triumph.

And there they stood, the only pair, as it seemed, who were yet hesitating on the verge of wickedness in this dark world. A basin was hollowed, naturally, in the rock. Did it contain water, reddened by the lurid light? or was it blood? or, perchance, a liquid flame? Herein did the shape of evil dip his hand and prepare to lay the mark of baptism upon their foreheads, that they might be partakers of the mystery of sin, more conscious of the secret guilt of others, both in deed and thought, than they could now be of their own. The husband cast one look at his pale wife, and Faith at him. What polluted wretches would the next glance show them to each other, shuddering alike at what they disclosed and what they saw!

"Faith! Faith!" cried the husband, "look up to heaven, and resist the wicked one."

Whether Faith obeyed he knew not. Hardly had he spoken when he found himself amid calm night and solitude, listening to a roar of the wind which died heavily away through the forest. He staggered against the rock, and felt it chill and damp; while a hanging twig, that had been all on fire, besprinkled his cheek with the coldest dew.

The next morning young Goodman Brown came slowly into the street of Salem village, staring around him like a bewildered man. The good old minister was taking a walk along the graveyard to get an appetite for breakfast and meditate his sermon, and bestowed a blessing, as he passed, on Goodman Brown. He shrank from the venerable saint as if to avoid an anathema. Old Deacon Gookin was at domestic worship, and the holy words of his prayer were heard through the open window. "What God doth the wizard pray to?" quoth Goodman Brown. Goody Cloyse, that excellent old Christian, stood in the early sunshine at her own lattice, catechizing a little girl who had brought her a pint of morning's milk. Goodman Brown snatched away the child as from the grasp of the fiend himself. Turning the corner by the meeting-house, he spied the head of Faith, with the pink ribbons, gazing anxiously forth, and bursting into such joy at sight of him that she skipped along the street and almost kissed her husband before the whole village. But Goodman Brown looked sternly and sadly into her face, and passed on without a greeting.

Had Goodman Brown fallen asleep in the forest and only dreamed a wild dream of a witch-meeting?

Be it so if you will; but, alas! it was a dream of evil omen for young Goodman Brown. A stern, a sad, a darkly meditative, a distrustful, if not a desperate man did he become from the night of that fearful dream. On the Sabbath day, when the congregation were singing a holy psalm, he could not listen because an anthem of sin rushed loudly upon his ear and drowned all the blessed strain. When the minister spoke from the pulpit with power and fervid eloquence, and, with his hand on the open *Bible*, of the sacred truths of our religion, and of saint-like lives and triumphant deaths, and of future bliss or misery unutterable, then did Goodman Brown turn pale, dreading lest the roof should thunder down upon the gray blasphemer and his hearers. Often, waking suddenly at midnight, he shrank from the bosom of Faith; and at morning or eventide, when the family knelt down at prayer, he scowled and muttered to himself, and gazed sternly at his wife, and turned away. And when he had lived long, and was borne to his grave a hoary corpse, followed by Faith, an aged woman, and children and grandchildren, a goodly procession, besides neighbors not a few, they carved no hopeful verse upon his tombstone, for his dying hour was gloom.

Notes

1. "Young Goodman Brown" is an allegorical tale, in which Hawthorne touches many themes, such as witchcraft, the sins of fathers, hypocrisy and Puritan guilt. The protagonist is a young man from Salem. His wife is named Faith. He sets off on a journey through the dark woods, and returns home a changed man after undergoing some horrible experiences.

2. Salem village: There was a witch trial here. The Salem witch trials were a series of hearings and prosecutions of people accused of witchcraft in colonial Massachusetts, between February 1692 and May 1693.

3. parting kiss: farewell kiss.

4. Faith: seems like a pure, good wife, but betrays her husband and attends the evil meeting. She might be faithless and disloyal.

5. aptly: in a suitable or appropriate manner.

6. pink ribbon: Pink ribbon is one of the important symbols in "Young Goodman Brown", which is closely associated with the theme, the man's original sin. Pink ribbon does appear several times at critical moments in the psychological development of Goodman Brown. It is the key symbol signifying his initial illusion about the true significance of his faith and belief. He believes his faith will lead him to heaven if he sticks to it after one more indulgence in sin. After his journey into the forest, the pink ribbons on his wife's head have also become as untruthful and absurd as the other faithful people in his cynical eyes.

7. prithee: It's an old English interjection formed from a corruption of the phrase "pray you".

8. troubled with such dreams and such thoughts: Faith's claim that she is "troubled with such dreams and such thoughts" is significant. For Puritans, one's thoughts and dreams pose a real danger to one's spiritual well-being because sin is not limited to physical actions. This claim suggests that Faith herself is not as innocent and pure as Goodman Brown believes her to be.

9. afeard: frightened; afraid.

10. tarry away from thee: stay away from you.

11. forth and back: move from one place to another and back again repeatedly.

12. dost thou: do you, from old English.

13. thy: you.

14. Methought: I think.

15. no, no: the repetition in "no, no" shows a small amount of suspicion on Goodman Brown's part, as if he has to persuade himself that Faith couldn't think about such things. This is the first indication of the suspicion he has for his Puritan community and faith.

16. cling to her skirts: stay with her together throughout his life.

17. peculiarity in such a solitude: This suggests that a traveler may believe himself alone but actually be watched by an "unseen multitude". This description creates tension and an apprehensive tone in the text and foreshadows the multitude to come.

18. the devil: It entices Goodman Brown to evil.

19. in grave and decent attire: well-dressed.

20. agone: ago.

21. King William: This is a reference to William III, also known as William of Orange, who ruled as king of England from 1689 to 1702, the time in which "Young Goodman Brown" is set.

22. thither: to or towards that place.

23. serpent: snake, symbolizes the evil.

24. covenant: It refers to an agreement, in particular one that is solemn and binding. The word has been historically associated with making a covenant with God to be a Christian. Because Goodman Brown had previously vowed to journey into the woods to meet the devil, his covenant is an inversion of his Puritan faith.

25. pitch-pine knot: A "knot" is usually a combining of parts of one or more ropes, strips of cloth, or anything flexible enough to bind. The compound adjective "pitch-pine" refers to the "pitch", or sap, from a "pine", a type of evergreen tree. A pitch-pine knot then is likely highly flammable, and such a thing could be thrown into a village and cause a fire — exactly like what the devil says Goodman Brown's father

did.

26. communion: At Christian masses or services, one of the acts that believers participate in is called "communion", a custom which emphasizes the personal sacrifice of Jesus Christ and his relationship to Christians.

27. Sabbath day and lecture day: Since the Puritans were Christian, the "Sabbath" refers to Sunday, a day of rest observed by Christians in prayer and service. The "lecture day" here possibly refers to a mid-week church meeting.

28. catechism: refers to a series of set religious questions and answers based on a book of instruction in the principles of the Christian faith. Puritans like Goodman Brown would have learned a series of questions and answers to confirm their faith and then use them during church services.

29. the minister and Deacon Gookin: seem like pious Puritans, but they attend the evil meeting.

30. Goody Cloyse: teaches catechism while attending the evil meeting.

31. Cory: The name "Cory" is a possible reference to Martha Corey, who was one of the women accused of witchcraft during the Salem witch trials. She was a respectable community member who was eventually hanged for witchcraft, despite Hawthorne's saying that she is "unhanged".

32. twinkling: it means the time required for a wink, which is instantaneous for the purpose of this expression.

33. ordination: refers to the ceremony in which an individual takes a vow to become a preacher or priest.

34. ecclesiastical council: refers to a meeting in which church administration or religious matters are discussed.

35. powwow: The word originates from North American Indian culture and tradition. It can refer to a religious or magical ceremony. It also can refer to a council or conference of Native Americans. Regardless of the nature of the meeting, the Puritan viewed powwow as a kind of non-Christian, or pagan, behavior.

36. spur up: means to increase speed. It comes from the practice of using spurs to prick a horse in order to make it go faster.

37. My Faith is gone: Brown emphasizes the relationship between his wife and his Puritan faith. Goodman Brown's beliefs rely on appearances and the behavior of

his peers, creating an extreme ideology that doesn't allow for nuance.

38. wilder and drearier: Here, by saying that the road has grown "wilder and drearier", Hawthorne conveys a lack of order, or a promotion of discord. That the road falls into disarray and eventually vanishes completely reflects what has happened to Goodman Brown's faith. Where once the road could take him safely back to Salem, now he has no clear path forward: Goodman Brown is a sinner.

39. congregation: the presence of a "congregation" in the "heart of the solitary woods" reveals the pervasiveness of evil. A "congregation" typically refers to a group of people who gather for a church service, giving this word religious and moral connotations.

40. convert: it is generally used as a religious term to refer to someone who accepts a new faith. Here, the meaning is twisted as the converts are not accepting Christianity; they are turning to the devil.

41. widows' weeds: likely refers to the mourning clothes worn after the death of a woman's husband. The devil continues to emphasize how many people have performed sinful deeds when not in the public eye.

42. dream: The choice of words here, "dream" specifically, suggests that the rest of the story may follow in a dream-like fashion.

Questions for Discussion

(1) What is the purpose of the writer in mentioning the similarity between Goodman Brown and his fellow traveler? What is the central idea behind this story? Explain in details to support your interpretation.

(2) Would the meaning of the story be different had the story been a mere dream? Explore and interpret the symbolic meanings of: Faith, Goodman, the forest, the staff, and the congregation in the forest.

(3) "Young Goodman Brown" is Nathaniel Hawthorne's representative short story. The use of metaphors of names in the story provides readers with ample space for imagination and thinking. A lot of Hawthorne's works, including "Young Goodman Brown", have close ties with the small town where he lives. Give some examples of names with metaphor and their connotative meanings.

(4) The implication of the story is profound, with symbolism in the description of scenes, things, colors, and characters. Give some specific examples on the symbolism of "pink" and "brown".

Suggested Reading

- Nathaniel Hawthorne. *Twice-Told Tales*. Modern Library Inc., 2001.
- 霍桑：《红字》，苏福忠译，上海：上海译文出版社，2011年。
- 文化部教育局编：《西方现代哲学与文艺思潮》，上海：上海文艺出版社，1987年。

8. Walt Whitman

Walt Whitman (1819–1892) was profoundly influenced by wars. The main theme of his living and writing is the growing importance of the city, industry and science in America. He pioneered new forms of poetry.

Whitman was born in Brooklyn, and after ten years, the family moved to Long Island. At a young age, Whitman took interest in reading and writing after being exposed to the printing industry. In fact, much of his learning was self-taught and by the time he was 12, he had already become proficient in several literary works including those of Shakespeare's, Homer's and Dante's. He worked in New York City as a printer, until he was forced to leave because of an accident. At the age of 17, he was employed to be a teacher in a school in Long Island and then decided to be a journalist and editor in New Orleans. It was here that he became aware of the harshness of slavery. While serving as an editor, Whitman expanded his horizons and became more fascinated with poetry. In 1855, he published his book called *Leaves of Grass* and subsequently revised it several times. During the Civil War, he took a keen interest in freelance journalism, always spending much time traveling and visiting wounded soldiers in the hospitals of New York City. It was during this time that he suffered from several tragedies, including poverty, his mother's death and a stroke.

But by 1882, he had saved enough money to buy his own house in Camden, New Jersey. Whitman died on March 26, 1892, and his tomb was designed by himself.

Walt Whitman is an American poet, journalist, and essayist whose verse collection *Leaves of Grass*, first published in 1855, is a landmark in the history of American literature. He is a poet with a strong sense of mission, having devoted himself to the creation of *Leaves of Grass*. The work has nine editions, the first one being published in 1855. This masterpiece portrays the sense of openness, freedom and individualism. His aim is to express new poetical feelings and to initiate a poetic tradition in which differences should be recognized. Whitman's chief concern in poetry is to show how humankind might achieve freedom through nature, for the mind and body through democracy, for heart through love, and for the soul through religion. He always applies repetition, parallelism, rhetorical methods, phrases instead of the foot as a unit of rhythm. His techniques have influenced later generations of poets.

Song of Myself

(Excerpt)

1

I[1] CELEBRATE myself, and sing myself,

And what I assume you shall assume,

For every atom belonging to me as good belongs to you.

I loafe and invite my soul[2],

I lean and loafe at my ease observing a spear of summer grass.

My tongue, every atom of my blood, form'd from this soil, this air,

Born here of parents born here from parents the same, and their parents the same,

I, now thirty-seven years old in perfect health begin,

Hoping to cease not till death.

Creeds and schools in abeyance[3],

Retiring back a while sufficed at what they are, but never forgotten,

I harbor for good or bad, I permit to speak at every hazard,

Nature without check with original energy.

2

Houses and rooms are full of perfumes, the shelves are crowded with perfumes,

I breathe the fragrance myself and know it and like it,

The distillation would intoxicate[4] me also, but I shall not let it.

The atmosphere is not a perfume, it has no taste of the distillation, it is odorless,

It is for my mouth forever, I am in love with it,

I will go to the bank by the wood and become undisguised[5] and naked,

I am mad for it to be in contact with me.

The smoke of my own breath,

Echoes, ripples[6], buzz'd whispers, love-root, silk-thread, crotch and vine,

My respiration and inspiration, the beating of my heart, the passing of blood and air through my lungs,

The sniff of green leaves and dry leaves, and of the shore and dark-color'd sea-rocks, and of hay in the barn,

The sound of the belch'd words of my voice loos'd to the eddies of the wind,

A few light kisses, a few embraces, a reaching around of arms,

The play of shine and shade on the trees as the supple boughs wag,

The delight alone or in the rush of the streets, or along the fields and hill-sides,

The feeling of health, the full-noon trill, the song of me rising from bed and meeting the sun.[7]

Notes

1. I: If the narrator "I" were completely self-absorbed, he would not be so interesting. Here, "I" is the self as part of the American nation, "a spear of summer grass" in the prairie. The narrator as the embodiment of American individualism, shows the typical character traits: he is a loafer who is free-spirited, optimistic and in glowing health.

2. I loafe and invite my soul: He speaks of his body as a way to universalize his self. "I am the poet of the body, /And I am the poet of the soul... I am the poet of the woman the same as the man." In a clearly transcendentalist ethos, he lets his soul record in a succession of vignettes and reflections the landscape wonder of America and he celebrates, through his songs, values of democracy. The tone is elevated.

3. abeyance: the condition of being temporarily set aside.

4. intoxicate: to excite by alcohol or a drug, especially to the point where physical and mental control is markedly diminished.

5. undisguised: not disguised or concealed.

6. ripple: to form or display little waves on the surface, as disturbed water does.

7. Whitman's major technical innovation in poetry is his use of "free verse". "Free verse" is the kind of poetry that does not follow a regular meter, does not rhyme, and does not use regular line lengths. Each line is end-stopped and is a rhythmic unit. In more conventionalized poetry, a poet sometimes stops a sentence and begins another in the middle of a line. This is often used to guarantee a designed rhythm pattern or rhyme scheme.

Questions for Discussion

(1) The first person pronoun "I" is used frequently in this poem. Does this show Whitman to be self-centered? Whitman's poetry is characterized by its enumerative style. Identify examples of this style in his poetry.

(2) Walt Whitman's *Song of Myself* is one of his longest and most representative poems, expressing his strong intention of seeking a definition of "self" and achieving self-consciousness. What attitudes are implied with this sense of "self"?

O Captain! My Captain![1]

1

O CAPTAIN! my Captain! our fearful trip[2] is done;
The ship has weather'd every rack[3], the prize[4] we sought is won;
The port is near, the bells I hear, the people all exulting,
While follow eyes the steady keel, the vessel grim and daring:
　　　But O heart! heart! heart!
　　　　O the bleeding drops of red,
　　　　　Where on the deck my Captain lies,
　　　　　　Fallen cold and dead.

2

O Captain! my Captain! rise up and hear the bells;

Rise up — for you the flag is flung — for you the bugle trills;

For you bouquets and ribbon'd wreaths — for you the shores a-crowding;

For you they call, the swaying mass, their eager faces turning;

    Here Captain! dear father!

    This arm beneath your head[5];

    It is some dream that on the deck,

    You've fallen cold and dead.

3

My Captain does not answer, his lips are pale and still;

My father does not feel my arm, he has no pulse nor will;

The ship is anchor'd safe and sound, its voyage closed and done;

From fearful trip, the victor ship, comes in with object won[6];

    Exult, O shores, and ring, O bells!

    But I, with mournful tread,

    Walk the deck my Captain lies,

    Fallen cold and dead.

Notes

1. "O Captain! My Captain!" is also a very famous poem by Whitman about a ship in war and how the crew love their Captain. This poem was written in honor of president Abraham Lincoln after his assassination. At the end of the Civil War in 1865, Abraham Lincoln, the symbol of democracy and progress, was assassinated by William Booth who did not agree with Lincoln in abolishing slavery. Lincoln's death shocked the whole country. The abolishment of slavery is not only a progress of America, but of the whole world. Lincoln's death is a great loss for Americans. In this poem, Whitman uses the "captain" to symbolize Lincoln at the helm, and the "ship" to represent the United States of America sailing into the harbor having survived the storm of the Civil War. Whitman skillfully uses conceptual metaphor by referring to daily visible ship activities that are vivid and easy to understand and remember yet concrete to associate with the suffering of the whole country.

2. our fearful trip: symbolizes the Civil War.

3. The ship has weather'd every rack: the ship has successfully come through all the storms and challenges.

4. the prize: refers to the abolition of slavery.

5. This arm beneath your head: note the abundance of images in the poem. After showing successive images, Whitman now creates a picture of a sorrowful son putting his arms under the head of his beloved father.

6. The ship is anchor'd... with object won: The two lines echo the beginning lines.

Questions for Discussion

(1) What is the significance of the American Civil War and the contribution of President Lincoln? In what way does Whitman express his profound love for Lincoln and his desperate sorrow for his death?

(2) "O Captain! My Captain!" is an extended metaphor poem written in 1865 by Walt Whitman about the death of American president Abraham Lincoln. The poem is popular among Americans. Much symbolism can be seen in the poem to express Whitman's deep sorrow for the death of Abraham Lincoln. Cite some examples that illustrate symbolism in this poem.

(3) Linguistically, allegory refers to an expressive style that uses fictional characters and events to describe some subjects by suggestive resemblances like an extended metaphor. This poem is written in the form of an allegory. How does this method add to the effect of the poem?

Suggested Reading

- 惠特曼：《草叶集》，北京：人民文学出版社，1987 年。
- 李野光：《惠特曼研究》，上海：上海外语教育出版社，2003 年。
- 张丹：《对惠特曼作品〈草叶集〉中隐喻的认知研究》，载《语文建设》，2015 年第 2 期。

9. Emily Dickinson

Emily Dickinson (1830–1886) is America's best-known female poet and writer in the 19th century. The main themes of her works include the essence of love, sexuality, the nature of death, the horrors of war, God and religious belief and so on.

She was born into a severely religious, puritanical family that had lived in New England for eight generations. To some extent, she lived in a quite wealthy family. Emily Dickinson's paternal grandfather, Samuel Dickinson, had almost single-handedly founded Amherst College. Her father Edward Dickinson was a very wealthy, successful, and prominent lawyer and politician. As a young girl, she was educated at Amherst Academy and Mount Holyoke Female Seminary in South Hadley, Massachusetts for only one year due to health problems. Around 1850, she began writing poetry. During her lifetime, she wrote 1,775 poems. In 1886, she found herself slowly becoming an invalid. Even though she was only 56 years old, she was suffering from Bright's disease. She died on May 15, 1886 and was buried in a white coffin in Amherst.

Her major works include "I Heard a Fly Buzz — When I Died —", "If You Were Coming in the Fall", "I Cannot Live with You", "I'm 'Wife' — I've Finished That", "Because I Could Not Stop for Death —", "This Is My Letter to the World", "I Like to See It Lap the Miles". Dickinson's poems are actually derived from her own experiences, sorrows, and joys. But within her little lyrics the main themes of those poems are religion, death, immortality, love and nature. Although she believed in God, she sometimes doubted His benevolence. Closely related to Dickinson's religious poetry are her poems concerning death and immortality, ranging over the physical as well as the psychological and emotional aspects of death. She looked at death from the point of view of both the living and the dying. She even imagined her own death, the loss of her own body, and the journey of her soul to the unknown. Perhaps Dickinson's greatest depiction of the moment of death is to be found in "I Heard a Fly Buzz — When I Died —", a poem universally considered to be one of her masterpieces.

I Heard a Fly Buzz — When I Died —

I heard a Fly buzz — when I died —
The stillness in the Room
Was like the stillness in the Air —
Between the Heaves of Storm —

The Eyes around — had wrung when them dry —
And breaths were gathering firm
For that last Onset[1] — when the King[2]
Be witnessed — in the Room —

I willed my keepsakes[3] — Signed away
What portion of me be
Assignable — and then it was
There interposed[4] a Fly —

With Blue — uncertain — stumbling Buzz —
Between the light — and me —
And then the windows failed — and then
I could not see to see —

Because I Could Not Stop for Death —[5]

Because I could not stop for Death —
He kindly stopped for me —
The carriage held but just ourselves —
And Immortality.

We slowly drove — he knew no haste
And I had put away
My labor and my leisure too,

For his civility —

We passed the school, where children strove
At recess — in the ring —
We passed the fields of gazing grain —
We passed the setting sun —

Or rather — he passed us —
The dews grew quivering and chill —
For only gossamer, my gown —
My tippet — only tulle —

We paused before a house that seemed
A swelling of the ground —
The roof was scarcely visible —
The cornice — but a mound —

Since then — 'tis centuries — and yet
Feels shorter than the day
I first surmised the horses' heads
Were toward eternity —

Wild Nights — Wild Nights!

Wild nights — Wild nights!
Were I with thee,
Wild nights should be
Our luxury!

Futile — the winds —
To a heart in port —
Done with the compass —

Done with the chart!

Rowing in Eden —
Ah — the sea!
Might I but moor — tonight —
In thee!

A Bird, Came down the Walk —

A bird, came down the walk —
He did not know I saw —
He bit an angle-worm in halves
And ate the fellow, raw,

And then, he drank a dew
From a convenient grass —
And then hopped sidewise to the wall
To let a beetle pass —

He glanced with rapid eyes
That hurried all abroad —
They looked like frightened beads, I thought,
He stirred his velvet head. —

Like one in danger, cautious,
I offered him a crumb,
And he unrolled his feathers,
And rowed him softer home —

Than oars divide the ocean,
Too silver for a seam,
Or butterflies, off banks of noon,

Leap, plashless as they swim.

This Is My Letter to the World

This is my letter[6] to the world,
That never wrote to me —
The simple news that Nature told —
With tender majesty.

Her message is committed
To hands I cannot see —
For love of her — sweet — countrymen —
Judge tenderly — of me

I Know That He Exists.

I know that He exists.
Somewhere — in Silence —
He has hid his rare life
From our gross eyes.

'Tis an instant's play —
'Tis a fond Ambush —
Just to make Bliss
Earn her own surprise!

But — should the play
Prove piercing earnest —
Should the glee — glaze —
In Death's — stiff — stare —

Would not the fun

Look too expensive!

Would not the jest —

Have crawled too far!

Notes

1. last Onset: It's an oxymoron. "Onset" means a beginning and "last" means an end. For Christians, death is the beginning of eternal life.

2. King: Probably refers to God in this context and they are all awaiting his entry to the room to take the soul of the narrator.

3. keepsakes: These keepsakes could be materials that the narrator collected during life, which would be useless in heaven. This line discusses the tradition of willing away property and material belongings.

4. interpose: means to come between or intervene.

5. Because I Could Not Stop for Death —: It is made up of 6 stanzas and uses a traditional meter called "common meter". The poem's lines are arranged in iambs.

6. letter: perhaps means this poem. Dickinson wants to express her ideas and feelings to the outer world through her poems, but the world does not understand her (as indicated by the second line).

Questions for Discussion

(1) The fly is the most important image in "I Heard a Fly Buzz — When I Died — ". It makes its appearance in the very beginning of the poem and dominates the last stanza. What does the fly suggest? Does the fly indicate that death has no spiritual significance, that there is no eternity or immortality for us?

(2) "With Blue — uncertain — stumbling Buzz — / Between the light — and me — / And then the windows failed — and then / I could not see to see — " In this stanza, what is the author's attitude towards immortality?

(3) "And breaths were gathering firm / For that last Onset — when the King / Be witnessed — in the Room — " In the three lines, we cannot find the fear of death, but only experiences the dead waiting for God. Why is Emily so calm?

(4) "This Is My Letter to the World" contains many vowels, so the rhythm is

slow and the tone is calm. In what way does the author express her inner feeling?

Suggested Reading

- Emily Dickinson. *The Poems of Emily Dickinson*. State College, PA: Pennsylvania State University Press, 2003.
- 狄金森：《狄金森诗选》（英汉对照），江枫译，北京：外语教学与研究出版社，2016 年。

10. Edgar Allan Poe

Edgar Allan Poe (1809–1849), American short-story writer, poet, critic, and editor. He is the father of modern short story, father of detective story, father of psychoanalytic criticism, forerunner of western decadent literature, forerunner of aesthetic literature, explorer of abnormal psychology.

On January 19, 1809, Poe was left an orphan after his mother passed away suddenly after childbirth. The young Poe was raised by John Allan of Richmond, Virginia. It was in Richmond where he grew up and flourished in his career. Poe studied at the University of Virginia for just one semester before turning his aspirations towards enlistment at West Point. Failing to be an officer's cadet at West Point did not slow down or deter Poe as he soon bounced back to embark on the next phase of his life as a writer. In 1827, he published his first collection *Tamerlane and Other Poems* under the name "a Bostonian".

Before settling down and marrying his 13-year old cousin Virginia Clemm in 1835, he had worked for talented writers and poets in Philadelphia, New York City and Baltimore. The newlyweds made Baltimore their home as both married life and Poe's literally career begun to flourish. Poe published the poem "The Raven" in 1845 which became his most highly received poem by the literary world. Two years after the release of this successful poem, Poe's wife died of tuberculosis. Poe passed away on October 7, 1849 at the age of 40, leaving behind the unproduced journal named

The Penn. This journal would later be entitled *The Stylus*. Poe's works eventually transcend for centuries to come and continue to receive both praise and acclaim today.

His major works include *Tales of the Grotesque and Arabesque*, "MS. Found in a Bottle", "The Murders in the Rue Morgue", "The Fall of the House of Usher", "The Raven", "Israfel", "Annabel Lee", "To Helen". His tale "The Murders in the Rue Morgue" initiated the modern detective story, and the atmosphere in his tales of horror is unrivaled in American fiction. His "The Raven" numbers among the best-known poems in the American literature.

Annabel Lee[1]

It was many and many a year ago,
 In a kingdom by the sea,
That a maiden there lived whom you may know
 By the name of Annabel Lee;
And this maiden she lived with no other thought
 Than to love and be loved by me.

I was a child and *she* was a child,
 In this kingdom by the sea,
But we loved with a love that was more than love —
 I and my Annabel Lee —
With a love that the wingèd seraphs of Heaven[2]
 Coveted her and me.

And this was the reason that, long ago,
 In this kingdom by the sea,
A wind blew out of a cloud, chilling
 My beautiful Annabel Lee;
So that her highborn kinsmen came
 And bore her away from me,
To shut her up in a sepulchre

In this kingdom by the sea.

The angels, not half so happy in Heaven,
  Went envying her and me —
Yes! — That was the reason (as all men know,
  In this kingdom by the sea)
That the wind came out of the cloud by night,
  Chilling and killing my Annabel Lee.

But our love it was stronger by far than the love
  Of those who were older than we —
  Of many far wiser than we —
And neither the angels in Heaven above,
  Nor the demons down under the sea,
Can ever dissever my soul form the soul
  Of the beautiful Annabel Lee;

For the moon never beams, without bringing me dreams[3]
  Of the beautiful Annabel Lee;
And the stars never rise, but I feel the bright eyes
  Of the beautiful Annabel Lee;
And so, all the night-tide, I lie down by the side
  Of my darling — my darling — my life and my bride,
  In her sepulchre there by the sea —
  In her tomb by the sounding sea.[4]

Notes

1. "Annabel Lee", like other poems of Edgar Allan Poe, describes the theme of the death of a beautiful woman which is called "the most poetical topic in the world" by the poet himself. In the poem, the narrator and Annabel Lee had an extremely strong love for each other since they were children. Unfortunately, their love is so

strong that even angels envy them and Annabel Lee was killed by them. However, the narrator retains a deep love for her even after her death. Just as the last stanza shows us, the narrator dreams about Annabel every day and lies by the side of her tomb at night. It seems that their love is beyond the grave and death. This poem is known for its melodious flow of sound and rhythm. The elaborately coined name by Poe "Annabel Lee", the frequent use of repetition, and some other poetic devices in the poem all make it musical.

2. wingèd seraphs of Heaven: angels of the highest rank standing in the presence of God, each with six wings.

3. In poetry, if rhyme occurs within a verse line, it is called internal rhyme. In this stanza, internal rhyme is used in several places: as in this line, "beams" rhymes with "dreams", and "rise" with "eyes" and "tide" with "side" in the following lines.

4. Poe believes that beauty is the sole purpose of the poem. He insists on an even metrical flow in versification. This poem is mainly written in anapestic trimeter, tetrameter, and sometimes dimeter. The poem consists of six stanzas and different stanzas are different in the number of lines and length, which creates melancholy and sad feeling to the readers. The rhyme scheme of the first stanza is ababcb; the second stanza is abcbdb; the third stanza is abcbdbcb; and rhyme schemes of the last three stanzas are abcbdb, abbabcb, abcbddbb. From here, you can see that rhyme scheme is not so regular among each stanza. So Poe stresses rhythm, and defines true poetry as "the rhythmical creation of beauty".

Questions for Discussion

(1) Most critics believe that this poem refers to Poe's wife, while others argue that the poem is about Elmira Shelton, a sweetheart of Poe's youth whose family had broken their early love affair. Poe was engaged to her again just before his death in 1849. What lines in the poem could have different interpretations according to each of these two possibilities?

(2) Repetition is one of the techniques often used in poetry. How is repetition used in this poem, that enhances emotional appeal, its simplicity of style as well as its sound effects?

Suggested Reading

- 埃德加·爱伦·坡：《爱伦·坡短篇故事全集》，上海：上海世界图书出版公司，2008 年。
- 刘象愚编选：《爱伦·坡精选集》，济南：山东文艺出版社，1999 年。
- 王李云：《〈安娜贝尔·李〉：爱情、死亡与唯美意境》，载《短篇小说》（原创版），2014 年第 35 期。

11. Henry Wadsworth Longfellow

Henry Wadsworth Longfellow (1807–1882), the most popular American poet in the 19th century, is known for such works as *The Song of Hiawatha* and "Paul Revere's Ride". Longfellow predominantly wrote lyrical poems which are known for their musicality and which often presented stories of mythology and legend. He became the most popular American poet of his day and also has success overseas.

Longfellow attended private schools and the Portland Academy. He graduated from Bowdoin College in 1825. At college, he was absorbed in Sir Walter Scott's romances and Washington Irving's *The Sketch Book*, and his verses appeared in American national magazines. He was so fluent in translating that on graduation he was offered a professorship in modern languages provided that he would first study in Europe. While in Europe he learned French, Spanish, and Italian but refused to accept a regimen of scholarship at any university. In 1829 he returned to the United States to be a professor and librarian at Bowdoin. He wrote and edited textbooks, translated poetry and prose, and wrote essays on French, Spanish, and Italian literature. However, he felt isolated. When he was offered a professorship at Harvard, with another opportunity to go abroad, he accepted it. During this trip, he visited England, Sweden, and the Netherlands. In 1835, he was saddened by the death of his first wife whom he had married in 1831. Then he settled in Heidelberg where he fell under the influence of German Romanticism.

His major works include *Voices of the Night, Ballads and Other Poems, The*

Song of Hiawatha. Though many of his works are featured as lyric poetry, Longfellow experimented with many other forms. His published poetry shows great versatility, varying in several subjects: European civilization, hardworking spirit, bravery and creativity of laboring people, peace and war, slavery and oppression. Filled with rich and colorful imagery, his poetry has a lyrical beauty with a vivid and beautiful rhyme and rhythm. Because of his simple language and his traditional style and subjects, his poems are widely popular with people of different walks of life.

The Tide Rises, the Tide Falls[1]

The tide rises, the tide falls[2],
The twilight darkens, the curlew calls[3];
Along the sea-sands damp and brown
The traveller hastens toward the town,
    And the tide rises, the tide falls.

Darkness settles on roofs and walls,
But the sea, the sea in the darkness calls;
The little waves, with their soft, white hands,
Efface the footprints in the sands,
    And the tide rises, the tide falls.

The morning breaks; the steeds in their stalls
Stamp and neigh, as the hostler calls;
The day returns, but nevermore
Returns the traveller to the shore[4],
    And the tide rises, the tide falls[5].

Notes

1. "The Tide Rises, the Tide Falls" has three stanzas of five lines each, and the rhyme scheme is aabba, aacca, aadda. The words and phrases "twilight", "traveller hastens" in stanza 1, "darkness", "efface the footprints" in stanza 2, "morning",

"nevermore returns" in stanza 3 show the changing time of a day. And the changing actually refers to the natural world as well as the life stages of human beings. It is the underlying cycle of life.

2. The rhymed words "falls" (stalls) and "calls" repeated in all the three stanzas are to make the transition between stanzas smoother. And with these repeated words, the whole poem is of tidy rhyme and pattern in order. The poem shows the poet's changing feelings. In the first two stanzas, the poet shows the traveller walks in darkness leaving even no footprints, which gives a feeling of sorrow and hopelessness to the readers.

3. "Call" is used many times in the poem, but they mean differently. The calls from curlew and the sea is nature calling, which show the charm of nature. The hostler calls for his real life.

4. "The tide rises, the tide falls" that repeat four times in the poem and "but nevermore/Returns the traveller to the shore" show that the sea and the world around us continue on no matter what we do or where we go. Time marches on as the tide rises and falls. Human beings are powerless before nature. Time and nature are eternal but human life is transient.

5. In the last stanza, "the day returns" and "the tide rises, the tide falls" show the poet's acceptance of nature's principles and realization of death as everyone's predetermined fate.

Questions for Discussion

(1) Longfellow wrote "The Tide Rises, the Tide Falls" as he was getting old and facing death, expressing his acceptance of eventual loss of fame and glory and facing calmly the approaching death. What is the figurative meaning of the title "The Tide Rises, the Tide Falls"?

(2) What message about the relationship between human beings and nature does the poem convey? What message about the differences between human beings and the natural world does it convey? What is the insight gained through the observation of nature?

(3) Both poetry and music function as the natural flow and expression of

experiences and emotions of human beings. "The Tide Rises, the Tide Falls" suggests its own musical logic including sound imitation, meter, and melody. What does the poet mean in stanza 3: "The day returns, but nevermore/Returns the traveller to the shore"?

The Arrow and the Song[1]

I shot an arrow in the air,
It fell to earth, I knew not where;
For so swiftly[2] it flew, the sight
Could not follow it in its flight[3].

I breathed a song into the air,
It fell to earth, I knew not where;
For who has sight so keen[4] and strong,
That it can follow the flight of song?

Long, long afterward, in an oak[5]
I found the arrow, still unbroke;
And the song, from beginning to end,
I found again in the heart of a friend.

Notes

1. In this poem, Longfellow compares the arrow to life, and the songs are compared to feelings. Even though songs (feelings) are unseen, they are still real. The arrow could also be compared to negative words shot from our mouths, and the song could be joyful words shared with others.

2. swiftly: in a swift manner.

3. flight: an instance of traveling by air.

4. keen: intense or sharp.

5. oak: the hard durable wood of the oak tree; used especially for furniture and flooring.

Questions for Discussion

(1) Describe the tone of the poem. What effect does the word "afterward" in line 9 have on the tone of the poem?

(2) The key to appreciate this poem is to understand the symbolic meanings of "arrow" and "song". What do "arrow" and "song" actually mean?

Suggested Reading

- Henry Wadsworth Longfellow. *Henry Wadsworth Longfellow: Representative Selections, with Introduction, Bibliography, and Notes.* Odell Shepard, ed. New York, NY: American Book Company, 1934.
- Newton Arvin. *Longfellow: His Life and Work.* New York, NY: Little, Brown and Company, 1963.
- 柳士军：《世界文学视域下的朗费罗诗歌研究》，北京：新华出版社，2016年。

Part Three

American Realism

12. Mark Twain

After American Civil War, American literature entered a new stage: romantic literature gradually declined and realistic literature rose. Mark Twain was an outstanding humorous and satirical writer of this realistic stage. With the ideals of bourgeois democracy, freedom and equality, he exposed and criticized American society with his humorous, comical, and satirical writings.

Mark Twain, or Samuel Langhorne Clemens (1835–1910) was born in Florida, Missouri. His parents settled in Hannibal, Missouri, on the Mississippi River in 1839. At the age of twelve, after his father's death, he was forced to leave school and apprenticed to a printer. In 1851, he went to work for his brother's newspaper. From 1856 to 1861, he supported himself on the Mississippi River as a steamboat pilot. And a wealth of material was accumulated for his masterworks during this period of time. It was from his job on the boat that he got to use "Mark Twain" as the pen name. He began to write satires and short stories in the 1860s. In 1865, he became famous with a humorous story "The Celebrated Jumping Frog of Calaveras County". During the Civil War, Mark Twain joined the Confederate army for a short while, then returned to his old business as a printer in Nevada and California, and later as a miner and journalist. In 1870, he married Olivia Langdon and soon settled in Hartford, Connecticut. From early 1870s to early 1890s, Mark Twain produced many works, and the major ones include *The Innocents Abroad*, *The Gilded Age: A Tale of Today*, *The Adventures of Tom Sawyer*, *A Tramp Abroad*, *The Prince and the Pauper*, *Life on the*

Mississippi, Adventures of Huckleberry Finn. These works, especially *The Adventures of Tom Sawyer* and *Adventures of Huckleberry Finn* with the exciting description of young characters experiencing particular horrors and joys, have been extremely popular readings among children and adults, and established Mark Twain's position in the literary world. In 1893, Mark Twain suffered a major bankruptcy from a failure in investment, and was forced to pay the debt by giving lectures around the world. The untimely death of his wife and two daughters inevitably led to the great change in his creative style: the humorous and comical elements were less evident in his works. "The Man That Corrupted Hadleyburg" is an obvious example of Twain's negativity and pessimism. Twain's thoughts gradually deepened, and the pessimistic views towards world conditions and human natures were largely contained in his works. In his later works like *Following the Equator*, Twain began to criticize the various colonial and aggressive behaviors of imperialism. Sarcasm revealed the author's dissatisfaction and anger. He died in Connecticut on April 21, 1910.

Mark Twain's humor is remarkable. He is rich in imagination, humor and exaggeration, and he often uses naive and innocent people as protagonists to make a contrast between phenomenon and essence, fantasy and reality. "Running for Governor" was such a satiric essay, where he exposed the deception of "democratic election" advertised by the bourgeoisie as "an expression of the people's free will". Mark Twain exaggerated to the extreme in this satire the tendency of bourgeois newspapers to disregard facts while specializing in spreading rumors, making it a wonderful political cartoon about democratic elections at that time.

Running for Governor

A few months ago I was nominated for Governor of the great State of New York, to run against Stewart L. Woodford and John T. Hoffman, on an independent ticket[1]. I somehow felt that I had one prominent advantage over these gentlemen, and that was, good character. It was easy to see by the newspapers, that if ever they had known what it was to bear a good name, that time had gone by. It was plain that in these latter years they had become familiar with all manner of shameful crimes. But at the very moment that I was exalting my advantage and joying in it in secret, there was a muddy undercurrent of discomfort "riling" the deeps of my happiness — and that was, the having to hear my name bandied about in familiar connection with those of such people. I grew more and more disturbed. Finally I wrote my grandmother about it. Her answer came quick and sharp[2]. She said:

You have never done one single thing in all your life to be ashamed of — not one. Look at the newspapers — look at them and comprehend what sort of characters Woodford and Hoffman are, and then see if you are willing to lower yourself to their level and enter a public canvass with them.

It was my very thought[3]! I did not sleep a single moment that night. But after all, I could not recede. I was fully committed and must go on with the fight. As I was looking listlessly over the papers at breakfast, I came across this paragraph, and I may truly say I never was so confounded[4] before:

PERJURY. — Perhaps, now that Mr. Mark Twain is before the people as a candidate for Governor, he will condescend to explain how he came to be convicted of perjury by thirty-four witnesses, in Wakawak, Cochin China[5], in 1863, the intent of which perjury was to rob a poor native widow and her helpless family of a meagre plantain patch, their only stay and support in their bereavement and their desolation. Mr. Twain owes it to himself, as well as to the great people whose suffrages[6] he asks, to clear this matter up. Will he do it?

I thought I should burst with amazement! Such a cruel, heartless charge — I never had seen Cochin China! I never had heard of Wakawak! I didn't know a plantain patch from a kangaroo! I did not know what to do. I was crazed and helpless. I let the day slip away without doing anything at all. The next morning the same paper had this — nothing more:

SIGNIFICANT. — Mr. Twain, it will be observed, is suggestively silent about the Cochin China perjury.

[Mem.[7] — During the rest of the campaign this paper never referred to me in any other way than as "the infamous perjurer Twain".]

Next came the "Gazette[8]," with this:

WANTED TO KNOW. — Will the new candidate for Governor deign to explain to certain of his fellow-citizens (who are suffering to vote for him!) the

little circumstance of his cabin-mates in Montana losing small valuables from time to time, until at last, these things having been invariably found on Mr. Twain's person or in his "trunk" (newspaper he rolled his traps in), they felt compelled to give him a friendly admonition for his own good, and so tarred and feathered him and rode him on a rail, and then advised him to leave a permanent vacuum in the place[9] he usually occupied in the camp. Will he do this?

Could anything be more deliberately malicious than that? For I never was in Montana in my life.

[After this, this journal customarily spoke of me as "Twain, the Montana Thief".]

I got to picking up papers apprehensively — much as one would lift a desired blanket which he had some idea might have a rattlesnake under it. One day this met my eye:

THE LIE NAILED! — By the sworn affidavits of Michael O'Flanagan, Esq.[10], of the Five Points, and Mr. Kit Burns and Mr. John Allen, of Water Street, it is established that Mr. Mark Twain's vile statement that the lamented grandfather of our noble standard-bearer[11], John T. Hoffman, was hanged for highway robbery, is a brutal and gratuitous LIE, without a single shadow of foundation in fact. It is disheartening to virtuous men to see such shameful means resorted to achieve political success as the attacking of the dead in their graves and defiling their honored names with slander. When we think of the anguish this miserable falsehood must cause the innocent relatives and friends of the deceased, we are almost driven to incite an outraged and insulted public to summary and unlawful vengeance upon the traducer. But no — let us leave him to the agony of a lacerating conscience — (though if passion should get the better of the public and in its blind fury they should do the traducer bodily injury, it is but too obvious that no jury could convict and no court punish the perpetrators of the deed).

The ingenious closing sentence had the effect of moving me out of bed with dispatch that night, and out at the back door, also, while the "outraged and insulted public" surged in the front way, breaking furniture and windows in their righteous indignation as they came, and taking off such property as they could carry when they went. And yet I can lay my hand upon the Book and say that I never slandered Governor Hoffman's grandfather. More — I had never even heard of him or mentioned him, up to that day and date.

[I will state, in passing, that the journal above quoted from always referred to me afterward as "Twain, the Body-Snatcher".]

The next newspaper article that attracted my attention was the following:

A SWEET CANDIDATE. — Mark Twain, who was to make such a blighting speech at the mass meeting of the Independents last night, didn't come to time! A telegram from his physician stated that he had been knocked down by a runaway team and his leg broken in two places — sufferer lying in great agony, and so forth, and so forth, and a lot more bosh[12] of the same sort. And the Independents tried hard to swallow the wretched subterfuge[13] and pretend that they did not know what was the real reason of the absence of the abandoned creature whom they denominate their standard-bearer. A certain man was seen to reel into Mr. Twain's hotel last night in state of beastly intoxication. It is the imperative duty of the Independents to prove that this besotted brute was not Mark Twain himself: We have them at last! This is a case that admits of no shirking. The voice of the people demands in thunder-tones: "WHO WAS THAT MAN?"

It was incredible, absolutely incredible, for a moment, that it was really my name that was coupled with this disgraceful suspicion. Three long years had passed over my head since I had tasted ale, beer, wine, or liquor of any kind.

[It shows what effect the times were having on me when I say that I saw myself confidently dubbed "Mr. Delirium Tremens[14] Twain" in the next issue of that journal without a pang — notwithstanding I knew that with monotonous fidelity the paper would go on calling me so to the very end.]

By this time anonymous letters were getting to be an important part of my mail matter. This form was common:

How about that old woman you kiked of your premises which was beging.
POL PRY[15].

And this:

There is things which you have done which is unbeknowens to anybody but me.

You better trot out a few dots, to yours truly, or you'll hear thro' the papers from
HANDY ANDY.

That is about the idea. I could continue them till the reader was surfeited, if desirable.

Shortly the principal Republican journal "convicted" me of wholesale bribery, and the leading Democratic paper "nailed" an aggravated case of blackmailing to me.

[In this way I acquired two additional names: "Twain, the Filthy Corruptionist", and "Twain, the Loathsome Embracer".]

By this time there had grown to be such a clamor for an "answer" to all the dreadful charges that were laid to me, that the editors and leaders of my party said it would be political ruin for me to remain silent any longer. As if to make their appeal the more imperative, the following appeared in one of the papers the very next day:

BEHOLD THE MAN! — The Independent candidate still maintains Silence. Because he dare not speak. Every accusation against him has been amply proved, and they have been endorsed and re-endorsed by his own eloquent silence till at this day he stands forever convicted. Look upon your candidate, Independents! Look upon the Infamous Perjurer! the Montana Thief! the Body-Snatcher! Contemplate your incarnate Delirium Tremens! Your Filthy Corruptionist! Your Loathsome Embracer![16] **Gaze upon him — ponder him well — and then say if you can give your honest votes to a creature who has earned this dismal array of titles by his hideous crimes, and dares not open his mouth in denial of any one of them!**

There was no possible way of getting out of it, and so, in deep humiliation, I set about preparing to "answer" a mass of baseless charges and mean and wicked falsehoods. But I never finished the task, for the very next morning a paper came out with a new horror, a fresh malignity, and seriously charged me with burning a lunatic asylum with all its inmates because it obstructed the view from my house. This threw me into a sort of panic. Then came the charge of poisoning my uncle to get his property, with an imperative demand that the grave should be opened. This drove me to the verge of distraction. On top of this I was accused of employing toothless and incompetent old relatives to prepare the food for the foundling hospital when I was warden. I was wavering — wavering. And at last, as a due and fitting climax to the shameless persecution that party rancor had inflicted upon me, nine little toddling children of all shades of color and degrees of raggedness were taught to rush on to the platform at a public meeting and clasp me around the legs and call me PA!

I gave up. I hauled down my colors and surrendered.[17] I was not equal to the requirements of a Gubernatorial campaign[18] in the State of New York, and so I sent in my withdrawal from the candidacy, and in bitterness of spirit signed it,

"Truly yours,

"Once a decent man, but now

"MARK TWAIN, I. P., M. T., B. S., D. T., F. C., and L. E.[19]"

Notes

1. on an independent ticket: an independent candidate who does not belong to a particular party.

2. sharp: sudden, critical and unsympathetic.

3. It was my very thought: That is exactly what I thought.

4. confounded: puzzled or confused by something.

5. Cochin China: the region that forms the southern part of present-day Vietnam.

6. suffrage: the right to vote in public elections.

7. Mem.: means the remark section.

8. Gazette: a newspaper, especially a local newspaper or the official paper of an organization.

9. leave a permanent vacuum in the place: leave the position empty forever.

10. Esq.: Esquire, a polite title written after a man's name, especially on an official letter addressed to him. If "Esq". is used, "Mr." is not then used.

11. standard-bearer: a leader in a political group or campaign.

12. bosh: tosh or nonsense.

13. subterfuge: a plan, action, or device designed to hide a real objective, or the process of hiding a real objective.

14. Delirium Tremens: a nervous and quivering situation, accompanied with symptoms of a psychiatric disorder which is caused by alcohol dependence and withdrawal.

15. POL PRY: a meddler or busy-body.

16. Look upon the Infamous… Loathsome Embracer!: Mr. Mark Twain, or "I" in this satire plays an honest people who felt that he himself had "prominent advantage" and "good character" than other candidates at the very beginning when he was nominated for Governor. But "I" started to lose joy and happiness as he was maliciously defamed by the array of crime titles got from different parties of newspaper though he had no connection with these committed charges.

17. I hauled down my colors and surrendered: I ceased all activities running for Governor.

18. Gubernatorial campaign: the campaign connected with the job of state governor.

19. I. P., M. T., B. S., D. T., F. C., and L. E.: the crime titles imposed on Mark Twain or the "I", were repeatedly mentioned here with their Capital letters, with the function of highlighting the ironic and satiric effect.

Questions for Discussion

(1) "Running for Governor" is not conceived in accord with the three elements of fiction writing. Mark Twain does not portray the direct conflict between "I" and "my" opponents through the character, event and environment description, nor does he describe the intense campaign. Still, the intensity and unfairness of the campaign and the strong attack and combat among the opponents are real. Discuss and analyze this unique feature of Mark Twain's writing conception in this short story.

(2) Mark Twain uses humorous language throughout the short story. His use of humor not only makes people laugh, but also allows people to see what is hidden in laughter, what is reflected in society and in human nature. Identify plots or situations that are funny, absurd and ridiculous while at the same time arouse readers' reflection.

(3) Mark Twain's short stories are good at using naive and innocent people to reveal the phenomenon and essence, fantasy and reality. The story of "Running for Governor" is also recounted by a good and senseless person. In addition to self-sarcasm, "I" also participated in the structural irony, which highlighted the irony effect of the whole story. If the narrator here is replaced instead by someone who is shrewd

and familiar with the rules of the campaign, will the irony effect be diminished? Why?

Suggested Reading

- Donald Pizer 编：《剑桥文学指南：美国现实主义和自然主义》，上海：上海外语教育出版社，2000 年。
- Forrest G. Robinson 编：《剑桥文学指南：马克·吐温》，上海：上海外语教育出版社，2001 年。
- Mark Twain. *The Signet Classic Book of Mark Twain's Short Stories*. Justin Kaplan and Debble Macomber, eds. Signet Classics, 2015.
- 马克·吐温：《哈克贝利·费恩历险记》，北京：外语教学与研究出版社，2020 年。
- 马克·吐温：《马克·吐温短篇小说集》，董强译，上海：上海三联书店，2010 年。

13. Bret Harte

Bret Harte (1836–1902) is an American writer who is known as one of the pioneers who initiated the "local color" writing in American literature, which focus on the life of miners in the West, imageries of remote forest areas, poor rural areas in the Midwest, ancient legends in the mountains, scenery of fishing islands, and stories of southern plantations, all of which have less been mentioned before American Civil War.

Harte was born in Albany, New York. His father was a Greek professor and died when Harte was nine years old, then his mother moved to California to reorganize her family. Harte dropped out of school at the age of thirteen and worked respectively as gold miner, printer, middle school teacher and editor. He worked for the journals *The Northern Californian*, *The Atlantic Monthly*, *The Golden Era* and some other publications as well. In 1868, after publishing a series of Spanish folklore, he was hired as the editor-in-chief of *Overland Monthly*, the first important publication in the West, which became a turning point in Harte's creative career. He successively published "The Luck of Roaring Camp" and "The Outcasts of Poker Flat", propelling him to fame nationwide. He also wrote the script to *Ah Sin* with Mark Twain. Till 1871, Harte won compliments among contemporaries like Henry Wadsworth Longfellow and Oliver Wendell Holmes. With his fame, he began lecturing and even working as a professor on literary creation at the University of California, but the lectures were not warmly welcomed with his growing reputation. His later works created after moving to New York were mediocre. After his retirement in 1885, he lived in England as a sojourner. He died on May 5, 1902 in London.

As a well-known writer on native American literature, Harte is very good at using a humorous and lyrical style to describe the joys of life of the ebullient gold diggers in the West. The gamblers, alcoholics, prostitutes and vagrants in his works may look rough, but they all have a golden heart; they are pure and innocent, full of dedication. It seems that these people always bring endless warmth to the world. This kind of romantic approach makes the description in realism more vivid and peculiar. As a result, he found a warmer critical reception for his tales of a mythic California, and his novels have been extensively translated and introduced to European countries.

The Luck of Roaring Camp

There was commotion in Roaring Camp. It could not have been a fight, for in 1850 that was not novel enough to have called together the entire settlement. The ditches and claims were not only deserted, but "Tuttle's grocery" had contributed its gamblers, who, it will be remembered, calmly continued their game the day that French Pete and Kanaka Joe shot each other to death over the bar in the front room. The whole camp was collected before a rude cabin on the outer edge of the clearing[1]. Conversation was carried on in a low tone, but the name of a woman was frequently repeated. It was a name familiar enough in the camp, — "Cherokee Sal[2]."

Perhaps the less said of her the better. She was a coarse and, it is to be feared[3], a very sinful woman. But at that time she was the only woman in Roaring Camp, and was just then lying in sore extremity[4], when she most needed the ministration of her own sex. Dissolute, abandoned, and irreclaimable, she was yet suffering a martyrdom[5] hard enough to bear even when veiled by sympathizing womanhood, but now terrible in her loneliness. The primal curse had come to her in that original isolation which must have made the punishment of the first transgression so dreadful. It was, perhaps, part of the expiation of her sin that, at a moment when she most lacked her sex's intuitive tenderness and care, she met only the half-contemptuous faces of her masculine associates. Yet a few of the spectators were, I think, touched by her sufferings. Sandy Tipton thought it was "rough on Sal", and, in the contemplation of her condition, for a moment rose superior to the fact that he had an ace and two bowers in his sleeve.

It will be seen also that the situation was novel. Deaths were by no means uncommon in Roaring Camp, but a birth was a new thing. People had been dismissed the camp effectively, finally, and with no possibility of return; but this was the first time that anybody had been introduced AB INITIO[6]. Hence the excitement.

"You go in there, Stumpy," said a prominent citizen known as "Kentuck", addressing one of the loungers. "Go in there, and see what you kin[7] do. You've had experience in them things."

Perhaps there was a fitness in the selection. Stumpy, in other climes, had been the putative head of two families; in fact, it was owing to some legal informality in these proceedings that Roaring Camp — a city of refuge — was indebted to his company. The crowd approved the choice, and Stumpy was wise enough to bow to the majority. The door closed on the extempore[8] surgeon and midwife, and Roaring Camp[9] sat down outside, smoked its pipe, and awaited the issue.

The assemblage numbered about a hundred men. One or two of these were actual fugitives from justice, some were criminal, and all were reckless. Physically they exhibited no indication of their past lives and character. The greatest scamp had a Raphael face[10], with a profusion of blonde hair; Oakhurst, a gambler, had the melancholy air and intellectual abstraction of a Hamlet; the coolest and most courageous man was scarcely over five feet in height, with a soft voice and an embarrassed, timid manner. The term "roughs" applied to them was a distinction rather than a definition. Perhaps in the minor details of fingers, toes, ears, etc., the camp may have been deficient, but these slight omissions did not detract from their aggregate force. The strongest man had but three fingers on his right hand; the best shot had but one eye.[11]

Such was the physical aspect of the men that were dispersed around the cabin. The camp lay in a triangular valley between two hills and a river. The only outlet was a steep trail over the summit of a hill that faced the cabin, now illuminated by the rising moon. The suffering woman might have seen it from the rude bunk whereon she lay, — seen it winding like a silver thread until it was lost in the stars above.

A fire of withered pine boughs added sociability to the gathering. By degrees the natural levity of Roaring Camp returned. Bets were freely offered and taken regarding the result. Three to five that "Sal would get through with it"; even that the child would survive; side bets as to the sex and complexion of the coming stranger. In the midst of an excited discussion an exclamation[12] came from those nearest the door, and the camp stopped to listen. Above the swaying and moaning of the pines, the swift rush of the river, and the crackling of the fire rose a sharp, querulous cry, — a cry unlike anything heard before in the camp. The pines stopped moaning, the river ceased to rush, and the fire to crackle. It seemed as if Nature had stopped to listen too.

The camp rose to its feet as one man! It was proposed to explode a barrel of gunpowder; but in consideration of the situation of the mother, better counsels prevailed, and only a few revolvers were discharged; for whether owing to the rude surgery of the camp, or some other reason, Cherokee Sal was sinking fast. Within an hour she had climbed, as it were, that rugged road that led to the stars, and so passed out of Roaring Camp, its sin and shame, forever. I do not think that the announcement disturbed them much, except in speculation as to the fate of the child. "Can he live now?" was asked of Stumpy. The answer was doubtful. The only other being of Cherokee Sal's sex and maternal condition in the settlement was an ass. There was some conjecture as to fitness, but the experiment was tried. It was less problematical than the ancient treatment of Romulus and Remus[13], and apparently as successful.

When these details were completed, which exhausted another hour, the door was opened, and the anxious crowd of men, who had already formed themselves into a queue, entered in single file. Beside the low bunk or shelf, on which the figure of the mother was starkly outlined below the blankets, stood a pine table. On this a candle-box was placed, and within it, swathed in staring red flannel, lay the last arrival at Roaring Camp. Beside the candle-box was placed a hat. Its use was soon indicated.

"Gentlemen," said Stumpy, with a singular mixture of authority and EX OFFICIO[14] complacency, — "gentlemen will please pass in at the front door, round the table, and out at the back door. Them as wishes to contribute anything toward the orphan will find a hat handy." The first man entered with his hat on; he uncovered, however, as he looked about him, and so unconsciously set an example to the next. In such communities good and bad actions are catching. As the procession filed in comments were audible, — criticisms addressed perhaps rather to Stumpy in the character of showman; "Is that him?" "Mighty small specimen"; "Has n't more 'n got the color"; "Ain't bigger nor a derringer."[15] The contributions were as characteristic[16]: A silver tobacco box; a doubloon; a navy revolver, silver mounted; a gold specimen; a very beautifully embroidered lady's handkerchief (from Oakhurst the gambler); a diamond breastpin; a diamond ring (suggested by the pin, with the remark from the giver that he "saw that pin and went two diamonds better"); a slung-shot; a *Bible* (contributor not detected); a golden spur; a silver teaspoon (the initials, I regret to say, were not the giver's); a pair of surgeon's shears; a lancet; a Bank of England note for 5 pounds; and about $200 in loose gold and silver coin. During these proceedings Stumpy maintained a silence as impassive as the dead on his left, a gravity as inscrutable as that of the newly born on his right. Only one incident occurred to break the monotony of the curious procession. As Kentuck bent over the candle-box half curiously, the child turned, and, in a spasm of pain, caught at his groping finger, and held it fast for a moment. Kentuck looked foolish and embarrassed. Something like a blush tried to assert itself in his weather-beaten cheek[17]. "The damned little cuss!" he said, as he extricated his finger, with perhaps more tenderness and care than he might have been deemed capable of showing. He held that finger a little apart from its fellows as he went out, and examined it curiously. The examination provoked the same original remark in regard to the child. In fact, he seemed to enjoy repeating it. "He rastled with my finger," he remarked to Tipton, holding up the member, "the damned little cuss!"

It was four o'clock before the camp sought repose[18]. A light burnt in the cabin where the watchers sat, for Stumpy did not go to bed that night. Nor did Kentuck. He drank quite freely, and related with great gusto his experience, invariably ending with his characteristic condemnation of the newcomer. It seemed to relieve him of any unjust implication of sentiment, and Kentuck had the weaknesses of the nobler sex. When everybody else had gone to bed, he walked down to the river and whistled reflectingly. Then he walked up the gulch[19] past the cabin, still whistling with demonstrative unconcern. At a large redwood-tree he paused and retraced his steps, and again passed the cabin. Halfway down to the river's bank he again paused, and then returned and knocked at the door. It was opened by Stumpy. "How goes it?" said Kentuck, looking past Stumpy toward the candle-box. "All serene[20]!" replied Stumpy. "Anything up?" "Nothing." There was a pause — an embarrassing one — Stumpy still holding the door. Then Kentuck had recourse to his finger, which he held up to Stumpy. "Rastled with it, — the damned little cuss," he said, and retired.

The next day Cherokee Sal had such rude sepulture as Roaring Camp afforded. After her body had been committed to the hillside, there was a formal meeting of the camp to discuss what should be done with her infant. A resolution to adopt it was unanimous and enthusiastic. But an animated discussion in regard to the manner and feasibility[21] of providing for its wants at once sprang up. It was remarkable that the argument partook of none of those fierce personalities with which discussions were usually conducted at Roaring Camp. Tipton proposed that they should send the child to Red Dog, — a distance of forty miles, — where female attention could be procured. But the unlucky suggestion met with fierce and unanimous opposition. It was evident that no plan which entailed parting from their new acquisition would for a moment be entertained. "Besides," said Tom Ryder, "them fellows at Red Dog would swap it, and ring in somebody else on us." A disbelief in the honesty of other camps prevailed at Roaring Camp, as in other places.

The introduction of a female nurse in the camp also met with objection. It was argued that no decent woman could be prevailed to accept Roaring Camp as her home, and the speaker urged that "they didn't want any more of the other kind". This unkind allusion to the defunct mother, harsh as it may seem, was the first spasm of propriety, — the first symptom of the camp's regeneration. Stumpy advanced nothing. Perhaps he felt a certain delicacy[22] in interfering with the selection of a possible successor in office. But when questioned, he averred stoutly that he and "Jinny" — the mammal before alluded to — could manage to rear the child. There was something original, independent, and heroic about the plan that pleased the camp. Stumpy was retained. Certain articles were sent for to Sacramento[23]. "Mind," said the treasurer, as he pressed a bag of gold-dust into the expressman's hand, "the best that can be got, — lace, you know, and filigree-work and frills, — damn the cost!"

Strange to say, the child thrived. Perhaps the invigorating climate of the mountain camp was compensation for material deficiencies. Nature took the foundling to her broader breast. In that rare atmosphere of the Sierra foothills, — that air pungent with balsamic odor, that ethereal cordial at once bracing and exhilarating, — he may have found food and nourishment, or a subtle chemistry that transmuted ass's milk to lime and phosphorus. Stumpy inclined to the belief that it was the latter and good nursing. "Me and that ass," he would say, "has been father and mother to him! Don't you," he would add, apostrophizing the helpless bundle before him, "never go back on us."

By the time he was a month old the necessity of giving him a name became apparent. He had generally been known as "The Kid", "Stumpy's Boy", "The Coyote" (an allusion to his vocal powers), and even by Kentuck's endearing diminutive of "The damned little cuss". But these were felt to be vague and unsatisfactory, and were at last dismissed under another influence. Gamblers and adventurers are generally superstitious, and Oakhurst one day declared that the baby had brought "the luck" to Roaring Camp. It was certain that of late they had been successful. "Luck" was the name agreed upon, with the prefix of Tommy for greater convenience. No allusion was made to the mother, and the father was unknown. "It's better," said the philosophical Oakhurst, "to take a fresh deal all round. Call him Luck, and start him fair." A day was accordingly set apart for the christening. What was meant by this ceremony the reader may imagine who has already gathered some idea of the reckless irreverence of Roaring Camp. The master of ceremonies was one "Boston", a noted wag, and the occasion seemed to promise the greatest facetiousness. This ingenious satirist had spent two days in preparing a burlesque of the Church service, with pointed local allusions. The choir was properly trained, and Sandy Tipton was to stand godfather. But after the procession had marched to the grove with music and banners, and the child had been deposited before a mock altar, Stumpy stepped before the expectant crowd. "It ain't my style to spoil fun, boys," said the little man, stoutly eyeing the faces around him, "but it strikes me that this thing ain't exactly on the squar. It's playing it pretty low down on this yer baby to ring in fun on him that he ain't goin' to understand. And ef there's goin' to be any godfathers round, I'd like to see who's got any better rights than me." A silence followed Stumpy's speech. To the credit of all humorists be it said that the first man to acknowledge its justice was the satirist thus stopped of his fun. "But," said Stumpy, quickly following up his advantage, "we're here for a christening, and we'll have it. I proclaim you Thomas Luck, according to the laws of the United States and the State of California, so help me God." It was the first time that the name of the Deity[24] had been otherwise uttered than profanely in the camp. The form of christening was perhaps even more ludicrous than the satirist had conceived; but strangely enough, nobody saw it and nobody laughed. "Tommy" was christened as seriously as he would have been under a Christian roof and cried and was comforted in as orthodox[25] fashion.

And so the work of regeneration[26] began in Roaring Camp. Almost imperceptibly a change came over the settlement. The cabin assigned to "Tommy Luck" — or "The Luck", as he was more frequently called — first showed signs of improvement. It was kept scrupulously clean and whitewashed. Then it was boarded, clothed, and papered. The rose wood cradle, packed eighty miles by mule, had, in Stumpy's way of putting it, "sorter killed the rest of the furniture." So the rehabilitation of the cabin became a necessity. The men who were in the habit of lounging in at Stumpy's to see "how 'The Luck' got on" seemed to appreciate the change, and in self-defense the rival establishment of "Tuttle's grocery" bestirred itself and imported a carpet and mirrors. The reflections of the latter on the appearance of Roaring Camp tended to produce stricter habits of personal cleanliness.[27] Again Stumpy imposed a kind of quarantine upon those who aspired to the honor and privilege of holding The Luck. It was a cruel mortification to Kentuck — who, in the carelessness of a large nature and the habits of frontier life, had begun to regard all garments as a second cuticle, which, like a snake's, only sloughed off through decay — to be debarred this privilege from certain prudential reasons. Yet such was the subtle influence of innovation that he thereafter appeared regularly every afternoon in a clean shirt and face still shining from his ablutions. Nor were moral and social sanitary laws neglected. "Tommy", who was supposed to spend his whole existence in a persistent attempt to repose, must not be disturbed by noise. The shouting and yelling, which had gained the camp its infelicitous title, were not permitted within hearing distance of Stumpy's. The men conversed in whispers or smoked with Indian gravity. Profanity was tacitly given up in these sacred precincts, and throughout the camp a popular form of expletive, known as "D — n the luck![28]" and "Curse the luck!" was abandoned, as having a new personal bearing[29]. Vocal music was not interdicted, being supposed to have a soothing, tranquilizing quality; and one song, sung by "Man-o'-War Jack", an English sailor from her Majesty's Australian colonies, was quite popular as a lullaby[30]. It was a lugubrious recital of the exploits of "the Arethusa, Seventy-four", in a muffled minor, ending with a prolonged dying fall at the burden of each verse, "On b-oo-o-ard of the Arethusa". It was a fine sight to see Jack holding The Luck, rocking from side to side as if with the motion of a ship, and crooning forth this naval ditty. Either through the peculiar rocking of Jack or the length of his song, — it contained ninety stanzas, and was continued with conscientious deliberation to the bitter end, — the lullaby generally had the desired effect. At such times the men would lie at full length under the trees in the soft summer twilight, smoking their pipes and drinking in the melodious utterances. An indistinct idea that this was pastoral happiness pervaded the camp. "This 'ere kind o'think[31]," said the Cockney Simmons, meditatively reclining on his elbow, "is'evingly[32]." It reminded him of Greenwich.

On the long summer days The Luck was usually carried to the gulch from whence the golden store of Roaring Camp was taken. There, on a blanket spread over pine boughs, he would lie while the men were working in the ditches below. Latterly there was a rude attempt to decorate this bower with flowers and sweet-smelling shrubs, and generally some one would bring him a cluster of wild honeysuckles, azaleas, or the painted blossoms of Las Mariposas. The men had suddenly awakened to the fact that there were beauty and significance in these trifles, which they had so long trodden carelessly beneath their feet. A flake of glittering mica, a fragment of variegated quartz, a bright pebble from the bed of the creek, became beautiful to eyes thus cleared and strengthened, and were invariably pat aside for The Luck. It was wonderful how many treasures the woods and hillsides yielded that "would do for Tommy". Surrounded by playthings such as never child out of fairyland had before, it is to he hoped that Tommy was content. He appeared to be serenely happy, albeit there was an infantine gravity about him, a contemplative light in his round gray eyes, that sometimes worried Stumpy. He was always tractable and quiet, and it is recorded that once, having crept beyond his "corral", — a hedge of tessellated pine boughs, which surrounded his bed, — he dropped over the bank on his head in the soft earth, and remained with his mottled legs in the air in that position for at least five minutes with unflinching gravity. He was extricated without a murmur. I hesitate to record the many other instances of his sagacity, which rest, unfortunately, upon the statements of prejudiced friends. Some of them were not without a tinge of superstition. "I crep' up the bank just now," said Kentuck one day, in a breathless state of excitement "and dern my skin if he was a-talking to a jay bird as was a-sittin' on his lap. There they was, just as free and sociable as anything you please, a-jawin' at each other just like two cherrybums." Howbeit, whether creeping over the pine boughs or lying lazily on his back blinking at the leaves above him, to him the birds sang, the squirrels chattered, and the flowers bloomed. Nature was his nurse and playfellow. For him she would let slip between the leaves golden shafts of sunlight that fell just within his grasp; she would send wandering breezes to visit him with the balm of bay and resinous gum; to him the tall redwoods nodded familiarly and sleepily, the bumblebees buzzed, and the rooks cawed a slumbrous accompaniment.[33]

 Such was the golden summer of Roaring Camp. They were "flush times", and the luck was with them. The claims had yielded enormously. The camp was jealous of its privileges and looked suspiciously on strangers. No encouragement was given to immigration[34], and, to make their seclusion more perfect, the land on either side of the mountain wall that surrounded the camp they duly preempted. This, and a reputation for singular proficiency with the revolver, kept the reserve of Roaring Camp inviolate. The expressman — their only connecting link with the surrounding world — sometimes told wonderful stories of the camp. He would say, "They've a street up there in 'Roaring' that would lay over any street in Red Dog.[35] They've got vines and flowers round their houses, and they wash themselves twice a day. But they're mighty rough on strangers, and they worship an Ingin baby."

 With the prosperity of the camp came a desire for further improvement. It was proposed to build a hotel in the following spring, and to invite one or two decent families to reside there for the sake of The Luck, who might perhaps profit by female companionship. The sacrifice that this concession to the sex cost these men, who were fiercely skeptical in regard to its general virtue and usefulness, can only be accounted for by their affection for Tommy. A few still held out. But the resolve could not be carried into effect for three months, and the minority meekly yielded in the hope that something might turn up to prevent it. And it did.

The winter of 1851 will long be remembered in the foothills. The snow lay deep on the Sierras[36], and every mountain creek became a river, and every river a lake. Each gorge and gulch was transformed into a tumultuous watercourse that descended the hillsides, tearing down giant trees and scattering its drift and debris along the plain. Red Dog had been twice under water, and Roaring Camp had been forewarned. "Water put the gold into them gulches," said Stumpy. "It been here once and will be here again!" And that night the North Fork suddenly leaped over its banks and swept up the triangular valley of Roaring Camp.

In the confusion of rushing water, crashing trees, and crackling timber, and the darkness which seemed to flow with the water and blot out the fair valley, but little could be done to collect the scattered camp. When the morning broke, the cabin of Stumpy, nearest the river-bank, was gone. Higher up the gulch they found the body of its unlucky owner; but the pride, the hope, the joy, The Luck, of Roaring Camp had disappeared. They were returning with sad hearts when a shout from the bank recalled them.

It was a relief-boat from down the river. They had picked up, they said, a man and an infant, nearly exhausted, about two miles below. Did anybody know them, and did they belong here?

It needed but a glance to show them Kentuck lying there, cruelly crushed and bruised, but still holding The Luck of Roaring Camp in his arms. As they bent over the strangely assorted pair, they saw that the child was cold and pulseless. "He is dead," said one. Kentuck opened his eyes. "Dead?" he repeated feebly. "Yes, my man, and you are dying too." A smile lit the eyes of the expiring Kentuck. "Dying!" he repeated; "he's a-taking me with him. Tell the boys I've got The Luck with me now;" and the strong man, clinging to the frail babe as a drowning man is said to cling to a straw, drifted away into the shadowy river that flows forever to the unknown sea.

Notes

1. clearing: a tract of land with few or no trees in the middle of a wooded area.
2. Cherokee Sal: the only woman in Roaring Camp, who offers prostitution to the

gold diggers there.

3. it is to be feared: I'm afraid to say.

4. in sore extremity: in extreme pain.

5. martyrdom: the use of this word implied that Cherokee Sal will be punished to death because of her adherence to the sin of violating morality and common ethics.

6. AB INITIO: at the beginning.

7. kin: can.

8. extempore: with little or no preparation or forethought.

9. Roaring Camp: "Roaring Camp" is taken to refer to all the males in Roaring Camp; here it is an adoption of metonymy.

10. Raphael face: the face of an angel.

11. The still mysterious western frontier is presented by the description of these "rough" men in a romantic writing.

12. exclamation: a short sound, word or phrase spoken suddenly to express an emotion.

13. Romulus and Remus: Roman legend has it that the abandoned twin brothers Romulus and Remus were nurtured by a mother wolf. Therefore Rome is also known as the country raised by wolves.

14. EX OFFICIO: An ex officio member of a committee or an organization is a member because the job he/she allows him/her to be involved. Stumpy played himself as the midwife for Cherokee Sal, now he naturally involved himself to the job of dealing with the following matters after Cherokee Sal passed away.

15. "Is that him?"... "Ain't bigger nor a derringer.": The words used by the crowd of men in appraising Stumpy's job express a variety of envy, jealousy, and mocking views.

16. as characteristic: characterized as the following.

17. weather-beaten cheek: The cheek is rough and damaged due to prolonged outdoor exposure.

18. repose: take some rest, sleep or keep calm.

19. gulch: a narrow valley with steep sides, that was formed by a fast flowing stream.

20. serene: tranquil, quiet, peaceful.

21. feasibility: possibility, viability or practicability.

22. delicacy: the need to be sensitive in order to avoid making people angry or upset.

23. Sacramento: capital city of California, located at the confluence of the Sacramento and American Rivers.

24. deity: a god.

25. orthodox: following closely to the traditional beliefs and practices of a religion.

26. regeneration: rebirth, renewal.

27. Almost imperceptibly... stricter habits of personal cleanliness: Baptizing the baby not only means that its birth is accepted and recognized by the orthodox religion, but also implies the expectation of these men that their lives can be on the right track again. Here in this paragraph, the depiction of the changes that have happened to them are just like new lives are born within each of them.

28. D — n the luck!: Damn the luck!

29. bearing: the way in which one stand, walk or behave.

30. lullaby: a soft gentle song sung to make a child sleep.

31. This 'ere kind o' think: This is the kind of what I think before.

32. is 'evingly: is evenly.

33. The baby got the best the men could give him, and they did their best to create the best for him.

34. No encouragement was given to immigration: No one was encouraged to move out from the Roaring Camp.

35. They have built a way to communicate with the outside world the Red Dog. They have become the envy of outsiders or strangers.

36. Sierras: a mountain range of Northern California.

Questions for Discussion

(1) The characters in Harte's writings cannot be judged simply by dichotomy. Just like the "round character" proposed by British novelist E. M. Forster, the characters in Harte's writings have more depth and complexity. Analyze multi-dimensional human nature from an individual or the group through the portrait of the characters in the

story.

(2) Harte's writing is in the period of transition from American naturalistic to realistic period. Are Harte's fictions considered to have inherited or refuted naturalistic environmental determinism? Why or why not?

(3) Harte's use of irony forms his unique style. In this story, how does he use irony to reinforce readers' aesthetic experience when depicting the life scenes of Roaring Camp?

Suggested Reading

- Bret Harte. *The Best of Bret Harte*. Boston, MA: Houghton Mifflin Company, 1947.
- Bret Harte. *The Best Stories of Bret Harte*. Robert N. Linscott, ed. New York, NY: The Modern Library, 1947.
- 陈许：《美国西部小说研究》，北京：北京大学出版社，2004 年。
- 何顺果：《美国边疆史：西部开发模式研究》，北京：北京大学出版社，2000 年。

14. Kate Chopin

Kate Chopin (1850–1904) is another important writer whose works have been recognized within the "local color" genre. Her works mainly reflect the life of the residents of Louisiana, the place that she is familiar with. The rural scenery and southern customs in Chopin's works are admirably exhibiting the unconventional, independence-pursuing and self-awakening perspectives by her fictional heroines.

Chopin was born in St. Louis, Missouri, to a wealthy family, all the members of the family of which are Catholics. After her father died when she was 4, Chopin grew up under the care of her great-grandmother. She received good education there, and read widely of European literature. She got married to a businessman Oscar

Chopin when she was 19. Chopin and Oscar were very happy together and had six children. However, their happiness did not last for long. In 1883 her husband died of an illness, leaving her with the responsibility of managing her husband's business for a year. Under the influence and encouragement of Dr. Kolbenheyer, Chopin decided to write and publish. Chopin began to write about the Creole and Cajun people she had observed in the South. Her first novel, *At Fault*, did not make her distinguished, but she was later widely recognized by her finely crafted short stories, which were included in the two collections *Bayou Folk* and *A Night in Acadie*. In 1899, she published the novel *The Awakening*, which caused a great deal of controversy and Chopin was consequently perceived as immoral. In the din of social consensus over *The Awakening*, Chopin wrote only seven short stories from 1900 to 1904. Chopin suffered a stroke and passed away on August 22, 1904.

Chopin started writing under the deep influence of French realist writers Flaubert and Maupassant, which always made her novels cleverly conceived, concise and full of surprises. *Désirée's Baby* and *The Story of an Hour* are two of these notable examples. Chopin is known for her ability to describe and reveal the rich and complex inner emotional world of women. Chopin believed that women as individuals, married or unmarried, should enjoy true love and lead an independent life. But the awakening of the consciousness in writing about sex appeared to be too advanced for the time, which was intolerable by the ethics of Puritanism. However, with the passage of time, Chopin's stories with the strong perspectives on female independence, especially *The Awakening*, have increasingly shown its value and won a large following, establishing her as pioneer of feminism in America.

The Story of an Hour

Knowing that Mrs. Mallard was afflicted with a heart trouble, great care was taken to break to her as gently as possible the news of her husband's death.

It was her sister Josephine who told her, in broken sentences; veiled hints that revealed in half concealing. Her husband's friend Richards was there, too, near her. It was he who had been in the newspaper office when intelligence of the railroad disaster was received, with Brently Mallard's name leading the list of "killed". He had only taken the time to assure himself of its truth by a second telegram, and had hastened to forestall[1] any less careful, less tender friend in bearing the sad message.[2]

She did not hear the story as many women have heard the same, with a paralyzed inability to accept its significance. She wept at once, with sudden, wild abandonment, in her sister's arms. When the storm of grief had spent itself she went away to her room alone. She would have no one follow her.

There stood, facing the open window, a comfortable, roomy armchair. Into this she sank, pressed down by a physical exhaustion that haunted her body and seemed to reach into her soul.

She could see in the open square before her house the tops of trees that were all aquiver[3] with the new spring life. The delicious breath of rain was in the air. In the street below a peddler was crying his wares. The notes of a distant song which some one was singing reached her faintly, and countless sparrows were twittering in the eaves.[4]

There were patches of blue sky showing here and there through the clouds that had met and piled one above the other in the west facing her window.

She sat with her head thrown back upon the cushion of the chair, quite motionless, except when a sob came up into her throat and shook her, as a child who has cried itself to sleep continues to sob in its dreams.

She was young, with a fair, calm face, whose lines bespoke repression and even a certain strength[5]. But now there was a dull stare in her eyes, whose gaze was fixed away off yonder on one of those patches of blue sky. It was not a glance of reflection, but rather indicated a suspension of intelligent thought.

There was something coming to her and she was waiting for it, fearfully. What was it[6]? She did not know; it was too subtle and elusive to name. But she felt it, creeping out of the sky, reaching toward her through the sounds, the scents, the color that filled the air.

Now her bosom rose and fell tumultuously. She was beginning to recognize this thing that was approaching to possess her, and she was striving to beat it back with her will — as powerless as her two white slender hands would have been.

When she abandoned herself a little whispered word escaped her slightly parted lips. She said it over and over under her breath: "free, free, free!" The vacant stare and the look of terror that had followed it went from her eyes. They stayed keen and bright. Her pulses beat fast, and the coursing blood warmed and relaxed every inch of her body.

She did not stop to ask if it were or were not a monstrous joy that held her. A clear and exalted perception enabled her to dismiss the suggestion as trivial.

She knew that she would weep again when she saw the kind, tender hands folded in death; the face that had never looked save with love upon her, fixed and gray and dead. But she saw beyond that bitter moment a long procession of years to come that would belong to her absolutely. And she opened and spread her arms out to them in welcome.

There would be no one to live for during those coming years; she would live for herself. There would be no powerful will bending hers in that blind persistence with which men and women believe they have a right to impose a private will upon a fellow-creature.[7] A kind intention or a cruel intention made the act seem no less a crime as she looked upon it in that brief moment of illumination.

And yet she had loved him — sometimes. Often she had not. What did it matter! What could love, the unsolved mystery, count for in face of this possession of self-assertion which she suddenly recognized as the strongest impulse of her being!

"Free! Body and soul free!" she kept whispering.

Josephine was kneeling before the closed door with her lips to the keyhole, imploring for admission. "Louise, open the door! I beg, open the door — you will make yourself ill. What are you doing Louise? For heaven's sake open the door."

"Go away. I am not making myself ill." No; she was drinking in a very elixir[8] of life through that open window.

Her fancy was running riot along those days ahead of her. Spring days, and summer days, and all sorts of days that would be her own. She breathed a quick prayer that life might be long. It was only yesterday she had thought with a shudder that life might be long.

She arose at length and opened the door to her sister's importunities[9]. There was a feverish triumph in her eyes, and she carried herself unwittingly like a goddess of Victory. She clasped her sister's waist, and together they descended the stairs. Richards stood waiting for them at the bottom.

Some one was opening the front door with a latchkey. It was Brently Mallard who entered, a little travel-stained, composedly carrying his grip-sack and umbrella. He had been far from the scene of accident, and did not even know there had been one. He stood amazed at Josephine's piercing cry; at Richards' quick motion to screen him from the view of his wife.

But Richards was too late.

When the doctors came they said she had died of heart disease — of joy that kills.[10]

Notes

1. forestall: to prevent something from happening by saying or doing something before it can happen.

2. He had only... the sad message: Richard knew that Mrs. Mallard could not bear sudden shock because of her heart trouble, so he could only uncover the news of his friend Mr. Mallard's death to the wife as tenderly as possible.

3. aquiver: quivering, especially from excitement or agitation.

4. She could see... in the eaves: The vibrant scenes, the new spring life of the trees, the delicious breath of rain, the crying from the paddler, etc., formed an open-and-shut contrast to Mrs. Mallard's grief over her husband.

5. bespoke repression and even a certain strength: The physical description of Mrs. Mallard seems to hint at her personality of embracing free choice.

6. it: The "it" which is emphasized in this paragraph indicates her self-consciousness.

7. There would be no one to live for... impose a private will upon a fellow-creature: The information conveyed from these two sentences is highly suggestive of the historical context. In particular, American wives in the late nineteenth century were legally bound to their husbands' power and status; but widows did not bear the responsibility of finding or following a husband, thus they could gain more legal freedom and recognition and often had more control over their own lives.

8. elixir: a magic liquid that is believed to cure illness or to make people live forever.

9. importunity: a demand made repeatedly or insistently.

10. The story does not end peacefully but instead creates a climactic twist. It's not Mrs. Mallard becoming free from her husband's death, but it is Mr. Mallard who becomes free of Mrs. Mallard.

Questions for Discussion

(1) Chopin is good at using symbolism. Identify the symbols used in the story to compare the current life and psychological development of the heroine.

(2) Describe how the heroine's independence consciousness went from budding to development to awakening?

(3) Chopin's attention to female independence consciousness in her works is not unrelated to her personal life experience and life choices. Describe the difference between male and female status during her time. Was she writing during the period of the feminist movement in the United States? In American history, how many feminist movements have happened?

(4) Critics believe that the ending of the story is designed to show that the best way for the heroine to pursue freedom is death. Provide support for such a sudden ending.

Suggested Reading

- Janet Beer, ed. *The Cambridge Companion to Kate Chopin*. Cambridge: Cambridge University Press, 2008.

15. Theodore Dreiser

Theodore Dreiser (1871–1945) is an American naturalist writer known for his consciousness of the harsh reality of American society. His unique dedication to American literature comes to his narrative weight, honesty to the reflection of human impulses, and his penetrative understanding of the sufferings of his characters. He is the cultural pioneer for the making of American Realism.

Theodore Dreiser was born in a poor and immigrant family at Terre Haute, Indiana. Among a dozen children, he was the second youngest one. He lived an unsettled life with the large family in various places in Indiana, and had attended some schools discontinuously. From the age of fifteen he started to work for a living from various odd jobs. When he was eighteen, he was funded to receive education at Indiana University, and a few months later he left for Chicago to work for a living. In 1892, he became a newspaper reporter for *Chicago Globe*, where he had the opportunity to learn how to observe the society from the reading of Charles Darwin, Thomas Huxley and Herbert Spencer. He began to write fictions at the time when he served as a magazine editor in New York in the year of 1894. In 1898 Dreiser married Sara White, but the marriage was not happy. In 1900, he published his first novel *Sister Carrie*, and the novel was based on the life of his sister Emma Dreiser, who ran off to New York City with a married man. Actually, the novel was reluctantly published with no advertising and got a dismal sales ultimately. The commercial failure subsequently sent Dreiser into depression and he was cured through almost one year's manual labor. Though *Sister Carrie* got many accusations and attacks from the critics, Dreiser persisted to reissue the novel in 1907 and eventually it was identified as an American classic. It was not until 1911 that he published his second novel *Jennie Gerhardt*. And almost all his main works were completed in the next fifteen years, including *The Financier*, *The Titan*, *The Genius*, *An American Tragedy*. Though generally recognized as a novelist, Dreiser also wrote and published some short stories and poems. His first collection of short stories, *Free and Other Stories* appeared in 1918, and his collected poems, *The Poetry Quartos* was published in 1929. In 1944, he received an Award of Merit from the Academy of Arts and Letters for his life achievement. Dreiser died from heart attack in Hollywood, California, on December 28, 1945.

Dreiser first came upon the literary scene at a time when both the press and popular literature often presented a false picture of life, one that overlooked its harsher aspects. With the empathy for the poor from his own Indiana poverty, and especially with the concerns to the lower classes, the minorities and the immigrants, Dreiser challenged the puritanical standards of American literature, and paved the way for American Realism, in which he believed that man's destiny is largely or even exclusively determined by heredity and environment — and has nothing to do with morality. That is why the readers are unwilling to accept that Sister Carrie succeeds with unconventional and immoral mode and her lovers exert their competence but decline in the Bourgeois competition. And the resulting personality of the individual, as combination are driven this way and that way in life, and have little or nothing to say about where to go. Hurstwood, once a proud manager of a popular saloon, slowly sinks into poverty and isolation, dies in the wretched cubicle of a hotel. Carrie, who desires comfort and nice clothes, is lured to the city and becomes Drouet's mistress, and then Hurstwood's. She becomes rich and famous but remains somehow unhappy. Dreiser's realism or naturalism was considered devastating in its exposure of the figures' fate. These tragic figures are average Americans, who wake up expecting the success of the American Dream and too often discover that it is instead an American Tragedy.

Sister Carrie

Chapter 1

The Magnet Attracting — A Walf Amid Forces

When Caroline Meeber boarded the afternoon train for Chicago, her total outfit consisted of a small trunk, a cheap imitation alligator-skin satchel, a small lunch in a paper box, and a yellow leather snap purse, containing her ticket, a scrap of paper with her sister's address in Van Buren Street, and four dollars in money. It was in August, 1889. She was eighteen years of age, bright, timid, and full of the illusions of ignorance and youth[1]. Whatever touch of regret at parting characterized her thoughts, it was certainly not for advantages now being given up[2]. A gush of tears at her mother's farewell kiss, a touch in her throat when the cars clacked by the flour mill where her father worked by the day, a pathetic sigh as the familiar green environs of the village passed in review, and the threads which bound her so lightly to girlhood and home were irretrievably broken.

To be sure there was always the next station, where one might descend and return. There was the great city, bound more closely by these very trains which came up daily. Columbia City was not so very far away, even once she was in Chicago.

What, pray, is a few hours — a few hundred miles? She looked at the little slip bearing her sister's address and wondered. She gazed at the green landscape, now passing in swift review, until her swifter thoughts replaced its impression with vague conjectures[3] of what Chicago might be.

When a girl leaves her home at eighteen, she does one of two things. Either she falls into saving hands and becomes better, or she rapidly assumes the cosmopolitan standard of virtue[4] and becomes worse. Of an intermediate balance, under the circumstances, there is no possibility[5]. The city has its cunning wiles, no less than the infinitely smaller and more human tempter. There are large forces which allure with all the soulfulness of expression[6] possible in the most cultured human. The gleam of a thousand lights is often as effective as the persuasive light in a wooing and fascinating eye. Half the undoing[7] of the unsophisticated and natural mind is accomplished by forces wholly superhuman. A blare of sound, a roar of life, a vast array of human hives, appeal to the astonished senses in equivocal terms. Without a counsellor at hand to whisper cautious interpretations, what falsehoods may not these things breathe into the unguarded ear! Unrecognized for what they are, their beauty, like music, too often relaxes, then weakens, then perverts the simpler human perceptions.

Caroline, or Sister Carrie, as she had been half affectionately termed by the family, was possessed of a mind rudimentary[8] in its power of observation and analysis. Self-interest with her was high, but not strong. It was, nevertheless, her guiding characteristic. Warm with the fancies of youth, pretty with the insipid prettiness of the formative period, possessed of a figure promising eventual shapeliness and an eye alight with certain native intelligence[9], she was a fair example of the middle American class — two generations removed from the emigrant[10]. Books were beyond her interest — knowledge a sealed book[11]. In the intuitive graces[12] she was still crude. She could scarcely toss her head gracefully. Her hands were almost ineffectual. The feet, though small, were set flatly. And yet she was interested in her charms, quick to understand the keener pleasures of life, ambitious to gain in material things. A half-equipped little knight she was, venturing to reconnoitre the mysterious city and dreaming wild dreams of some vague, far-off supremacy, which should make it prey and subject — the proper penitent, grovelling at a woman's slipper.[13]

"That," said a voice in her ear, "is one of the prettiest little resorts in Wisconsin."

"Is it?" she answered nervously.

The train was just pulling out of Waukesha. For some time she had been conscious of a man behind. She felt him observing her mass of hair. He had been fidgeting, and with natural intuition she felt a certain interest growing in that quarter. Her maidenly reserve, and a certain sense of what was conventional under the circumstances, called her to forestall and deny this familiarity, but the daring and magnetism of the individual, born of past experiences and triumphs, prevailed. She answered.

He leaned forward to put his elbows upon the back of her seat and proceeded to make himself volubly agreeable.

"Yes, that is a great resort for Chicago people. The hotels are swell. You are not familiar with this part of the country, are you?"

"Oh, yes, I am," answered Carrie. "That is, I live at Columbia City. I have never been through here, though."

"And so this is your first visit to Chicago," he observed.

All the time she was conscious of certain features out of the side of her eye. Flush, colourful cheeks, a light moustache, a grey fedora[14] hat. She now turned and looked upon him in full, the instincts of self-protection and coquetry mingling confusedly in her brain.

"I didn't say that," she said.

"Oh," he answered, in a very pleasing way and with an assumed air of mistake, "I thought you did."

Here was a type of the travelling canvasser[15] for a manufacturing house — a class which at that time was first being dubbed by the slang of the day "drummers[16]". He came within the meaning of a still newer term, which had sprung into general use among Americans in 1880, and which concisely expressed the thought of one whose dress or manners are calculated to elicit the admiration of susceptible young women — a "masher[17]". His suit was of a striped and crossed pattern of brown wool, new at that time, but since become familiar as a business suit. The low crotch of the vest revealed a stiff shirt bosom of white and pink stripes. From his coat sleeves protruded a pair of linen cuffs of the same pattern, fastened with large, gold plate buttons, set with the common yellow agates known as "cat's-eyes". His fingers bore several rings —

one, the ever-enduring heavy seal — and from his vest dangled a neat gold watch chain, from which was suspended the secret insignia of the Order of Elks[18]. The whole suit was rather tight-fitting, and was finished off with heavy-soled tan shoes, highly polished, and the grey fedora hat. He was, for the order of intellect represented, attractive, and whatever he had to recommend him, you may be sure was not lost upon Carrie, in this, her first glance.

Lest this order of individual should permanently pass, let me put down some of the most striking characteristics of his most successful manner and method. Good clothes, of course, were the first essential, the things without which he was nothing. A strong physical nature, actuated by a keen desire for the feminine, was the next. A mind free of any consideration of the problems or forces of the world and actuated not by greed, but an insatiable love of variable pleasure. His method was always simple. Its principal element was daring, backed, of course, by an intense desire and admiration for the sex. Let him meet with a young woman once and he would approach her with an air of kindly familiarity, not unmixed with pleading, which would result in most cases in a tolerant acceptance. If she showed any tendency to coquetry he would be apt to straighten her tie, or if she "took up" with him at all, to call her by her first name. If he visited a department store it was to lounge familiarly over the counter and ask some leading questions. In more exclusive circles, on the train or in waiting stations, he went slower. If some seemingly vulnerable object appeared he was all attention — to pass the compliments of the day, to lead the way to the parlor car, carrying her grip, or, failing that, to take a seat next her with the hope of being able to court her to her destination. Pillows, books, a footstool, the shade lowered; all these figured in the things which he could do. If, when she reached her destination he did not alight and attend her baggage for her, it was because, in his own estimation, he had signally failed.

A woman should some day write the complete philosophy of clothes. No matter how young, it is one of the things she wholly comprehends. There is an indescribably faint line[19] in the matter of man's apparel which somehow divides for her those who are worth glancing at and those who are not. Once an individual has passed this faint line on the way downward he will get no glance from her. There is another line at which the dress of a man will cause her to study her own. This line the individual at her elbow now marked for Carrie. She became conscious of an inequality. Her own plain blue dress, with its black cotton tape trimmings, now seemed to her shabby. She felt the worn state of her shoes.

"Let's see," he went on, "I know quite a number of people in your town. Morgenroth the clothier and Gibson the dry goods man."

"Oh, do you?" she interrupted, aroused by memories of longings their show windows had cost her.

At last he had a clew to her interest[20], and followed it deftly. In a few minutes he had come about into her seat. He talked of sales of clothing, his travels, Chicago, and the amusements of that city.

"If you are going there, you will enjoy it immensely. Have you relatives?"

"I am going to visit my sister," she explained.

"You want to see Lincoln Park," he said, "and Michigan Boulevard[21]. They are putting up great buildings there. It's a second New York — great. So much to see — theatres, crowds, fine houses — oh, you'll like that."

There was a little ache in her fancy of all he described. Her insignificance in the presence of so much magnificence faintly affected her. She realized that hers was not to be a round of pleasure, and yet there was something promising in all the material prospect he set forth. There was something satisfactory in the attention of this individual with his good clothes. She could not help smiling as he told her of some popular actress of whom she reminded him. She was not silly, and yet attention of this sort had its weight.

"You will be in Chicago some little time, won't you?" he observed at one turn of the now easy conversation.

"I don't know," said Carrie vaguely — a flash vision of the possibility of her not securing employment rising in her mind.

"Several weeks, anyhow," he said, looking steadily into her eyes.

There was much more passing now than the mere words indicated. He recognized the indescribable thing that made up for fascination and beauty in her. She realized that she was of interest to him from the one standpoint which a woman both delights in and fears. Her manner was simple, though for the very reason that she had not yet learned the many little affectations with which women conceal their true feelings.

Some things she did appeared bold. A clever companion — had she ever had one — would have warned her never to look a man in the eyes so steadily.

"Why do you ask?" she said.

"Well, I'm going to be there several weeks. I'm going to study stock at our place and get new samples. I might show you 'round."

"I don't know whether you can or not. I mean I don't know whether I can. I shall be living with my sister, and — "

"Well, if she minds, we'll fix that." He took out his pencil and a little pocket note-book as if it were all settled. "What is your address there?"

She fumbled her purse which contained the address slip.

He reached down in his hip pocket and took out a fat purse. It was filled with slips of paper, some mileage books, a roll of greenbacks. It impressed her deeply. Such a purse had never been carried by any one attentive to her. Indeed, an experienced traveller, a brisk man of the world, had never come within such close range before. The purse, the shiny tan shoes, the smart new suit, and the air with which he did things, built up for her a dim world of fortune, of which he was the centre. It disposed her pleasantly toward all he might do.

He took out a neat business card, on which was engraved Bartlett, Caryoe & Company, and down in the left-hand corner, Chas. H. Drouet.

"That's me," he said, putting the card in her hand and touching his name. "It's pronounced Drew-eh. Our family was French, on my father's side."

She looked at it while he put up his purse. Then he got out a letter from a bunch in his coat pocket. "This is the house I travel for," he went on, pointing to a picture on it, "corner of State and Lake." There was pride in his voice. He felt that it was something to be connected with such a place, and he made her feel that way.

"What is your address?" he began again, fixing his pencil to write.

She looked at his hand.

"Carrie Meeber," she said slowly. "Three hundred and fifty-four West Van Buren Street, care S. C. Hanson."

He wrote it carefully down and got out the purse again. "You'll be at home if I come around Monday night?" he said.

"I think so," she answered.

How true it is that words are but the vague shadows of the volumes we mean. Little audible links, they are, chaining together great inaudible feelings and purposes. Here were these two, bandying little phrases, drawing purses, looking at cards, and both unconscious of how inarticulate all their real feelings were. Neither was wise enough to be sure of the working of the mind of the other. He could not tell how his luring succeeded. She could not realize that she was drifting, until he secured her address. Now she felt that she had yielded something — he, that he had gained a victory. Already they felt that they were somehow associated. Already he took control in directing the conversation. His words were easy. Her manner was relaxed.

They were nearing Chicago. Signs were everywhere numerous. Trains flashed by them. Across wide stretches of flat, open prairie[22] they could see lines of telegraph poles stalking across the fields toward the great city. Far away were indications of suburban towns, some big smokestacks towering high in the air.

Frequently there were two-story frame houses standing out in the open fields, without fence or trees, lone outposts of the approaching army of homes.

To the child, the genius with imagination, or the wholly untravelled, the approach to a great city for the first time is a wonderful thing. Particularly if it be evening — that mystic period between the glare and gloom of the world when life is changing from one sphere or condition to another. Ah, the promise of the night. What does it not hold for the weary! What old illusion of hope is not here forever repeated! Says the soul of the toiler to itself, "I shall soon be free. I shall be in the ways and the hosts of the merry. The streets, the lamps, the lighted chamber set for dining, are for me. The theatre, the halls, the parties, the ways of rest and the paths of song — these are mine in the night." Though all humanity be still enclosed in the shops, the thrill runs abroad. It is in the air. The dullest feel something which they may not always express or describe. It is the lifting of the burden of toil.

Sister Carrie gazed out of the window. Her companion, affected by her wonder, so contagious are all things, felt anew some interest in the city and pointed out its marvels.

"This is Northwest Chicago," said Drouet. "This is the Chicago River," and he pointed to a little muddy creek, crowded with the huge masted wanderers from far-off waters nosing the black-posted banks. With a puff, a clang, and a clatter of rails it was gone. "Chicago is getting to be a great town," he went on. "It's a wonder. You'll find lots to see here."

She did not hear this very well. Her heart was troubled by a kind of terror. The fact that she was alone, away from home, rushing into a great sea of life and endeavour, began to tell. She could not help but feel a little choked for breath — a little sick as her heart beat so fast. She half closed her eyes and tried to think it was nothing, that Columbia City was only a little way off.

"Chicago! Chicago!" called the brakeman, slamming open the door. They were rushing into a more crowded yard, alive with the clatter and clang of life[23]. She began to gather up her poor little grip and closed her hand firmly upon her purse. Drouet arose, kicked his legs to straighten his trousers, and seized his clean yellow grip.

"I suppose your people will be here to meet you?" he said. "Let me carry your grip."

"Oh, no," she said. "I'd rather you wouldn't. I'd rather you wouldn't be with me when I meet my sister."

"All right," he said in all kindness. "I'll be near, though, in case she isn't here, and take you out there safely."

"You're so kind," said Carrie, feeling the goodness of such attention in her strange situation.

"Chicago!" called the brakeman, drawing the word out long. They were under a great shadowy train shed, where the lamps were already beginning to shine out, with passenger cars all about and the train moving at a snail's pace. The people in the car were all up and crowding about the door.

"Well, here we are," said Drouet, leading the way to the door. "Good-bye, till I see you Monday."

"Good-bye," she answered, taking his proffered hand.

"Remember, I'll be looking till you find your sister."

She smiled into his eyes.

They filed out, and he affected to take no notice of her. A lean-faced, rather commonplace woman recognised Carrie on the platform and hurried forward.

"Why, Sister Carrie!" she began, and there was embrace of welcome.

Carrie realised the change of affectional atmosphere at once. Amid all the maze, uproar, and novelty she felt cold reality taking her by the hand. No world of light and merriment. No round of amusement. Her sister carried with her most of the grimness of shift and toil.

"Why, how are all the folks at home?" she began; "how is father, and mother?"

Carrie answered, but was looking away. Down the aisle, toward the gate leading into the waiting-room and the street, stood Drouet. He was looking back. When he saw that she saw him and was safe with her sister he turned to go, sending back the shadow of a smile. Only Carrie saw it. She felt something lost to her when he moved away. When he disappeared she felt his absence thoroughly. With her sister she was much alone, a lone figure in a tossing, thoughtless sea.

Notes

1. illusions of ignorance and youth: illusions resulting from her being young and little knowledge of the world.

2. it was certainly not for advantages now being given up: it was certainly not for the idea of leaving because of the comfort and ease at home.

3. conjecture: a conclusion, judgment based on incomplete or indefinite information.

4. assumes the cosmopolitan standard of virtue: to accept the cosmopolitan standard of morality without checking or confirming.

5. there is no possibility: possibly there is no in-between of the two things.

6. the soulfulness of expression: the potential and unanticipated trap of expression.

7. undoing: the ruin or destruction of somebody or something.

8. rudimentary: premature, underdeveloped.

9. native intelligence: natural or inborn gift of noticing or understanding something.

10. two generations removed from the emigrant: excluding the generation of the emigrant, Carrie is the third generation.

11. knowledge a sealed book: nothing of book knowledge can get into her mind.

12. in the intuitive graces: in the graces that happened to be seen at a glance.

13. A half-equipped... at a woman's slipper: Sister Carrie's desire and pursuit for material comforts is compared to the Knight's adventure for women's love. This metaphor indicates that her dream is bound to fail and she will make herself a victim in the city of adventure.

14. fedora: a low soft hat with a curled brim.

15. canvasser: a salesman.

16. drummer: a traveling salesperson.

17. masher: a man who pays his attention to a woman.

18. Order of Elks: the full title of which is The Benevolent and Protective Order of Elks (BPOE), an organization founded in New York City in 1868, which has formed a quiet network of people doing good deeds for youngsters, college-bound students, old or handicapped people, active-duty armed forces — anyone who needs assistance.

19. faint line: an indication or a marking line.

20. had a clew to her interest: worked out the clues to her interest.

21. Michigan Boulevard: the street wall of Michigan Avenue defines the western edge of Grant Park and forms one of the most distinguished images of downtown Chicago. It is the backdrop to lakefront festivals and concerts.

22. prairie: a large flat area in central North America covered with grass and farmland but without trees.

23. the clatter and clang of life: refers to the noise and excitement in real life. Clatter refers to loud noise made from the knocking of hard objects; clang refers to a loud ringing sound caused by hitting metal.

Questions for Discussion

(1) When *Sister Carrie* came out, the public was unwilling to accept this book. But with *Sister Carrie*'s success some critics agree that Dreiser's moral values embodied in this novel is anti-traditional. What does the "traditional" here refer to? Is the morality embodied in *Sister Carrie* a total denial of tradition or a neglect of it? Why?

(2) American literary critics V. L. Parrington summarizes several principles of

naturalism, which include objectivity, frankness, attitude without moral judgement toward material, a philosophy of Determinism, and a bias toward pessimism in selecting details. Apply at least one of the above principles in analyzing Dreiser's writing in *Sister Carrie*.

(3) In accordance with the characters' desire and dependence on the material, tracing the chronological characteristics of the work, please discuss the social changes which have been taken place in the United States. What were the developmental trends of big cities like New York, Los Angeles and Chicago?

(4) As one of the most important power of Dreiser's writing, the representation of imperfect humanity is depicted by the complete difference between the surface of real life experienced by the characters and their actual pursuit of life. How do you feel in this regard?

Suggested Reading

- Donald Pizer 编：《剑桥文学指南：美国现实主义和自然主义》，上海：上海外语教育出版社，2000 年。
- 德莱塞：《嘉莉妹妹》，北京：外语教学与研究出版社，2020 年。

16. Jack London

Jack London is a very important writer in the history of American literature. He is so prolific that in less than twenty years (1899–1916) he produced almost forty books and a thousand articles. Many of these excellent works have the critical power of realism and unique artistic styles.

London was born in San Francisco on 12 January, 1876. He was the stepson of John London, to whom his mother Flora got married when he was eight months old. London's childhood, before age of nine, passed with little fun and fresh memories. It was characterized by much restlessness with his mother's ambition of becoming rich, forcing them to move repeatedly and change household business. It was not until nine did young London get something to read. Reading like *Captain James Cook's Voyage*, *The Alhambra*, *Ouida Signa* and *Explorations and Adventures* took him to the world of his imagination. These works allowed him to enjoy the adventures, and also triggered his later desire and determination to use his writing to change the living situation of lower-class citizens. His time in Oakland from 1886 to 1891 was a period lived fully and freely, as he continued to extend his reading in the Oakland Free Library. But he also got himself into the street life, fighting and drinking. At the age of fifteen, only after three years of schooling, he resigned himself to his fate and was trapped in the toughest period of life. In order to ease his family predicament, he was forced to work as a child laborer in a cannery which ruthlessly squeezed him both in health and spirit. Before he was able to get out of the low stage of life, London had also worked as an adventurer, pirate, sailor, prospector and explorer. He drank a lot and nearly killed himself. In 1895, he enrolled in Oakland High School. One year later, he was admitted into the University of California but dropped out after a semester for lack of funds. After leaving university, in the summer of 1897, London joined the gold rush in Alaskan Klondike. He was not the one came back rich on fortune but the one accumulated much material for his life–long writing. His writing attempt in 1898 shocked him with success and attracted the attention of publishers. He was then sponsored to bring out a series of his Alaska short stories. And on 7 April of 1900, London got married to Elizabeth Mae Madern, who gave birth to two daughters for London in the year of 1901 and 1902. In the process of bringing out new works, London started to write novels. In 1903, London brought out his masterpiece *The Call of the Wild*, which became a runaway best seller and made London an international celebrity. The novels and short stories he later published were well received among the readers unsuprisingly. Till the advent of *Martin Eden*, London has firmly established himself as America's premier writer. Martin Eden's fate in his semi-biographical novel foreshadowed the disillusionment which London confronted during the last decade of his life. His sickness punched his great desire for challenge and adventure; he was hit by the abortion of his second wife Charmian; the loss of his dreamed family and home — all of these unbearable sufferings tortured him mentally and physically. He died, at age of forty, on 12 November 1916.

  Jack London's early publishing are mostly short stories describing the common gold prospectors and the life of people in northern America with such works as *The Son of the Wolf: Tales of the Far North*, "The God of His Father", *Children of the Frost*, "Love of Life" and so on. His middle-stage works were novels reflecting his struggle and integration to the society under the influence of social Darwinism, socialism, Nietzsche philosophy, etc. *The Call of the Wild, White Fang, The Sea Wolf, Iron Heel* and *Martin Eden* are the representative works of this period. His later works, including some excellent short stories and novels created after the year of 1910, continue to highlight his concern over social reality and express his pursuit of personal happiness. As a writer from the low-level proletarian, London can be considered as the most class-conscious writer in his era, because he has created a lot of works related to it. He was equally a chaser of American Dream who desired to be on the side of social justice and progress but forever avid for individual fortune and fame, therefore presented much contradiction and antagonism in his writings.

Love of Life

"This out of all will remain —
They have lived and have tossed:
So much of the game will be gain,
Though the gold of the dice has been lost.[1]"

THEY limped painfully down the bank, and once the foremost of the two men staggered among the rough-strewn rocks. They were tired and weak, and their faces had the drawn expression of patience which comes of hardship long endured. They were heavily burdened with blanket packs which were strapped to their shoulders. Head-straps, passing across the forehead, helped support these packs. Each man carried a rifle. They walked in a stooped posture, the shoulders well forward, the head still farther forward, the eyes bent upon the ground.

"I wish we had just about two of them cartridges that's layin' in that cache of ourn[2]," said the second man.

His voice was utterly and drearily expressionless. He spoke without enthusiasm; and the first man, limping into the milky stream that foamed over the rocks, vouchsafed no reply.

The other man followed at his heels. They did not remove their foot-gear, though the water was icy cold — so cold that their ankles ached and their feet went numb. In places the water dashed against their knees, and both men staggered for footing.

The man who followed slipped on a smooth boulder[3], nearly fell, but recovered himself with a violent effort, at the same time uttering a sharp exclamation of pain. He seemed faint and dizzy and put out his free hand while he reeled, as though seeking support against the air. When he had steadied himself he stepped forward, but reeled again and nearly fell. Then he stood still and looked at the other man, who had never turned his head.

The man stood still for fully a minute, as though debating with himself. Then he called out:

"I say, Bill, I've sprained my ankle."

Bill staggered on through the milky water. He did not look around. The man watched him go, and though his face was expressionless as ever, his eyes were like the eyes of a wounded deer.

The other man limped up the farther bank and continued straight on without looking back. The man in the stream watched him. His lips trembled a little, so that the rough thatch of brown hair which covered them was visibly agitated. His tongue even strayed out to moisten them.[4]

"Bill!" he cried out.

It was the pleading cry of a strong man in distress, but Bill's head did not turn. The man watched him go, limping grotesquely and lurching forward with stammering gait up the slow slope toward the soft sky-line of the low-lying hill. He watched him go till he passed over the crest and disappeared. Then he turned his gaze and slowly took in the circle of the world that remained to him now that Bill was gone.

Near the horizon the sun was smouldering[5] dimly, almost obscured by formless mists and vapors, which gave an impression of mass and density without outline or tangibility. The man pulled out his watch, the while resting his weight on one leg. It was four o'clock, and as the season was near the last of July or first of August, — he did not know the precise date within a week or two, — he knew that the sun roughly marked the northwest. He looked to the south and knew that somewhere beyond those bleak hills lay the Great Bear Lake[6]; also, he knew that in that direction the Arctic

Circle cut its forbidding way across the Canadian Barrens. This stream in which he stood was a feeder to the Coppermine River[7], which in turn flowed north and emptied into Coronation Gulf[8] and the Arctic Ocean. He had never been there, but he had seen it, once, on a Hudson Bay Company[9] chart.

Again his gaze completed the circle of the world about him. It was not a heartening spectacle. Everywhere was soft sky-line. The hills were all low-lying. There were no trees, no shrubs, no grasses — naught but a tremendous and terrible desolation that sent fear swiftly dawning into his eyes[10].

"Bill!" he whispered, once and twice; "Bill!"

He cowered in the midst of the milky water, as though the vastness were pressing in upon him with overwhelming force, brutally crushing him with its complacent awfulness. He began to shake as with an ague-fit, till the gun fell from his hand with a splash. This served to rouse him. He fought with his fear and pulled himself together[11], groping in the water and recovering the weapon. He hitched his pack farther over on his left shoulder, so as to take a portion of its weight from off the injured ankle. Then he proceeded, slowly and carefully, wincing with pain, to the bank.

He did not stop. With a desperation that was madness, unmindful of the pain, he hurried up the slope to the crest of the hill over which his comrade had disappeared — more grotesque and comical by far than that limping, jerking comrade. But at the crest he saw a shallow valley, empty of life. He fought with his fear again, overcame it, hitched the pack still farther over on his left shoulder, and lurched on down the slope.

The bottom of the valley was soggy with water, which the thick moss held, spongelike, close to the surface. This water squirted out from under his feet at every step, and each time he lifted a foot the action culminated in a sucking sound as the wet moss reluctantly released its grip. He picked his way from muskeg to muskeg, and followed the other man's footsteps along and across the rocky ledges which thrust like islets through the sea of moss.

Though alone, he was not lost. Farther on he knew he would come to where dead spruce and fir, very small and weazened, bordered the shore of a little lake, the TITCHIN-NICHILIE[12], in the tongue of the country, the "land of little sticks". And into that lake flowed a small stream, the water of which was not milky. There was rush-grass on that stream — this he remembered well — but no timber, and he would follow it till its first trickle ceased at a divide. He would cross this divide to the first trickle of another stream, flowing to the west, which he would follow until it emptied into the river Dease, and here he would find a cache under an upturned canoe and piled over with many rocks. And in this cache would be ammunition for his empty gun, fish-hooks and lines, a small net — all the utilities for the killing and snaring of food[13]. Also, he would find flour, — not much, — a piece of bacon, and some beans.

Bill would be waiting for him there, and they would paddle away south down the Dease to the Great Bear Lake. And south across the lake they would go, ever south, till they gained the Mackenzie[14]. And south, still south, they would go, while the winter raced vainly after them, and the ice formed in the eddies, and the days grew chill and crisp, south to some warm Hudson Bay Company post, where timber grew tall and generous and there was grub without end.

These were the thoughts of the man as he strove onward. But hard as he strove with his body, he strove equally hard with his mind, trying to think that Bill had not deserted him, that Bill would surely wait for him at the cache. He was compelled to think this thought, or else there would not be any use to strive, and he would have lain down and died. And as the dim ball of the sun sank slowly into the northwest he covered every inch — and many times — of his and Bill's flight south before the downcoming winter. And he conned the grub of the cache and the grub of the Hudson Bay Company post over and over again. He had not eaten for two days; for a far longer time he had not had all he wanted to eat. Often he stooped and picked pale muskeg berries, put them into his mouth, and chewed and swallowed them. A muskeg berry is a bit of seed enclosed in a bit of water. In the mouth the water melts away and the seed chews sharp and bitter. The man knew there was no nourishment in the berries, but he chewed them patiently with a hope greater than knowledge and defying experience.

At nine o'clock he stubbed his toe on a rocky ledge, and from sheer weariness and weakness staggered and fell. He lay for some time, without movement, on his side. Then he slipped out of the pack-straps and clumsily dragged himself into a sitting posture. It was not yet dark, and in the lingering twilight he groped about among the rocks for shreds of dry moss. When he had gathered a heap he built a fire, — a smouldering, smudgy fire, — and put a tin pot of water on to boil.

He unwrapped his pack and the first thing he did was to count his matches. There were sixty-seven. He counted them three times to make sure. He divided them into several portions, wrapping them in oil paper, disposing of one bunch in his empty tobacco pouch, of another bunch in the inside band of his battered hat, of a third bunch under his shirt on the chest. This accomplished, a panic came upon him, and he unwrapped them all and counted them again. There were still sixty-seven.

He dried his wet foot-gear by the fire. The moccasins[15] were in soggy shreds. The blanket socks were worn through in places, and his feet were raw and bleeding. His ankle was throbbing, and he gave it an examination. It had swollen to the size of his knee. He tore a long strip from one of his two blankets and bound the ankle tightly. He tore other strips and bound them about his feet to serve for both moccasins and socks. Then he drank the pot of water, steaming hot, wound his watch, and crawled between his blankets.

He slept like a dead man. The brief darkness around midnight came and went. The sun arose in the northeast — at least the day dawned in that quarter[16], for the sun was hidden by gray clouds.

At six o'clock he awoke, quietly lying on his back. He gazed straight up into the gray sky and knew that he was hungry. As he rolled over on his elbow he was startled by a loud snort, and saw a bull caribou[17] regarding him with alert curiosity. The animal was not more than fifty feet away, and instantly into the man's mind leaped the vision and the savor of a caribou steak sizzling and frying over a fire. Mechanically he reached for the empty gun, drew a bead, and pulled the trigger. The bull snorted and leaped away, his hoofs rattling and clattering as he fled across the ledges.

The man cursed and flung the empty gun from him. He groaned aloud as he started to drag himself to his feet. It was a slow and arduous task.

His joints were like rusty hinges. They worked harshly in their sockets, with much friction, and each bending or unbending was accomplished only through a sheer exertion of will. When he finally gained his feet, another minute or so was consumed in straightening up, so that he could stand erect as a man should stand.

He crawled up a small knoll[18] and surveyed the prospect. There were no trees, no bushes, nothing but a gray sea of moss scarcely diversified by gray rocks, gray lakelets, and gray streamlets. The sky was gray. There was no sun nor hint of sun. He had no idea of north, and he had forgotten the way he had come to this spot the night before. But he was not lost. He knew that. Soon he would come to the land of the little sticks. He felt that it lay off to the left somewhere, not far — possibly just over the next low hill.

He went back to put his pack into shape for travelling. He assured himself of the existence of his three separate parcels of matches, though he did not stop to count them. But he did linger, debating, over a squat moose-hide sack. It was not large. He could hide it under his two hands. He knew that it weighed fifteen pounds, — as much as all the rest of the pack, — and it worried him. He finally set it to one side and proceeded to roll the pack. He paused to gaze at the squat moose-hide sack[19]. He picked it up hastily with a defiant glance about him, as though the desolation were trying to rob him of it; and when he rose to his feet to stagger on into the day, it was included in the pack on his back.

He bore away to the left, stopping now and again to eat muskeg berries. His ankle had stiffened, his limp was more pronounced, but the pain of it was as nothing compared with the pain of his stomach. The hunger pangs were sharp. They gnawed and gnawed until he could not keep his mind steady on the course he must pursue to gain the land of little sticks. The muskeg berries did not allay this gnawing, while they made his tongue and the roof of his mouth sore with their irritating bite.

He came upon a valley where rock ptarmigan[20] rose on whirring wings from the ledges and muskegs. Ker — ker — ker was the cry they made. He threw stones at them, but could not hit them. He placed his pack on the ground and stalked them as a cat stalks a sparrow. The sharp rocks cut through his pants' legs till his knees left a trail of blood; but the hurt was lost in the hurt of his hunger. He squirmed[21] over the wet moss, saturating his clothes and chilling his body; but he was not aware of it, so great was his fever for food. And always the ptarmigan rose, whirring, before him, till their ker — ker — ker became a mock to him, and he cursed them and cried aloud at them with their own cry.

Once he crawled upon one that must have been asleep. He did not see it till it shot up in his face from its rocky nook. He made a clutch as startled as was the rise of the ptarmigan, and there remained in his hand three tail-feathers. As he watched its flight he hated it, as though it had done him some terrible wrong. Then he returned and shouldered his pack.

As the day wore along he came into valleys or swales where game[22] was more plentiful. A band of caribou passed by, twenty and odd animals, tantalizingly within rifle range. He felt a wild desire to run after them, a certitude that he could run them down. A black fox came toward him, carrying a ptarmigan in his mouth. The man shouted. It was a fearful cry, but the fox, leaping away in fright, did not drop the ptarmigan.

Late in the afternoon he followed a stream, milky with lime, which ran through sparse patches of rush-grass. Grasping these rushes firmly near the root, he pulled up what resembled a young onion-sprout no larger than a shingle-nail. It was tender, and his teeth sank into it with a crunch that promised deliciously of food. But its fibers were tough. It was composed of stringy filaments saturated with water, like the berries, and devoid of nourishment. He threw off his pack and went into the rush-grass on hands and knees, crunching and munching, like some bovine[23] creature.

He was very weary and often wished to rest — to lie down and sleep; but he was continually driven on — not so much by his desire to gain the land of little sticks as by his hunger. He searched little ponds for frogs and dug up the earth with his nails for worms, though he knew in spite that neither frogs nor worms existed so far north.

He looked into every pool of water vainly, until, as the long twilight came on, he discovered a solitary fish, the size of a minnow, in such a pool. He plunged his arm in up to the shoulder, but it eluded him. He reached for it with both hands and stirred up the milky mud at the bottom. In his excitement he fell in, wetting himself to the waist. Then the water was too muddy to admit of his seeing the fish, and he was compelled to wait until the sediment had settled.

The pursuit was renewed, till the water was again muddied. But he could not wait. He unstrapped the tin bucket and began to bale the pool. He baled wildly at first, splashing himself and flinging the water so short a distance that it ran back into the pool. He worked more carefully, striving to be cool, though his heart was pounding against his chest and his hands were trembling. At the end of half an hour the pool was nearly dry. Not a cupful of water remained. And there was no fish. He found a hidden crevice among the stones through which it had escaped to the adjoining and larger pool — a pool which he could not empty in a night and a day. Had he known of the crevice, he could have closed it with a rock at the beginning and the fish would have been his.

Thus he thought, and crumpled up and sank down upon the wet earth. At first he cried softly to himself, then he cried loudly to the pitiless desolation that ringed him around; and for a long time after he was shaken by great dry sobs.[24]

He built a fire and warmed himself by drinking quarts of hot water, and made camp on a rocky ledge in the same fashion he had the night before. The last thing he did was to see that his matches were dry and to wind his watch. The blankets were wet and clammy. His ankle pulsed with pain. But he knew only that he was hungry, and through his restless sleep he dreamed of feasts and banquets and of food served and spread in all imaginable ways.

He awoke chilled and sick. There was no sun. The gray of earth and sky had become deeper, more profound. A raw wind was blowing, and the first flurries[25] of snow were whitening the hilltops. The air about him thickened and grew white while he made a fire and boiled more water. It was wet snow, half rain, and the flakes were large and soggy. At first they melted as soon as they came in contact with the earth, but ever more fell, covering the ground, putting out the fire, spoiling his supply of moss-fuel.

This was a signal for him to strap on his pack and stumble onward, he knew not where. He was not concerned with the land of little sticks, nor with Bill and the cache under the upturned canoe by the river Dease. He was mastered by the verb "to eat". He was hunger-mad. He took no heed of[26] the course he pursued, so long as that course led him through the swale bottoms. He felt his way through the wet snow to the watery muskeg berries, and went by feel as he pulled up the rush-grass by the roots. But it was tasteless stuff and did not satisfy. He found a weed that tasted sour and he ate all he could find of it, which was not much, for it was a creeping growth, easily hidden under the several inches of snow.

He had no fire that night, nor hot water, and crawled under his blanket to sleep the broken hunger-sleep. The snow turned into a cold rain. He awakened many times to feel it falling on his upturned face. Day came — a gray day and no sun. It had ceased raining. The keenness of his hunger had departed. Sensibility, as far as concerned the yearning for food, had been exhausted. There was a dull, heavy ache in his stomach, but it did not bother him so much. He was more rational, and once more he was chiefly interested in the land of little sticks and the cache by the river Dease.

He ripped the remnant of one of his blankets into strips and bound his bleeding feet. Also, he recinched the injured ankle and prepared himself for a day of travel. When he came to his pack, he paused long over the squat moose-hide sack, but in the end it went with him.

The snow had melted under the rain, and only the hilltops showed white. The sun came out, and he succeeded in locating the points of the compass, though he knew now that he was lost. Perhaps, in his previous days' wanderings, he had edged away too far to the left. He now bore off to the right to counteract the possible deviation from his true course.

Though the hunger pangs were no longer so exquisite, he realized that he was weak. He was compelled to pause for frequent rests, when he attacked the muskeg berries and rush-grass patches. His tongue felt dry and large, as though covered with a fine hairy growth, and it tasted bitter in his mouth. His heart gave him a great deal of trouble. When he had travelled a few minutes it would begin a remorseless thump, thump, thump, and then leap up and away in a painful flutter of beats that choked him and made him go faint and dizzy.

In the middle of the day he found two minnows in a large pool. It was impossible to bale it, but he was calmer now and managed to catch them in his tin bucket. They were no longer than his little finger, but he was not particularly hungry. The dull ache in his stomach had been growing duller and fainter. It seemed almost that his stomach was dozing. He ate the fish raw, masticating with painstaking care, for the eating was an act of pure reason[27]. While he had no desire to eat, he knew that he must eat to live.

In the evening he caught three more minnows, eating two and saving the third for breakfast. The sun had dried stray shreds of moss, and he was able to warm himself with hot water. He had not covered more than ten miles that day; and the next day, travelling whenever his heart permitted him, he covered no more than five miles. But his stomach did not give him the slightest uneasiness. It had gone to sleep. He was in a strange country, too, and the caribou were growing more plentiful, also the wolves. Often their yelps drifted across the desolation, and once he saw three of them slinking away before his path.

Another night; and in the morning, being more rational, he untied the leather string that fastened the squat moose-hide sack. From its open mouth poured a yellow stream of coarse gold-dust and nuggets. He roughly divided the gold in halves, caching one half on a prominent ledge, wrapped in a piece of blanket, and returning the other half to the sack.[28] He also began to use strips of the one remaining blanket for his feet. He still clung to his gun, for there were cartridges in that cache by the river Dease.

This was a day of fog, and this day hunger awoke in him again. He was very weak and was afflicted with a giddiness which at times blinded him. It was no uncommon thing now for him to stumble and fall; and stumbling once, he fell squarely into a ptarmigan nest. There were four newly hatched chicks, a day old — little specks of pulsating life no more than a mouthful; and he ate them ravenously, thrusting them alive into his mouth and crunching them like egg-shells between his teeth. The mother ptarmigan beat about him with great outcry. He used his gun as a club with which to knock her over, but she dodged[29] out of reach. He threw stones at her and with one chance shot broke a wing. Then she fluttered away, running, trailing the broken wing, with him in pursuit.

The little chicks had no more than whetted his appetite[30]. He hopped and bobbed clumsily along on his injured ankle, throwing stones and screaming hoarsely at times; at other times hopping and bobbing silently along, picking himself up grimly and patiently when he fell, or rubbing his eyes with his hand when the giddiness threatened to overpower him.

The chase led him across swampy ground in the bottom of the valley, and he came upon footprints in the soggy moss. They were not his own — he could see that. They must be Bill's. But he could not stop, for the mother ptarmigan was running on. He would catch her first, then he would return and investigate.

He exhausted the mother ptarmigan; but he exhausted himself. She lay panting on her side. He lay panting on his side, a dozen feet away, unable to crawl to her. And as he recovered she recovered, fluttering out of reach as his hungry hand went out to her. The chase was resumed. Night settled down and she escaped. He stumbled from weakness and pitched head foremost on his face, cutting his cheek, his pack upon his back. He did not move for a long while; then he rolled over on his side, wound his watch, and lay there until morning.

Another day of fog. Half of his last blanket had gone into foot-wrappings. He failed to pick up Bill's trail. It did not matter. His hunger was driving him too compellingly — only — only he wondered if Bill, too, were lost. By midday the irk of his pack became too oppressive. Again he divided the gold, this time merely spilling half of it on the ground. In the afternoon he threw the rest of it away, there remaining to him only the half-blanket, the tin bucket, and the rifle.[31]

An hallucination[32] began to trouble him. He felt confident that one cartridge remained to him. It was in the chamber of the rifle and he had overlooked it. On the other hand, he knew all the time that the chamber was empty. But the hallucination persisted. He fought it off for hours, then threw his rifle open and was confronted with emptiness. The disappointment was as bitter as though he had really expected to find the cartridge.

He plodded on for half an hour, when the hallucination arose again. Again he fought it, and still it persisted, till for very relief he opened his rifle to unconvince himself[33]. At times his mind wandered farther afield, and he plodded on, a mere automaton, strange conceits and whimsicalities gnawing at his brain like worms. But these excursions out of the real were of brief duration, for ever the pangs of the hunger-bite called him back. He was jerked back abruptly once from such an excursion by a sight that caused him nearly to faint. He reeled and swayed, doddering like a drunken man to keep from falling. Before him stood a horse. A horse! He could not believe his eyes. A thick mist was in them, intershot with sparkling points of light. He rubbed his eyes savagely to clear his vision, and beheld, not a horse, but a great brown bear. The animal was studying him with bellicose[34] curiosity.

The man had brought his gun halfway to his shoulder before he realized. He lowered it and drew his hunting-knife from its beaded sheath at his hip. Before him was meat and life. He ran his thumb along the edge of his knife. It was sharp. The point was sharp. He would fling himself upon the bear and kill it. But his heart began its warning thump, thump, thump. Then followed the wild upward leap and tattoo of flutters, the pressing as of an iron band about his forehead, the creeping of the dizziness into his brain.

His desperate courage was evicted by a great surge of fear. In his weakness, what if the animal attacked him? He drew himself up to his most imposing stature, gripping the knife and staring hard at the bear. The bear advanced clumsily a couple of steps, reared up, and gave vent to a tentative growl. If the man ran, he would run after him; but the man did not run. He was animated now with the courage of fear. He, too, growled, savagely, terribly, voicing the fear that is to life germane and that lies twisted about life's deepest roots.[35]

The bear edged away to one side, growling menacingly, himself appalled by this mysterious creature that appeared upright and unafraid. But the man did not move. He stood like a statue till the danger was past, when he yielded to a fit of trembling and sank down into the wet moss.

He pulled himself together and went on, afraid now in a new way. It was not the fear that he should die passively from lack of food, but that he should be destroyed violently before starvation had exhausted the last particle of the endeavor in him that made toward surviving.[36] There were the wolves. Back and forth across the desolation drifted their howls, weaving the very air into a fabric of menace that was so tangible that he found himself, arms in the air, pressing it back from him as it might be the walls of a wind-blown tent.

Now and again the wolves, in packs of two and three, crossed his path. But they sheered clear of him. They were not in sufficient numbers, and besides they were hunting the caribou, which did not battle, while this strange creature that walked erect might scratch and bite.

In the late afternoon he came upon scattered bones where the wolves had made a kill. The debris had been a caribou calf an hour before, squawking and running and very much alive. He contemplated the bones, clean-picked and polished, pink with the cell-life in them which had not yet died. Could it possibly be that he might be that ere[37] the day was done! Such was life, eh? A vain and fleeting thing. It was only life that pained. There was no hurt in death. To die was to sleep. It meant cessation, rest. Then why was he not content to die?[38]

But he did not moralize long. He was squatting in the moss, a bone in his mouth, sucking at the shreds of life that still dyed it faintly pink. The sweet meaty taste, thin and elusive almost as a memory, maddened him. He closed his jaws on the bones and crunched. Sometimes it was the bone that broke, sometimes his teeth. Then he crushed the bones between rocks, pounded them to a pulp, and swallowed them. He pounded his fingers, too, in his haste, and yet found a moment in which to feel surprise at the fact that his fingers did not hurt much when caught under the descending rock.

Came frightful days of snow and rain. He did not know when he made camp, when he broke camp. He travelled in the night as much as in the day. He rested wherever he fell, crawled on whenever the dying life in him flickered up and burned less dimly. He, as a man, no longer strove. It was the life in him, unwilling to die, that drove him on. He did not suffer. His nerves had become blunted, numb, while his mind was filled with weird visions and delicious dreams.

But ever he sucked and chewed on the crushed bones of the caribou calf, the least remnants of which he had gathered up and carried with him. He crossed no more hills or divides, but automatically followed a large stream which flowed through a wide and shallow valley. He did not see this stream nor this valley. He saw nothing save visions. Soul and body walked or crawled side by side, yet apart, so slender was the thread that bound them.

He awoke in his right mind, lying on his back on a rocky ledge. The sun was shining bright and warm. Afar off he heard the squawking of caribou calves. He was aware of vague memories of rain and wind and snow, but whether he had been beaten by the storm for two days or two weeks he did not know.

For some time he lay without movement, the genial sunshine pouring upon him and saturating his miserable body with its warmth. A fine day, he thought. Perhaps he could manage to locate himself. By a painful effort he rolled over on his side. Below him flowed a wide and sluggish river. Its unfamiliarity puzzled him. Slowly he followed it with his eyes, winding in wide sweeps among the bleak, bare hills, bleaker and barer and lower-lying than any hills he had yet encountered. Slowly, deliberately, without excitement or more than the most casual interest, he followed the course of the strange stream toward the sky-line and saw it emptying into a bright and shining sea. He was still unexcited. Most unusual, he thought, a vision or a mirage[39] — more likely a vision, a trick of his disordered mind. He was confirmed in this by sight of a ship lying at anchor in the midst of the shining sea. He closed his eyes for a while, then opened them. Strange how the vision persisted! Yet not strange. He knew there were no seas or ships in the heart of the barren lands, just as he had known there was no cartridge in the empty rifle.

He heard a snuffle behind him — a half-choking gasp or cough. Very slowly, because of his exceeding weakness and stiffness, he rolled over on his other side. He could see nothing near at hand, but he waited patiently. Again came the snuffle and cough, and outlined between two jagged rocks not a score of feet away he made out the gray head of a wolf. The sharp ears were not pricked so sharply as he had seen them on other wolves; the eyes were bleared and bloodshot, the head seemed to droop limply and forlornly. The animal blinked continually in the sunshine. It seemed sick. As he looked it snuffled and coughed again.

This, at least, was real, he thought, and turned on the other side so that he might see the reality of the world which had been veiled from him before by the vision. But the sea still shone in the distance and the ship was plainly discernible[40]. Was it reality, after all? He closed his eyes for a long while and thought, and then it came to him. He had been making north by east, away from the Dease Divide and into the Coppermine Valley. This wide and sluggish river was the Coppermine. That shining sea was the Arctic Ocean. That ship was a whaler, strayed east, far east, from the mouth of the Mackenzie, and it was lying at anchor in Coronation Gulf. He remembered the Hudson Bay Company chart he had seen long ago, and it was all clear and reasonable to him.

He sat up and turned his attention to immediate affairs. He had worn through the blanket-wrappings, and his feet were shapeless lumps of raw meat. His last blanket was gone. Rifle and knife were both missing. He had lost his hat somewhere, with the bunch of matches in the band, but the matches against his chest were safe and dry inside the tobacco pouch and oil paper. He looked at his watch. It marked eleven o'clock and was still running. Evidently he had kept it wound.

He was calm and collected. Though extremely weak, he had no sensation of pain. He was not hungry. The thought of food was not even pleasant to him, and whatever he did was done by his reason alone. He ripped off his pants' legs to the knees and bound them about his feet. Somehow he had succeeded in retaining the tin bucket. He would have some hot water before he began what he foresaw was to be a terrible journey to the ship.

His movements were slow. He shook as with a palsy[41]. When he started to collect dry moss, he found he could not rise to his feet. He tried again and again, then contented himself with crawling about on hands and knees. Once he crawled near to the sick wolf. The animal dragged itself reluctantly out of his way, licking its chops with a tongue which seemed hardly to have the strength to curl. The man noticed that the tongue was not the customary healthy red. It was a yellowish brown and seemed coated with a rough and half-dry mucus.

After he had drunk a quart of hot water the man found he was able to stand, and even to walk as well as a dying man might be supposed to walk. Every minute or so he was compelled to rest. His steps were feeble and uncertain, just as the wolf's that trailed him were feeble and uncertain; and that night, when the shining sea was blotted out by blackness, he knew he was nearer to it by no more than four miles.

Throughout the night he heard the cough of the sick wolf, and now and then the squawking of the caribou calves. There was life all around him, but it was strong life, very much alive and well, and he knew the sick wolf clung to the sick man's trail in the hope that the man would die first. In the morning, on opening his eyes, he beheld it regarding him with a wistful and hungry stare. It stood crouched, with tail between its legs, like a miserable and woe-begone dog. It shivered in the chill morning wind, and grinned dispiritedly when the man spoke to it in a voice that achieved no more than a hoarse whisper.

The sun rose brightly, and all morning the man tottered and fell toward the ship on the shining sea. The weather was perfect. It was the brief Indian Summer[42] of the high latitudes. It might last a week. To-morrow or next day it might be gone.

In the afternoon the man came upon a trail. It was of another man, who did not walk, but who dragged himself on all fours. The man thought it might be Bill, but he thought in a dull, uninterested way. He had no curiosity. In fact, sensation and emotion had left him. He was no longer susceptible to pain. Stomach and nerves had gone to sleep. Yet the life that was in him drove him on.[43] He was very weary, but it refused to die. It was because it refused to die that he still ate muskeg berries and minnows, drank his hot water, and kept a wary eye on the sick wolf.

He followed the trail of the other man who dragged himself along, and soon came to the end of it — a few fresh-picked bones where the soggy moss was marked by the foot-pads of many wolves. He saw a squat moose-hide sack, mate to his own, which had been torn by sharp teeth. He picked it up, though its weight was almost too much for his feeble fingers. Bill had carried it to the last. Ha! ha! He would have the laugh on Bill. He would survive and carry it to the ship in the shining sea. His mirth was hoarse and ghastly[44], like a raven's croak, and the sick wolf joined him, howling lugubriously. The man ceased suddenly. How could he have the laugh on Bill if that were Bill; if those bones, so pinky-white and clean, were Bill?

He turned away. Well, Bill had deserted him; but he would not take the gold, nor would he suck Bill's bones. Bill would have, though, had it been the other way around, he mused as he staggered on.

He came to a pool of water. Stooping over in quest of minnows, he jerked his head back as though he had been stung. He had caught sight of his reflected face. So horrible was it that sensibility awoke long enough to be shocked. There were three minnows in the pool, which was too large to drain; and after several ineffectual attempts to catch them in the tin bucket he forbore. He was afraid, because of his great weakness, that he might fall in and drown. It was for this reason that he did not trust himself to the river astride one of the many drift-logs which lined its sand-spits.

That day he decreased the distance between him and the ship by three miles; the next day by two — for he was crawling now as Bill had crawled; and the end of the fifth day found the ship still seven miles away and him unable to make even a mile a day. Still the Indian Summer held on, and he continued to crawl and faint, turn and turn about; and ever the sick wolf coughed and wheezed at his heels. His knees had become raw meat like his feet, and though he padded them with the shirt from his back it was a red track he left behind him on the moss and stones. Once, glancing back, he saw the wolf licking hungrily his bleeding trail, and he saw sharply what his own end might be — unless — unless he could get the wolf. Then began as grim a tragedy of existence as was ever played — a sick man that crawled, a sick wolf that limped, two creatures dragging their dying carcasses across the desolation and hunting each other's lives.

Had it been a well wolf, it would not have mattered so much to the man; but the thought of going to feed the maw of that loathsome and all but dead thing was repugnant to him. He was finicky. His mind had begun to wander again, and to be perplexed by hallucinations, while his lucid intervals grew rarer and shorter.

He was awakened once from a faint by a wheeze[45] close in his ear. The wolf leaped lamely back, losing its footing and falling in its weakness. It was ludicrous, but he was not amused. Nor was he even afraid. He was too far gone for that. But his mind was for the moment clear, and he lay and considered. The ship was no more than four miles away. He could see it quite distinctly when he rubbed the mists out of his eyes, and he could see the white sail of a small boat cutting the water of the shining sea. But he could never crawl those four miles. He knew that, and was very calm in the knowledge. He knew that he could not crawl half a mile. And yet he wanted to live. It was unreasonable that he should die after all he had undergone. Fate asked too much of him. And, dying, he declined to die. It was stark madness, perhaps, but in the very grip of Death he defied Death and refused to die.

He closed his eyes and composed himself with infinite precaution. He steeled himself to keep above the suffocating languor[46] that lapped like a rising tide through all the wells of his being. It was very like a sea, this deadly languor, that rose and rose and drowned his consciousness bit by bit. Sometimes he was all but submerged, swimming through oblivion with a faltering stroke; and again, by some strange alchemy of soul, he would find another shred of will and strike out more strongly.

Without movement he lay on his back, and he could hear, slowly drawing near and nearer, the wheezing intake and output of the sick wolf's breath. It drew closer, ever closer, through an infinitude of time, and he did not move. It was at his ear. The harsh dry tongue grated like sandpaper against his cheek. His hands shot out — or at least he willed them to shoot out. The fingers were curved like talons, but they closed on empty air. Swiftness and certitude require strength, and the man had not this strength.

The patience of the wolf was terrible. The man's patience was no less terrible. For half a day he lay motionless, fighting off unconsciousness and waiting for the thing that was to feed upon him and upon which he wished to feed. Sometimes the languid sea rose over him and he dreamed long dreams; but ever through it all, waking and dreaming, he waited for the wheezing breath and the harsh caress of the tongue.

He did not hear the breath, and he slipped slowly from some dream to the feel of the tongue along his hand. He waited. The fangs pressed softly; the pressure increased; the wolf was exerting its last strength in an effort to sink teeth in the food for which it had waited so long. But the man had waited long, and the lacerated hand closed on the jaw. Slowly, while the wolf struggled feebly and the hand clutched feebly, the other hand crept across to a grip. Five minutes later the whole weight of the man's body was on top of the wolf. The hands had not sufficient strength to choke the wolf, but the face of the man was pressed close to the throat of the wolf and the mouth of the man was full of hair. At the end of half an hour the man was aware of a warm trickle in his throat. It was not pleasant. It was like molten lead being forced into his stomach, and it was forced by his will alone. Later the man rolled over on his back and slept.

* * * * *

There were some members of a scientific expedition on the whale-ship *Bedford*. From the deck they remarked a strange object on the shore. It was moving down the beach toward the water. They were unable to classify it, and, being scientific men, they climbed into the whale-boat alongside and went ashore to see. And they saw something that was alive but which could hardly be called a man. It was blind, unconscious. It squirmed along the ground like some monstrous worm. Most of its efforts were ineffectual, but it was persistent, and it writhed and twisted and went ahead perhaps a score of feet an hour.

* * * * *

Three weeks afterward the man lay in a bunk on the whale-ship *Bedford*, and with tears streaming down his wasted cheeks told who he was and what he had undergone. He also babbled[47] incoherently of his mother, of sunny Southern California, and a home among the orange groves and flowers.

The days were not many after that when he sat at table with the scientific men and ship's officers. He gloated over the spectacle of so much food, watching it anxiously as it went into the mouths of others. With the disappearance of each mouthful an expression of deep regret came into his eyes. He was quite sane, yet he hated those men at mealtime. He was haunted by a fear that the food would not last. He inquired of the cook, the cabin-boy, the captain, concerning the food stores. They reassured him countless times; but he could not believe them, and pried cunningly about the lazarette to see with his own eyes.

It was noticed that the man was getting fat. He grew stouter with each day. The scientific men shook their heads and theorized. They limited the man at his meals, but still his girth increased and he swelled prodigiously under his shirt.

The sailors grinned. They knew. And when the scientific men set a watch on the man, they knew too. They saw him slouch for'ard after breakfast, and, like a mendicant, with outstretched palm, accost a sailor. The sailor grinned and passed him a fragment of sea biscuit. He clutched it avariciously, looked at it as a miser looks at gold, and thrust it into his shirt bosom. Similar were the donations from other grinning sailors.

The scientific men were discreet. They let him alone. But they privily examined his bunk. It was lined with hardtack; the mattress was stuffed with hardtack; every nook and cranny was filled with hardtack. Yet he was sane[48]. He was taking precautions against another possible famine — that was all. He would recover from it, the scientific men said; and he did, ere the *Bedford*'s anchor rumbled down in San Francisco Bay.

Notes

1. At the very beginning of the article, this four-line poem reveals that the power of life enables the protagonist to put aside the desire for material things and finally survives trials and tribulations.

2. I wish we... cache of ourn: I wish we had just about two of the cartridges that are laying in the cache of our own.

3. boulder: a very large rock which has been shaped by water or the weather.

4. His lips... agitated. His tongue... them: The sentences describe the second man's anger and dissatisfaction with his peer, and further reveal his fears and worries about his isolation as he was left by his peer.

5. smolder: to burn slowly and gently, usually with some smoke, but without a flame.

6. the Great Bear Lake: a large lake in the Northwest Territories of Canada.

7. the Coppermine River: a river in the Mackenzie District of the Northwest Territories of Canada.

8. Coronation Gulf: a gulf between Victoria Island and the mainland of Canada.

9. Hudson Bay Company: Hudson Bay Company controlled most of the fur trade

in the British-occupied North American region for centuries. It also undertook the development and exploration of North American continent. Its post network which later became official institutions can be found everywhere in Canada and the western United States. When the fur businesses declined, the company entered the commodity market, selling daily necessities to new immigrants in western Canada.

10. ... that sent fear swiftly dawning into his eyes: that threatened him and the air of fear moved swiftly into his eyes.

11. pulled himself together: bestir himself; to cheer up.

12. TITCHIN-NICHILIE: the natives used the word "TITCHIN-NICHILIE" to mean the "land of little sticks".

13. snaring of food: the food that is both alluring and dangerous, especially kept in a trap with a device to catch something.

14. Mackenzie: a river system in the northwest of Canada; the second largest river system of North America.

15. moccasin: a kind of native North American heelless shoe made of deerskin or other soft leather wrapped around the foot and stitched on top.

16. that quarter: one of the four directions, i.e. northeast.

17. caribou: a large deer with long thin legs and horns on its head that lives in northern North America.

18. knoll: a small rounded hill or mound.

19. the squat moose-hide sack: short, wide or fat bag that is made of deer skin. Here it is not known of what's in this bag or sack, but the importance of it is obviously second only to the matches.

20. ptarmigan: a type of bird with a fat body and feathers on its legs, found in mountain areas and in Arctic region.

21. squirm: to move by twisting and turning in a small space.

22. game: the wild animals or birds which can be hunted for sport or food.

23. bovine: looking or displaying slowly, and slightly stupid, just like a cow or related animals.

24. Thus he thought... dry sobs.: He strived to get some eats, but again and again ends in fruitless, which is enough to make him feel isolated and helpless, and make him emotionally collapse.

25. flurry: a sudden short period of snowfall.

26. take no heed of: disregard; regardless of.

27. for the eating was an act of pure reason: for the eating was purely a rational choice and act.

28. The squat moose-hide sack in which gold dust and nuggets were kept has become less important in his rational consciousness of surviving.

29. dodge: to move quickly and suddenly to one side to avoid being caught or hit by somebody or something.

30. whetted his appetite: increased his desire for food, or regained his interest in eating.

31. Nothing is more important than life, and he felt that the pack with gold was imposing a burdensome and cruel domination against his instincts for survival.

32. hallucination: a symptom of psychiatric disorder of seeming to see or hear somebody/something that is not really there.

33. till for very relief he opened his rifle to unconvince himself: till the relief from hallucination he opened his rifle to convince himself that its chamber was empty.

34. bellicose: ready or inclined to quarrel, fight, or go to war.

35. At this very moment, extreme bravery was brought out from extreme fear of being attacked by the bear.

36. He is not afraid of dying because of lack of food, but he is afraid that his willpower and the intrinsic nature of pursuing life will be destroyed.

37. ere: (old English) means before; ere the day was done: before the day was over.

38. He is not very clear about the meaning of being alive. But in the face of the bones, he is more willing to let his life continue to bear the pain, because only by living can he have the right to feel pain.

39. mirage: a strange effect in a desert or on the ocean in which you see something that is not really there; something that seems to be real or true but is not really so.

40. discernible: able to be seen or noticed.

41. palsy: loss of control or feeling of moving part or all of the body.

42. Indian Summer: a period of warm weather in autumn.

43. Yet the life that was in him drove him on: The unyielding of life and

willpower are showed here once again in this expression.

44. His mirth was hoarse and ghastly: His happiness/enjoyment with laughter was rough, unpleasant and shocking, because the mirth involved the man's pain and fear of being destroyed like Bill.

45. wheeze: the noisy and difficult breathing, or the hoarse whistling sound that accompanied to the breath.

46. languor: the weariness or weakness heaved up before the fire of life goes out.

47. babble: to reveal something thoughtlessly or impulsively with a continuous low murmuring or bubbling sound.

48. sane: be able to think and speak in a reasonable way and to behave normally.

Questions for Discussion

(1) Jack London was deeply influenced by Darwin's theory of survival of the fittest and he interpreted his creative understanding of Darwin's theory in his works. In "Love of Life", when the protagonist was abandoned by his companions, he was such a weak person who was on the verge of being eliminated. Later, he was gradually inspired by the instinct for life. Besides the strong instinct for life, what are the other instincts of the protagonist conveyed in the story?

(2) The "wilderness" is the most representative image in London's creation. What does the "wilderness" symbolize? Does it symbolize despair, hope, the inner spiritual world of human beings? Or is it a symbol of the indifference and mercilessness of the world?

Suggested Reading

- Donald Pizer 编：《剑桥文学指南：美国现实主义和自然主义》，上海：上海外语教育出版社，2000 年。
- Jack London. *Love of Life and other Stories* (English Edition). Hoboken, NJ: Start Publishing LLC, 2012.
- 杰克·伦敦（Jack London）：《当世界还年轻时：杰克·伦敦最好的短篇小说》(*When the World Was Young: Best Short Stories of Jack London*)，天津：天津人民出版社，2015 年。

17. Edwin Arlington Robinson

Edwin Arlington Robinson is generally regarded as one of the the greatest American poets of the late 19th century, and he maintained a prominent position in American literature into the latter decades of the 20th century.

Robinson was born in the town of Head Tide, Maine, on December 22, 1869, the third son of the family. He was given a female's name because his mother had expected a daughter and no male name was prepared for a possible son. When Robinson was eighteen months old, the family moved to Gardiner where his father was offered the directorship of a bank. Growing up, he was unhappy with the family's habit of calling him "Win" and after he grew into adulthood, he would use "E. A." for his name. Robinson was a shy and quiet child, but he would always join the neighbor's brothers picking apples and swimming in the river. But his greatest joy was on the sound of words; he took much pride in his ability to sound out difficult words. Robinson finally realized his keen interest in poetry in 1889. He then got the chance to introduce his gift of poetry to Dr. Alanson Tucker Schumann, a homeopathic physician, who immediately recognized Robinson's unique literary talent. Dr. Schumann agreed to personally tutor Robinson in formal poetic forms such as sonnet, ballad, and villanelle. After high school, Robinson attended Harvard College where his intellectual interests and his circle of friends broadened. But his studies came to an abrupt end two years later when his family suffered severe financial losses in the panic of 1893. After returning to Gardiner, he formed a small poetry and philosophy group that often read drafts of his poems to the members. In 1896 he published at his own cost his first book, *The Torrent and the Night Before*, which received several positive reviews. Robinson soon reworked on the collection into his first commercial publication, *The Children of the Night*, the publication of which was guaranteed by Laura E. Richards. Then tragedy struck when Robinson's father, mother and his beloved elder brother all died within the next three years of each other. After the second eldest brother Herman's death, Robinson had no choice but to earn enough money to support his brother's family. When Robinson was down and out, it was Laura E. Richards, one of his most important lifelong friends who gave him continuous support. But Robinson's life did not start to turn until his poems were submitted to Theodore Roosevelt, then-president of the United States. Theodore Roosevelt admired the poems so much that he wrote a review for *The Children of the Night* and persuaded a publisher to reprint it. Later on, Robinson dedicated his *The Town Down the River* to the president. In 1922 he received his first Pulitzer Prize, followed by two more in 1925 and 1928. In all, Robinson published twenty-eight books of poetry in his lifetime. He died of cancer on April 6, 1935.

Robinson's early poems were mostly written in traditional poetic forms, like sonnet and villanelle, mainly describing local conditions, customs and various characters in "Tilbury", which is the archetype of Gardiner, the town where he lived for more than 27 years. Among these poems, the fictional "portrait" poems are especially popular, like "Richard Cory", "Mr. Flood's Party", "The Tree in Pamela's Garden" and "Miniver Cheevy". The later works are long narrative poems based on the legend of King Arthur and the Knights of the Round Table: *Merlin*, *Lancelot*, and *Tristram*, all in iambic pentameter without rhyme. Although Robinson uses traditional rhythms in the forms, his poems are more modern in contents. He embraces novel ideas and images, pays attention to the characters' innermost things, and combines passion, cynicism and humor as one in his poetry. He is often criticized of being obscure in his works, but the fault usually lays in the inability of his readers to detect subtleties and ironies. From the ways Robinson makes his presentation, he is considered as someone who tries to get rid of the influence of British romantic poetry by exploring failure, anti-materialism, and alienation among the people, themes which have similarities to American modernistic poetry. The well-known critic Collins Brooks says that Robinson both relies on and deviates from the American literary tradition.

Richard Cory[1]

Whenever Richard Cory went down town,
We people on the pavement looked at him:
He was a gentleman from sole to crown,
Clean-favoured and imperially slim.[2]

And he was always quietly arrayed,
And he was always human when he talked;[3]
But still he fluttered pulses when he said,
"Good Morning!" and he glittered when he walked.[4]

And he was rich, yes, richer than a king[5],
And admirably schooled[6] in every grace:
In fine — we thought that he was everything
To make us wish that we were in his place.[7]

So on we worked and waited for the light,
And went without the meat and cursed the bread[8],
And Richard Cory, one calm summer night,
Went home and put a bullet in his head.[9]

Notes

1. Richard Cory: a fictive name given to the hero of the poem. Richard: the meaning of Richard is "powerful leader". It is a Norman name commonly used for the last 900 years except in the 19th century. Cory: a prominent surname for male. So, from the name the readers can get a glimpse into the author's deliberations in portraying his characters.

2. He was... imperially slim: from sole to crown means from foot to head; clean-favored: the preferred clean and refreshing; imperially slim: tall and handsome like an emperor. Robinson shapes Cory as such a special being, even the words used to describe his appearance are extremely exquisite, thus constructing the distinction between Cory and the narrator "we".

3. And he was always quietly... when he talked: arrayed means dressed in a particular way, especially in beautiful clothes; human: means Cory has the same feeling and emotion as "we" the ordinary people.

4. But still... when he talked: fluttered pulses mean his heart beats very quickly and not regularly; glittered: with shiny light around. Cory's natural beauty sets him apart the other ordinary people.

5. And he was rich, yes, richer than a king: With the usage of comparison, Cory in ordinary people's regard is still surprisingly more different.

6. schooled: acquired, studied.

7. From the begining to the end of the third stanza, Cory is portrayed as someone with all the advantages in life. Naturally his life becomes an ideal that is the envy of ordinary people.

8. This line again highlights the conflict between Richard Cory and the narrator "we" — the ordinary people.

9. That Cory shot himself reveals his real situation — he was not as happy as he makes out to be. It follows that what he wants is not to be admired and honored by others. His death overturns all the foreshadowing of the first three stanzas, and constructs the ultimate irony.

Miniver Cheevy[1]

Miniver Cheevy, child of scorn,
Grew lean while he assailed the seasons;[2]
He wept that he was ever born,
And he had reasons.

Miniver loved the days of old
When swords were bright and steeds were prancing;[3]
The vision of a warrior bold
Would set him dancing.

Miniver sighed for what was not,
And dreamed, and rested from his labors[4];
He dreamed of Thebes and Camelot,
And Priam's neighbors.[5]

Minever mourned the ripe renown
That made so many a name so fragrant;[6]

He mourned Romance, now on the town,
And Art, a vagrant[7].

Miniver loved the Medici,
Albeit he had never seen one;[8]
He would have sinned incessantly
Could he have been one.

Miniver cursed the commonplace
And eyed a khaki suit with loathing;[9]
He missed the mediæval grace
Of iron clothing.

Miniver scorned the gold he sought,
But sore annoyed was he without it;
Miniver thought, and thought, and thought,
And thought about it.[10]

Miniver Cheevy, born too late,
Scratched his head and kept on thinking;
Miniver coughed, and called it fate,
And kept on drinking[11].

Notes

1. This is a narrative poem about a character chosen from Robinson's fictional portrait poems. The title of the poem "Miniver Cheevy" can sufficiently arouse the curiosity of readers.

2. Miniver... the seasons: For "child of scorn", critics have it that Robinson or the narrator's point in using this phrase to describe Miniver Cheevy can have two meanings. One is that the character scorns the modern world because it is not the world of the past. The second is that his behavior makes him worthy of scorn. Grew

lean: became thin; assailed the seasons: highly critical of the modern world.

3. Miniver loved... prancing: The days of old refer to the age when warriors can fight on the battlefield with swords and mount on horses; steeds: war-horse; prancing: refers to the scene when a war-horse walks lively and raises legs high in the air, which shows a noble bearing.

4. his labors: his labors in reality. In the first stanza, Miniver "wept" that he was in the wrong stage; and then in the second stanza, Miniver misses and highly appreciates the heroic spirit in the past. So here in the third stanza, "rested from his labors" actually reflects Miniver's disdain and rejection of reality.

5. He dreamed of... neighbors: Thebes is one of the famed cities of antiquity, the capital of the ancient Egyptian empire in its heyday; Camelot: in the legend, King Arthur's palace was seated in Camelot in which King Arthur and his Knights sat on the round table to discuss state affairs; Priam: in Greek mythology, Priam was the last king of Troy. He ruled the city during the Trojan War and had ties to both its beginning and end. Thebes, Camelot and Priam all represent the classical and medieval grandeur.

6. Minever... so fragrant: Minever is the variant spelling of Miniver; made so many a name so fragrant: made so many names with good reputation for ages.

7. vagrant: a person who has no home or job, especially one who begs. Here art is personified as a vagrant, which implies the decline of art in the modern world.

8. Minever loved... seen one: Medici refers to the Medici family, a prominent family in Italy, which is a symbol of power and wealth. The House of Medici had strongly supported the arts and humanities in Italian Renaissance. Albeit: although, even if.

9. Miniver cursed... with loathing: commonplace refers to the things that commonly happen or ordinary things in the modern world. Khaki: a strong greenish or yellowish cloth, used especially for making military uniforms; here it is used for the comparison of suit of armor in medieval times.

10. Miniver scorned... about it: Gold represents the pursuit of material. In this stanza, Miniver is described as a contradictory existence: he not only mocks the pursuit of material, but also pursues material enthusiastically.

11. And kept on drinking: Such an ending leaves space for interpretation to the readers, because no result is given based on Miniver's attitude towards life. Will he accept destiny optimistically? Or he just shows a kind of courage in despair?

Questions for Discussion

(1) What theme do you think Robinson wants to express in "Richard Cory"? Is it loneliness? Does it reflect loss in the modern world? Or is it just a portrayal of his psychological journey in his adulthood? What is your opinion?

(2) In the poem "Richard Cory", Robinson successfully depicts the life of a "big man" within only sixteen lines, and he also shows the readers the unique charm of his portrait poem by highlighting the tension of contrast in both form and contents. How do you understand the poem from any of the following pair perspectives — the appearance and the substance, perfection and imperfection, the Cory in the eyes of others and the Cory in his own eyes, the stated and unstated, material abundance and spiritual void?

(3) Robinson has experienced many hardships in his life before he was discovered by president Roosevelt. His personal experience has given him a deep understanding of social reality. Do you think Miniver's resistance to the reality in "Miniver Cheevy" is negative or positive? Why?

(4) Some critics consider that Robinson's poems use traditional rhythms in form, but are more modern in contents and presentation. How would you analyze Robinson's two poems on the principles of modernistic poetry?

Suggested Reading

- Lloyd R. Morris. *The Poetry of Edwin Arlington Robinson: An Essay in Appreciation*. Port Washington: Kennikat Press, 1969.

Part Four

Modern American Literature

18. Ezra Pound

Ezra Pound is widely considered one of the most influential American poets of the 20th century; his contributions to modernist poetry were enormous. He is an early champion of a number of avant-garde and modernist poets; develops important channels of intellectual and aesthetic exchange between the United States and Europe; and contributes to important literary movements such as Imagism[1] and Vorticism.

Pound was born in Hailey, on October 30, 1885. In June 1889, following his father Homer Pound's appointment to the U.S. Mint in Philadelphia, they settled in nearby Wyncote, where Pound lived a typical middle-class childhood. He got his bachelor degree at Hamilton College in 1905, received an M.A. in June 1906 but withdrew from the university after working one more year toward his doctorate. He left with a knowledge of Latin, Greek, French, Italian, German, Spanish, Provençal, and Anglo-Saxon, as well as of English literature and grammar.

He lived in London from 1908 to 1920, where he connected with many writers, such as T. S. Eliot, whose known masterpiece *Waste Land* was edited and improved by Pound. Similar to his friend, T. S. Eliot was also a prolific critic as well as a poet. In 1912, Pound helped create a movement that he and others called "Imagism" which signaled a new literary direction for the poet. Imagism originated in England and America in the early twentieth century. As leader of the Imagist movement from 1912 to 1914, successor of the "school of images", he drew up the first Imagist manifesto, with its emphasis on direct and sparse language and precise images in poetry, and he edited the first Imagist anthology *Des Imagistes*.

In 1920, after 12 years in London, Pound left England for a new start in Paris. But his tolerance for French life, it seemed, was limited. In 1924, tired of the Parisian scene, he moved to Rapallo, Italy, where he would remain for the next two decades. It was there that Pound's life changed significantly. In 1925, he had a daughter, Maria, with the American violinist Olga Rudge; the following year he had a son, Omar, with his wife, Dorothy. But it is in this period that Pound became involved in fascist politics, and did not return to the United States until 1945, when he was arrested on charges of treason for broadcasting fascist propaganda by radio to the United States during World War II. In 1946, he was acquitted, but declared mentally ill and was committed to St. Elizabeth's Hospital in Washington, D.C. After the treason charges were dismissed in 1958, Pound returned to Italy and settled in Venice, where he died on November 1, 1972.

Professionally, Pound had turned his full attention to *The Cantos*, an ambitious long-form poem he had begun in 1915. A work he self-described as his "poem including history", *The Cantos* reveals Pound's interest in economics and in the world's changing financial landscape in the wake of World War I, in which he explored poetic traditions from different cultures ranging from ancient Greece, China, and the continent, to current-day England and America.

The first section of the poem was published in 1925, with later editions appeared later (*Eleven New Cantos*, 1934; *The Fifth Decade of Cantos*, 1937; *Cantos LII-LXXI*, 1940). Pound's poetry is best known for its clear, visual images, fresh rhythms, and muscular, intelligent, unusual lines; "In a Station of the Metro" is an example. This poem is an absolute representative of Ezra Pound's Imagism.

In a Station of the Metro[2]

The apparition[3] of these faces in the crowd:
Petals on a wet, black bough[4].

Notes

1. Imagism: A reactionary movement against Romanticism and Victorian poetry,

Imagism emphasizes simplicity, clarity of expression, and precision through the use of exacting visual images. Ezra Pound has been noted as the founder of Imagism.

2. In a Station of the Metro: One day in Paris in a cold winter of 1912, Pound was leaving a metro station. All of a sudden, he saw several beautiful faces of stunning women and children. And Pound decided to write a poem about what he saw. It is said that Pound had written a thirty-line poem, only to destroy it as a work of "second intensity". Six months later, he rewrote the poem in fifteen lines, using the same theme — a moment of sudden emotion at seeing beautiful faces in a metro station in Paris. After another year, he had reduced the poem to its final, two-line form.

3. apparition: This word has a two-fold meaning. On the one hand, it means the "appearance" of something Pound actually saw; on the other hand, it may refer to an image of a ghostly sight, an unreal appearance.

4. bough: a main branch of a tree.

Questions for Discussion

(1) Imagism makes this poem intriguing and leaves readers with the urge to probe further. Find a Chinese translation by yourself and try to find out what figure of speech is applied in the translation. Identify one or two Chinese poems that are similar to "In a Station of the Metro" in figure of speech.

(2) Many critics consider this poem to be impressionist by the way modern life is captured by extremely symbolic images. Pound leaves readers a broad space for thinking, making the poem shine and become a classic in modern British and American literature. Identify the impressionistic element in the poem.

Suggested Reading

- Donald Gallup. *Ezra Pound: A Bibliography*. Charlottesville, VA: The University Press of Virginia, 1983.
- Ezra Pound. *Personae: The Shorter Poems of Ezra Pound*. London: Faber & Faber, 2001.

19. Robert Frost

As a well-known and often-quoted poet, Robert Frost was highly honored in his life time with 4 Pulitzer Prizes, and is believed to be the most popular modern poet in America. He received more literary awards, recognition, and institutional honors than any other poets of the 20th century.

Frost was born in San Francisco, 1874 and spent his childhood in the Far West. He moved to New Hampshire at the age of eleven after his father's death. With an enduring dislike for academic education, he tried college but soon left without graduating. And for the next twelve years Frost supported himself by teaching and farming while writing till 1912. He decided to pursue his career in literature, thus he left New Hampshire for England. In the next year, Frost published his first book titled *A Boy's Will*. More importantly, he made contacts with T. E. Hulme, Edward Thomas, and Ezra Pound, who were the first Americans to write a favorable review of Robert Frost's works and helped him publish his poetry collection *North of Boston*. The collection contains some of his most excellent pieces, including "Mending Walls" and "After Apple-Picking". It was then he became known in the United States. In 1917, he took a teaching position at Amherst College, Massachusetts.

What's worth noting are the personal tragedies he went through. He suffered from his father's untimely death at the age of eleven, the illnesses of his daughters, the suicide of his son Carol, and eventually the loss of his beloved wife. So overall, Robert Frost was very successful in the public eye, yet a tragic figure as well.

The reason's why the general audience find Robert Frost's works appealing might be the universal subjects in his poems, his frequent use of rhyme, and the profound meaning behind his poems. Robert Frost's works are highly associated with rural life in New England. He employs the plain speech of rural residence in New England and prefers the short, traditional forms in his poems. Frost's works are often deceptively simple. Many poems, without doubt, suggest a deeper meaning. For example, in "Stopping by Woods on a Snowy Evening", a quiet snowy evening depicted by an almost hypnotic rhyme scheme may suggest the not entirely unwelcome approach of death.

"The Road Not Taken" is quite a popular poem; however, its popularity comes mainly from the misreading of the poem. With this poem, Frost gives the world a piece of writing that every individual can relate to, especially when it comes to the concept of choices and opportunities in life.

Most of the time, this poem is quoted and used with an interpretation that is not exactly "correct". The poem describes how the narrator struggles to choose between two roads diverging in the yellowish woods on an autumn morning. The narrator is aware of the futility of making a choice, since his current path will bring about separate paths in itself, disallowing any consequent reversal. The narrator concludes on a melancholic note of how different circumstances and outcomes would have been, had it been the "other" path.

The poem "Stopping by Woods on a Snowy Evening", published in 1923 in his collection *New Hampshire*, also narrates the account of a man standing deep in the woods torn between two choices. The narrator stops his horse in a winter night to observe the beauty of the scenery in the forest, and then is moved to continue his journey.

The Road Not Taken

Two roads diverged in a yellow wood[1],
And sorry I could not travel both
And be one traveler, long I stood
And looked down one[2] as far as I could
To where it bent[3] in the undergrowth; [4]

Then took the other, as just as fair[5],
And having perhaps the better claim
Because it was grassy and wanted wear[6];
Though as for that, the passing[7] there
Had worn them really about the same, [8]

And both that morning equally lay

In leaves no step had trodden black⁹.
Oh, I marked the first for another day!
Yet knowing how way leads on to way
I doubted if I should ever come back¹⁰.

I shall be telling this with a sigh
Somewhere ages and ages hence¹¹:
Two roads diverged in a wood, and I,
I took the one less traveled by,
And that has made all the difference.¹²

Notes

1. Two roads diverged in a yellow wood: to diverge is to split off in a different direction. In other words, the narrator is describing a fork in the road; Yellow wood: a forest in autumn ("yellow" refers to the color of autumn leaves). Referring to a forest as a "wood" is also an example of synecdoche.

2. looked down one: looked along one of the two roads.

3. bent: disappeared.

4. Two roads... in the undergrowth: These lines present an archetypal human situation where man is faced with the difficulty of making choices. In one sense, Frost — or the narrator of his poem — seems to suggest that the choice would "[make] all the difference"; but the poet is too deep and too wise to be so absolute about life and people.

5. as just as fair: It is as reasonable as the choice of the first road to choose the second one.

6. wanted wear: lacked. To say that the road "wanted wear" means that it wasn't worn. Frost's use of the word "wanted" here also has a subtle second meaning: it suggests that the road was calling him, as though it "wanted" him to choose it.

7. passing: walking or traveling. The narrator is saying that the two roads, in fact, had been walked on about the same amount.

8. Though as... about the same: What the narrator is saying is probably this:

ultimately one would look back in retrospect and see that both roads have the same prospects as they are equally worn.

9. In leaves no step had trodden black: The fallen leaves of trees had not been trodden black; trodden: the past participle of "tread", meaning to crush or flatten something with the feet. To say that the leaves had not been trodden black means that they had not been turned black by the wear of foot traffic.

10. I should ever come back: Each choice may be a beginning, but it is also an ending; and having to choose cuts off the knowledge of another choice, such that the person who is choosing will never know if he has made the "right" choice.

11. hence: in the future.

12. The poem ends with the narrator imagining the far future, when he or she thinks back to this choice and believes that it has made "all the difference". But the rest of the poem has shown that the narrator doesn't (and can never) know what it would have been like to travel down the other road — and can't even know if the road taken is indeed the one less traveled. And, further, the final line is a subtle reminder that the only thing one can know about the choices one makes in life is that they make "all the difference" — but how, or from what? Neither the poem nor life provides any answer.

Questions for Discussion

(1) How does the apparent contradiction of the narrator in the poem taking the road "less traveled by", "the passing there/Had worn them really about the same", affect the meaning of the poem?

(2) "The Road Not Taken" is an example of an extended metaphor. Name several lines to support the argument.

Suggested Reading

- George Monteiro. *Robert Frost & the New England Renaissance.* Cambridge: Cambridge University Press, 1991.
- 弗罗斯特:《弗罗斯特集》, 理查德·普瓦里耶、马克·理查森编, 曹明伦译, 沈阳: 辽宁教育出版社, 2002 年。

20. William Carlos Williams

William Carlos Williams was born on September 17, 1883, in Rutherford, New Jersey. He is considered to be an American poet who succeeded in making the ordinary appear extraordinary through the clarity and discreteness of his imagery. Being the eldest child of the family, he attended a private school in Switzerland and went on to the University of Pennsylvania where he got his medical degree in 1906. He was a practicing pediatrician throughout his life, delivering over 2000 babies while writing poems on his prescription pads. He did his graduate work at the University of Leipzig.

He received his M.D. from the University of Pennsylvania, where he met and befriended Ezra Pound. Pound became a great influence in Williams' writing, and in 1913 he arranged for the publication of Williams' second collection in London, *The Tempers*. Following Pound, Williams was one of the principal poets of the Imagist movement, and his early poetry also revealed the influence of Imagism. However, as time went on, he began to increasingly disagree with the values put forth in the works of Pound and T. S. Eliot, who he felt were too attached to European culture and traditions. Unlike Eliot's frequent use of allusions to foreign languages and classical sources, as in *The Waste Land*, Williams preferred drawing his themes from what he called "the local".

Returning to Rutherford, where he continued his medical practice throughout his life, Williams began publishing his works in small magazines and embarked on a prolific career as a poet, novelist, essayist, and playwright. Meanwhile, Williams sought to invent an entirely fresh — and singularly American — poetic, whose subject matter was centered on the everyday circumstances of life and the lives of common people. His influence as a poet spread slowly in 1920s and 1930s, overshadowed, he felt, by the immense popularity of Eliot's *The Waste Land*. However, his works received increasingly more attention in the 1950s and 1960s as younger poets, including Beats poets with Allen Ginsberg as the representative, were impressed by the accessibility of his language and his openness as a mentor. His major works include *Kora in Hell*, *Spring and All*, and *Pictures from Brueghel and Other Poems*.

Unfortunately, Williams' health began to decline after a heart attack in 1948 and the subsequent series of strokes. He continued writing until his death in New Jersey in 1963.

Williams tries to create a fresh-new poetic form, an American form with the theme of daily living environment and common people's life full of ordinary people's dialogue. They are placed in nearby streets, hospitals and backyards. His goal is to reproduce the rhythm of American speech and the words of ordinary people. He emphasizes images or things and avoids expressing ideas directly. Williams' poetry shows a kind of fortitude and control, which is masculine and anti-perceptual. His themes are very broad, including the emergence of life, the essence of poetry, unfortunate human nature in various disguises, sex and pornography, rich daily experience, and, most importantly, the reality of industrial America.

Williams has a famous maxim, "No ideas but in things". It means, instead of speaking about and expressing ideas, emotions, and abstractions, we must root them firmly in the things of the world. All but the first two lines of "The Red Wheelbarrow" is devoted to his theory. In the very short poem, the poet depicts two things — wheelbarrow and chicken, using sole and simple enough adjectives — red and white, which would certainly interest readers to probe further.

The Red Wheelbarrow[1]

so much depends
upon[2]

a red wheel
barrow

glazed[3] with rain
water

beside the white
chickens[4]

This Is Just to Say[5]

I have eaten

the plums[6]

that were in

the icebox[7]

and which

you were probably

saving

for breakfast

Forgive me

they were delicious

so sweet

and so cold

Notes

1. William Carlos Williams published "The Red Wheelbarrow" in his 1923 poetry collection, *Spring and All*. In this collection, the poem does not have a title, but is merely marked "XXII" (the Roman numeral for the number 22). "The Red Wheelbarrow" is considered one of the most prominent poems of the Imagist movement. A wheelbarrow is a gardening and construction tool. It consists of a single wheel and a cart with two handles on either side, and is used to lift and transport heavy loads. In the poem, the word is broken in two words, but it is most often spelled as a compound word.

2. The first two lines of the poem are its most vague, and in turn, the most suggestive lines. The lines constitute a mysterious cliffhanger: "so much depends upon" what exactly? In this moment, it could be anything; four short words open up endless possibilities.

3. glazed: when used here, it refers to being covered with a smooth or shiny finish. After the rainfall, the wheelbarrow is now wet, and the wetness has given the

wheelbarrow a sheen.

4. This short poem consists entirely of a single sentence, which is drawn out over the course of eight lines using enjambment. Each line spills over into the next, creating a casual, free-flowing sensation that contributes to the poem's calm, meditative tone. Note how quickly the image would rush by were the lines not enjambed: so much depends upon a red wheelbarrow glazed with rainwater beside the white chickens. The enjambment slows down the poem, ensuring that the reader is surveying the scene with the same focus and intent as the narrator.

5. William Carlos Williams published "This Is Just to Say" in 1934. In the poem, the narrator confesses to having sneakily eaten plums from an icebox (a kind of precursor to the modern refrigerator). Because of its casual style, some readers believe it was originally written as a note from Williams to his wife.

6. plum: a soft round fruit with smooth red or purple skin, sweet flesh and a large flat seed inside. The poet's use of the present perfect tense ("have eaten") instead of the past tense ("ate") makes the entire confession seem somehow more immediate, as if the act of eating the plums is still bringing itself to bear on the present, making it seem as if the eating of the plums isn't completely over and done with.

7. icebox: a chilled box or cupboard used to keep food cold before the invention of refrigerators. In the first stanza, the pairing of consonant "n" and sibilant sounds "s" is very euphonic, creating an almost tactile sound that reflects the pleasure the narrator seems to have derived from eating the plums.

Questions for Discussion

(1) In Williams' poems, ordinary objects are chosen to be the main targets. For example, in "The Red Wheelbarrow", only a red wheelbarrow and white chickens are presented in four stanzas. What is the deal with that red wheelbarrow and those white chickens? What kind of picture does the poet try to describe for us?

(2) "This Is Just to Say" is believed to be a note written by Williams to his wife. Why does he use "sweet" and "cold" simultaneously to describe the plums he ate?

Suggested Reading

● William Carlos Williams. *The Collected Earlier Poems of William Carlos Williams.* New York, NY: New Directions, 1951.

● 威廉·卡洛斯·威廉斯：《威廉·卡洛斯·威廉斯诗选》，傅浩译，上海：上海译文出版社，2015年。

21. Carl Sandburg

Carl Sandburg was born into a poor family in Galesburg, Illinois. He was the son of Swedish immigrants August and Clara Anderson Sandburg. The elder Sandburg, a blacksmith's helper for the nearby Chicago, Burlington and Quincy Railroad, purchased a cottage in 1873. Carl, called "Charlie" by the family, was born the second of seven children in 1878. A year later the Sandburgs sold the small cottage in favor of a larger house in Galesburg.

Carl Sandburg worked from the time he was a young boy. He quit school following his graduation from eighth grade in 1891 and spent a decade working on a variety of jobs. He delivered milk, harvested ice, laid bricks, threshed wheat in Kansas, and shined shoes in Galesburg's Union Hotel before traveling as a hobo in 1897. His working and traveling experiences greatly influenced his writing and political views. As a hobo he learned a number of folk songs, which he later performed at speaking engagements. He saw first-hand the sharp contrast between rich and poor, a dichotomy that instilled in him a distrust of capitalism.

When the Spanish-American war broke out in 1898, Sandburg volunteered to join the army. At the age of 20, he was sent to Puerto Rico, where he struggled with heat and mosquitoes only for a few days. When he returned to his hometown later that year, he entered Lombard college and became a firefighter on his own. In 1914, a group of Sandburg's poems appeared in *Poetry* magazine. At that time, the literary world knew almost nothing about him. Two years later, the publication of his poetry collection *Chicago Poems* brought him international reputation. Sandburg published another collection of poetry *Cornhuskers* in 1918 and made an in-depth analysis of the racial riots in Chicago in 1919.

Following Whitman, Sandburg depicts a sweeping landscape of American life, western and eastern, as well as a sketch of the modern city. In Sandburg's language of poetry, directness of statement is used more frequently than subtleties and rhythms. Instead of achieving regular stanza patterns and traditional blank verse, Sandburg writes an utterly free verse. Sandburg's most ambitious attempt to achieve his goal is *The People, Yes*, consisting of prose vignettes and anecdotes, beginning with the two-volume *Abraham Lincoln: The Prairie Years* and culminating in *The War Years*, a four-volume work which won him the Pulitzer Prize in 1940. In 1951, he also got another Pulitzer Prize for his *Complete Poems*.

The poem "Fog" first appeared in *Chicago Poems*, which was published in the year of 1916. The poem consists of 2 stanzas of different length. The first stanza is made up of 2 lines, while the second stanza is made up of 4 lines. Hence, the entire poem consists of 6 lines in total. The poet depicts the fog as a cat as a rhetorical device, presenting a picture of fog hovering over a city and moving on in a plain and direct way.

Fog[1]

The fog comes
on little cat feet.[2]

It sits looking
over harbor and city[3]
on silent haunches
and then moves on.[4]

Notes

1. The poem "Fog" is inspired by haiku, a kind of traditional Japanese poem. Carl Sandburg states that he writes the poem with the intention of creating an "American haiku". The poem does not have a set rhyming scheme, making it a free verse. As a

result, the poem is like the unfiltered thoughts of the narrator, expressing the sincere feelings of the author.

2. The fog... cat feet: The poem begins with the narrator stating that the fog arrives "on little cat feet". Cats are often associated with lithe, quiet, and graceful movements. By comparing the fog to a cat, the narrator ascribes these characteristics to the fog as well. The narrator specifically states that the fog has "little cat feet", which evokes the image of the agile way in which cats move.

3. It sits looking... and city: The narrator describes how the fog sits looking over the city. This once again adds characterization to the fog as a living entity. When fog forms over a location, it often lingers over the landscape for a few hours. The narrator is pointing out that this natural phenomenon almost seems deliberate, as though the fog is actually watching over the city that it has settled over.

4. on silent haunches... moves on: The author once again characterizes the fog as a living creature. "Haunches" are the back leg area of an animal. Because the narrator has earlier stated that the fog comes in on "little cat feet", we can infer that the "haunches" here refer specifically to those of a cat. This once again characterizes the fog as a feline-like entity. The word "silent" further emphasizes that it is quiet, lithe, and peaceful.

Questions for Discussion

(1) Sandburg depicts the shape of fog in image. Compare Sandburg's "Fog" with Frost's and Williams' poems. What are the similarities and distinctions?

(2) This poem was published in 1916, at the height of World War I. What is the theme of the poem? "Chicago" is another representative poem by Carl Sandburg, in which he praises the beauty of Chicago. The poem reflects his unique opinion on the image of Chicago: it is a city of the future. Discuss whether there is any link between the war or the historical context and Sandburg's poems, like "Fog" and "Chicago".

Suggested Reading

- Carl Sandburg. *Complete Poems*. San Diego, CA: Harcourt Brace & Company, 1950.

- 桑德堡：《桑德堡诗选》，北京：人民文学出版社，1987 年。

22. Wallace Stevens

Wallace Stevens is an American modernist poet. He won the Pulitzer Prize for Poetry for his *Collected Poems* in 1955. Some of his best-known poems include "Anecdote of the Jar", "Disillusionment of Ten O'Clock", "The Snow Man" and "Thirteen Ways of Looking at a Blackbird". Literary critic Harold Bloom calls Stevens the best and most representative American poet of the time, and claims no western writer since Sophocles has had such a late flowering of artistic genius.

Wallace Stevens was born and raised in Pennsylvania. His father was a prosperous attorney, and advised him to take on law after his study at Harvard. During his stay in New York, Stevens became connected with lots of young and ambitious writers, including William Carlos Williams and Marianne Moore. In 1923, he was persuaded to publish a book of poems, *Harmonium*. But its poor reception was a blow for him and almost discouraged him to quit writing poems. The reprinting of *Harmonium* in 1931 resulted in positive critical attention to Stevens' skill of use of extraordinary vocabulary, having a flair for memorable phrasing, and accomplished sense of imagery. After that Stevens began his years of steady publication. Eventually, he received the National Book Award and the Pulitzer Prize for the publication of his *Collected Poems*.

Stevens has a unique writing style. Although his language is often difficult and abstract, his poems have an extraordinary richness of imagery and sound. Stevens' poetry dwells upon themes of the imagination, the necessity for aesthetic form and the belief that the order of art corresponds with an order in nature. With rich, various and philosophical vocabulary, his poems celebrate the natural scenes in a variety of experiments. He creates poetic surfaces of elegance, exotic imagery, old sounds, curious analogies, and inscrutable titles. Stevens adopts traditional values and seeks to come to terms with the confusions of his time, which explains why Stevens' major theme is the relationship between the mind and physical reality. In his view, people constantly face the disorder of the world and the certainty of their own death. They are rescued from this potentially tragic situation by the use of imagination. Imagination can give meaning to the confusion of reality and can also discover the beauty in nature and joy in the face of death. Because Stevens believes that only the imagination can make sense of the universe, he thinks that God and the imagination are one.

"Anecdote of the Jar" is a poem that expresses, through the story of "a jar" and "a hill", the progressive overtaking of industry over nature. In the final stanza, that overtaking is revealed to be a sad and absurd prospect since Stevens' comparisons make it clear that he believes nature is far more remarkable than industry will ever be. While there are other explanations that could be applied to this poem, the heart of the plot is a reflection of this absurdity, making the three-stanzas a combined lament of the forsaking of nature for what was misinterpreted as betterment.

Anecdote of the Jar

I placed a jar in Tennessee,
And round it was, upon a hill.
It made the slovenly[1] wilderness[2]
Surround that hill.[3]

The wilderness rose up to it,
And sprawled[4] around, no longer wild.
The jar was round upon the ground
And tall and of a port in air[5].[6]

It took dominion[7] everywhere.
The jar was gray and bare.
It did not give of[8] bird or bush,
Like nothing else in Tennessee.[9]

Notes

1. slovenly: disordered, untidy, and/or careless.

2. wilderness: a wild and uncultivated area of land.

3. I placed... that hill: The narrator begins "Anecdote of the Jar" by the simple proclamation that he "placed a jar in Tennessee... upon a hill". This is a very clear and nondescript action, and even this "jar" is treated in a less than vivid manner. The reader does not know how big this "jar" is, or what color it is. Rather, the reader can only know that it is "round". Despite the simple design and description, however, this "jar" turns into something of massive importance since "[i]t made the slovenly wilderness [s]urround that hill".

4. sprawl: spread out over a large area.

5. a port in air: a port is a transportation hub, typically where harbor ships dock. A "port in air" suggests that the jar is in some way a kind of harbor in the air. This might be because it's empty (and thus air, only air, fills it).

6. The wilderness... port in air: Early in the second stanza, the sway of this "jar" over "[t]he wilderness" increases so that "wilderness" does not just "[s]urround the hill" this "jar" is "on", but "[rises] up to" "[t]he jar" itself. This progress is so strong and impacting that "wilderness" is "no longer wild" by the time the transition is finished.

7. dominion: ruling power.

8. give of: an ambiguous moment in the poem that probably means either "create" or "care for".

9. It took... in Tennessee: The third stanza begins with the blunt declaration that this simple jar "took dominion everywhere", which extends the influence of "[t]he jar" beyond the "hill".

Questions for Discussion

(1) "Anecdote of the Jar" was published in Stevens' first book, *Harmonium*, in 1923. What does the "jar" symbolize if the publication time is taken into account? And why is it "gray and bare"?

(2) Wallace Stevens usually writes poems with imagination. Yet, certain critics

believe Stevens' poems contain conflict among reality, imagination and aestheticism. What is your thought on the comment? What is the theme of "Anecdote of the Jar"?

Suggested Reading

● John N. Serio. *The Cambridge Companion to Wallace Stevens.* Cambridge: Cambridge University Press, 2007.

● 华莱士·史蒂文斯：《我可以触摸的事物》，马永波译，北京：商务印书馆，2018年。

23. Edward Estlin Cummings

Edward Estlin (E. E.) Cummings is an American poet, painter, essayist, author, and playwright. He wrote approximately 2,900 poems, two autobiographical novels, four plays, and several essays. He is often regarded as one of the most important American poets of the 20th century. Cummings is associated with modernist free-form poetry. Much of his work has idiosyncratic syntax and uses lower-case spellings for poetic expression.

E. E. Cummings is the son of a famous minister, born in Cambridge, Massachusetts. He obtained his Bachelor's degree and Master's degree by 1916 at Harvard University. Then he went on to serve in World War I overseas as a volunteer for the ambulance corps. As a pacifist, Cummings was imprisoned for several months by the French authorities for suspicion of treason due to the letters he had written. He later recounted his jail experiences in the autobiographical novel *The Enormous Room*, published in 1922. Critical reaction was overwhelmingly positive, although Cummings' account of his imprisonment was oddly cheerful in tone and freewheeling in style. He depicted his internment camp stay as a period of inner growth.

The early 1920s was an extremely productive time for Cummings. Cummings' first collection of poems, *Tulips and Chimneys*, appeared in 1923. His eccentric use of grammar and punctuation are evident in the volume, though many of the poems are written in conventional language. A car accident in 1926 killed his father and injured his mother severely. His father's death had a profound effect on him, leading to an entirely new period in his artistic life. He paid homage to his father in his poem "my father moved through dooms of love".

Clearly influenced by Gertrude Stein's syntactical and Amy Lowell's imagistic experiments, Cummings' early poems had nevertheless discovered an original way of describing the chaotic immediacy of sensuous experience. The games they play with language (adverbs functioning as nouns, for instance) and lyric form combine with their deliberately simplistic view of the world (the individual and spontaneity versus collectivism and rational thought) to give them the gleeful and precocious tone which became, a hallmark of his work. Love poems, satirical squibs, and descriptive nature poems would always be his forms of choice.

As one of the most innovative poets of his time, Cummings experimented with poetic form and language to create a distinct personal style. A typical Cummings' poem is spare and precise, employing a few key words eccentrically placed on the page. Some of these words were invented by Cummings, often by combining two common words into a new synthesis. He also revised grammatical and linguistic rules to suit his own purposes, using such words as "if", "am", and "because" as nouns, for example, or assigning his own private meanings to words.

In Cummings' poems, each line is no more than four words long which gives his poems a choppy effect that portrays the narrator's feelings about what he has just done. Even though no words in the poem outright state his feelings of guilt, the message still comes through loud and clear because of the way in which it is written. He doesn't put in any unnecessary words at all; each word he puts in there is essential to the sentence and would be meaningless without it.

Our brains make mandatory a certain amount of thought pertaining to each situation we are involved in; we can't just block out everything even if we'd like to. Cummings is just giving the minimal thought to the situation that he cannot block out. That shows how he is feeling and what is going in his head. His poems are broken up because his thoughts are broken up and uneven.

(Me up at does)[1]

Me up at does

out of the floor
quietly Stare[2]

a poisoned mouse

still who alive

is asking What
have i done that

You wouldn't have[3]

Notes

1. E. E. Cummings invites readers to "put yourself in someone else's shoes" in his 1963 poem "(Me up at does)". The whole poem can be written into a sentence: a poisoned mouse, who, still alive, is asking "what have i done" that you wouldn't have, does quietly stare out of the floor up at me.

2. stare: two things done by the mouse — to stare and to ask.

3. The rhyme of the poem is abbaabba. All of the rhymes are slant rhymes — for example, "does" and "mouse" are two different words that sound similar, but they are not the same. The use of rhyme mirrors the fact that the mouse and the narrator are two different creatures that are similar but not the same.

Questions for Discussion

(1) Cummings writes his poems in a simple but unique way, which is visually aesthetic to readers. What do you think "Me" and "mouse" stand for in this poem? What is the relation between them?

(2) Go through the poem once more, and notice how Cummings capitalizes some of the words, but not others. Is there any referential or symbolic meaning in this kind of writing technique? Why are "Me" and "You" capitalized?

Suggested Reading

- E. E. Cummings. *The Enormous Room: Large Print.* Scotts Valley, CA: CreateSpace Independent Publishing Platform, 2017.
- E. E. 卡明斯：《卡明斯诗选》，邹仲之译，上海：上海译文出版社，2016 年。
- 董广坤：《卡明斯的视觉诗》，南昌：江西人民出版社，2019 年。

24. Francis Scott Fitzgerald

F. Scott Fitzgerald (1896–1940) is an American short-story writer and novelist. He is widely considered the literary spokesman of the Jazz Age.

His private life with his wife, Zelda, in both America and France, became almost as celebrated as his novels. His life is just like a fairy tale. During World War I, Fitzgerald enlisted in the U.S. Army and fell in love with a beautiful and rich girl named Zelda Sayre, who lived near Montgomery, Alabama. And then Zelda broke off their engagement because he was very poor. After he was discharged from the army, he went to New York to pursue his literary dream in order to marry her. His first novel, *This Side of Paradise* sold well and they got married. But due to their inability to handle the stresses from success and fame, they squandered all their wealth. In 1924, they moved to France for seven years. Zelda became mentally unstable and had to be hospitalized; Fitzgerald himself became an alcoholic and died very young.

His major works include novels: *This Side of Paradise, The Beautiful and Damned, The Great Gatsby, Tender Is the Night*; short-story collections: *Flappers and Philosophers, Tales of the Jazz Age, All the Sad Young Men, Taps at Reveille. The Great Gatsby* tells of the American dream of the self-made man with a brilliant and economical structure. The protagonist, the mysterious Jay Gatsby discovers the devastating cost of success in terms of personal fulfillment and love. Another great work of Fitzgerald — *Tender Is the Night* tells a miserable story of a young psychiatrist and his marriage to an unstable woman. Fitzgerald captures the glittering, desperate life of the 1920s better than any other writers. *This Side of Paradise* is very popular with the voice of modern American youth. The book describes Fitzgerald's sense of failure with his academic performance and the frustration of his dreams at Princeton. It portrays at the same time "a generation grown up to find all gods dead, all wars fought, all faith in man shaken". His second novel, *The Beautiful and Damned*, continues his exploration of the self-destructive extravagance of his time.

The Great Gatsby[1]

Chapter 1

In my younger and more vulnerable years my father gave me some advice that I've been turning over in my mind ever since.

"Whenever you feel like criticizing any one," he told me, "just remember that all the people in this world haven't had the advantages that you've had."

He didn't say any more but we've always been unusually communicative in a reserved way, and I understood that he meant a great deal more than that. In consequence I'm inclined to reserve all judgments, a habit that has opened up many curious natures to me and also made me the victim of not a few veteran[2] bores. The abnormal mind is quick to detect and attach itself to this quality when it appears in a normal person, and so it came about that in college I was unjustly accused of being a politician, because I was privy[3] to the secret griefs of wild, unknown men. Most of the confidences were unsought[4] — frequently I have feigned[5] sleep, preoccupation[6], or a hostile levity[7] when I realized by some unmistakable sign that an intimate revelation was quivering[8] on the horizon[9] — for the intimate revelations of young men or at least the terms in which they express them are usually plagiaristic and marred by obvious suppressions[10]. Reserving judgments is a matter of infinite hope. I am still a little afraid of missing something if I forget that, as my father snobbishly[11] suggested, and I snobbishly repeat a sense of the fundamental decencies[12] is parcelled out[13] unequally[14] at birth.

And, after boasting this way of my tolerance, I come to the admission that it has a limit. Conduct may be founded on the hard rock[15] or the wet marshes[16] but after a certain point I don't care what it's founded on. When I came back from the East last autumn I felt that I wanted the world to be in uniform[17] and at a sort of moral attention[18] forever; I wanted no more riotous[19] excursions[20] with privileged[21] glimpses into the human heart. Only Gatsby, the man who gives his name to this book, was exempt from my reaction — Gatsby who represented everything for which I have an unaffected scorn. If personality is an unbroken series of successful gestures, then there was something gorgeous about him, some heightened sensitivity to the promises of life, as if he were related to one of those intricate machines that register earthquakes ten thousand miles away. This responsiveness had nothing to do with that flabby[22] impressionability which is dignified under the name of the "creative temperament" — it was an extraordinary gift for hope, a romantic readiness such as I have never found in any other person and which it is not likely I shall ever find again. No — Gatsby turned out all right at the end; it is what preyed on Gatsby, what foul dust floated in the wake of his dreams that temporarily closed out my interest in the abortive sorrows and short-winded[23] elations[24] of men.

My family have been prominent, well-to-do people in this middle-western city for three generations. The Carraways are something of a clan[25] and we have a tradition that we're descended from the Dukes of Buccleuch[26], but the actual founder of my line was my grandfather's brother who came here in fifty-one, sent a substitute to the Civil War and started the wholesale hardware business that my father carries on today.

I never saw this great-uncle but I'm supposed to look like him — with special reference to the rather hard-boiled[27] painting that hangs in Father's office. I graduated from New Haven[28] in 1915, just a quarter of a century after my father, and a little later I participated in that delayed Teutonic migration known as the Great War. I enjoyed the counter-raid[29] so thoroughly that I came back restless. Instead of being the warm center of the world the middle-west now seemed like the ragged[30] edge of the universe — so I decided to go east and learn the bond business. Everybody I knew was in the bond business so I supposed it could support one more single man. All my aunts and uncles talked it over as if they were choosing a prep-school[31] for me and finally said, "Why — ye-es" with very grave, hesitant faces. Father agreed to finance me for a year and after various delays I came east, permanently, I thought, in the spring of twenty-two.[32]

The practical thing was to find rooms in the city but it was a warm season and I had just left a country of wide lawns and friendly trees, so when a young man at the office suggested that we take a house together in a commuting town it sounded like a great idea. He found the house, a weather beaten cardboard bungalow at eighty a month, but at the last minute the firm ordered him to Washington and I went out to the country alone. I had a dog, at least I had him for a few days until he ran away, and an old Dodge and a Finnish woman who made my bed and cooked breakfast and muttered[33] Finnish wisdom to herself over the electric stove.

It was lonely for a day or so until one morning some man, more recently arrived than I, stopped me on the road.[34]

"How do you get to West Egg[35] village?" he asked helplessly.

I told him. And as I walked on I was lonely no longer. I was a guide, a pathfinder[36], an original settler. He had casually conferred on me the freedom of the neighborhood.

And so with the sunshine and the great bursts of leaves growing on the trees — just as things grow in fast movies — I had that familiar conviction that life was beginning over again with the summer.

There was so much to read for one thing and so much fine health to be pulled down out of the young breath-giving air.[37] I bought a dozen volumes on banking and credit and investment securities and they stood on my shelf in red and gold like new money from the mint, promising to unfold the shining secrets that only Midas[38] and Morgan[39] and Maecenas[40] knew. And I had the high intention[41] of reading many other books besides. I was rather literary in college — one year I wrote a series of very solemn and obvious editorials for the "Yale News" — and now I was going to bring back all such things into my life and become again that most limited of all specialists, the "well-rounded man". This isn't just an epigram — life is much more successfully looked at from a single window, after all.

It was a matter of chance[42] that I should have rented a house in one of the strangest communities in North America. It was on that slender riotous island which extends itself due east[43] of New York and where there are, among other natural curiosities[44], two unusual formations of land. Twenty miles from the city a pair of enormous eggs, identical in contour and separated only by a courtesy bay, jut out into the most domesticated body of salt water in the Western Hemisphere, the great wet barnyard of Long Island Sound. They are not perfect ovals — like the egg in the Columbus story they are both crushed flat at the contact end — but their physical resemblance must be a source of perpetual confusion to the gulls that fly overhead. To the wingless a more arresting phenomenon is their dissimilarity in every particular except shape and size.

I lived at West Egg, the — well, the less fashionable of the two, though this is a most superficial tag to express the bizarre and not a little sinister contrast between them. My house was at the very tip of the egg, only fifty yards from the Sound[45], and squeezed between two huge places that rented for twelve or fifteen thousand a season. The one on my right was a colossal affair by any standard — it was a factual imitation of some Hôtel de Ville in Normandy[46], with a tower[47] on one side, spanking new under a thin beard of raw ivy, and a marble swimming pool and more than forty acres of lawn and garden. It was Gatsby's mansion. Or rather, as I didn't know Mr. Gatsby it was a mansion inhabited by a gentleman of that name. My own house was an eye-sore, but it was a small eye-sore, and it had been overlooked, so I had a view of the water, a partial view of my neighbor's lawn, and the consoling proximity of millionaires — all for eighty dollars a month.

Across the courtesy bay the white palaces of fashionable East Egg glittered along the water, and the history of the summer really begins on the evening I drove over there to have dinner with the Tom Buchanans. Daisy was my second cousin once removed and I'd known Tom in college. And just after the war I spent two days with them in Chicago.

Her husband, among various physical accomplishments, had been one of the most powerful ends that ever played football at New Haven — a national figure in a way, one of those men who reach such an acute limited excellence at twenty-one that everything afterward savors of anti-climax. His family were enormously wealthy — even in college his freedom with money was a matter for reproach — but now he'd left Chicago and come east in a fashion that rather took your breath away: for instance he'd brought down a string of polo ponies from Lake Forest[48]. It was hard to realize that a man in my own generation was wealthy enough to do that.

Why they came east I don't know. They had spent a year in France, for no particular reason, and then drifted here and there unrestfully wherever people played polo and were rich together. This was a permanent move, said Daisy over the telephone, but I didn't believe it — I had no sight into Daisy's heart but I felt that Tom would drift on forever seeking a little wistfully for the dramatic turbulence of some irrecoverable football game.

Notes

1. *The Great Gatsby*: It is a short novel of just nine chapters, each built around a party scene — though the final "party" is a funeral. The story itself is about a poor boy from a farming background becomes fabulously wealthy. It is also a love story. The novel is fascinating but perhaps, at its deepest level, it is an examination of the American Dream that reaches a pessimistic conclusion. The accumulation of great wealth and the aspiration to win the lady end in tragedy because the Dream does not live up to what it promises. The concept of money, which is at the center of the Dream is complex. There is a tension between "old money" and "new money", represented in the novel by the towns of East Egg where the old rich, including the Buchanans, live, and the downmarket West Egg, where Gatsby's mansion is. In the end Gatsby is killed as a result of the events they are all involved in, and the Buchanans survive unharmed by retreating into the privileged society that will always protect them.

2. veteran: a person who has had long service or experience in a particular occupation.

3. privy: know about something secret.

4. unsought: not desired or unrequested.

5. feign: not genuine or pretended.

6. preoccupation: with all attention.

7. hostile levity: very unfriendly or aggressive.

8. quivering: shaking or trembling.

9. horizon: the furthest that you can see.

10. suppression: the state of being suppressed.

11. snobbishly: thinking that having a high social class is very important.

12. decency: honest, polite behavior that follows accepted moral standards and shows respect for others.

13. parcel out: to divide sth. into parts or between several people.

14. unequally: with people being treated in different ways.

15. hard rock: it is a metaphor.

16. marsh: an area of low land that is always soft and wet.

17. uniform: the type of clothes that soldiers usually wear.

18. attention: the position soldiers take when they stand very straight with their feet together and their arms at their sides.

19. riotous: violent, especially in a public place.

20. excursion: a short journey made for pleasure.

21. privileged: having special rights or advantages that most people do not have.

22. flabby: loose fat or soft.

23. short-winded: having difficulty breathing after exercise or physical effort.

24. elation: a feeling of great happiness and excitement.

25. something of a clan: a sort of aristocratic family.

26. Dukes of Buccleuch: Scottish noble.

27. hard-boiled: indifferent.

28. New Haven: where Yale University is located.

29. counter-raid: sudden fight.

30. ragged: (of clothes) old and torn.

31. prep-school: it's a private boarding school only for the children of rich families.

32. Father agreed to... of twenty-two: "My" father agreed to fund "me" for a year, but after a long delay "I" came to the west side in the spring of my life, thinking this time was gone forever.

33. mutter: to speak or say something in a quiet voice that is difficult to hear.

34. It was lonely... on the road: These days were a bit lonely until someone who came a few days later than me stopped me on the road.

35. West Egg: it's where the newly rich lives, while the old aristocracy lives in East Egg. Gatsby lives in West Egg.

36. pathfinder: a person, group or thing that goes before others and shows the way over unknown land.

37. There was so... breath-giving air: On the one hand, there are a lot of books to read; on the other hand, there is a new smell in the air that stimulates me to learn.

38. Midas: the King of Greek mythology who asked God for the Golden Touch.

39. Morgan: an American financial magnate.

40. Maecenas: a wealthy patron in ancient Rome.

41. high intention: the desire or strength of mind to be successful, rich, powerful, etc.

42. a matter of chance: by accident.

43. due east: directly towards the east.

44. natural curiosities: marvellous natural.

45. the Sound: Long Island Sound, a narrow finger of the Atlantic Ocean between Long Island and the state of Connecticut on the mainland, just east of New York City.

46. Normandy: a geographical and cultural region in northwestern Europe. It comprises mainland Normandy (a part of France) and insular Normandy (mostly the British Channel Islands).

47. tower: diving platform.

48. Lake Forest: a small town in northeastern Illinois.

Questions for Discussion

(1) What is the role of women in *The Great Gatsby*? What kind of life does Gatsby live judging from his parties? From whose point of view is the story told? How does the first person narrator affect the way the reader responds?

(2) The use of many symbolic techniques in the novel greatly influences the comprehensive portrayal of the American society in the Jazz Age. It plays an important role in fully demonstrating the shattering of the American Dream for most people in the 1920s. What aspects of life do these symbols suggest? How does Gatsby, as well as F. Scott Fitzgerald himself, depict the disillusionment with the American Dream and illustrate its paradox?

(3) Women's images are usually influenced by patriarchal culture. If women want

to rebel against society or men, they will be punished and treated as aliens by society. Discuss how women are portrayed in this work.

Suggested Reading

- F. S. 菲茨杰拉德：《崩溃》，黄昱宁、包慧怡译，上海：上海译文出版社，2011 年。
- Matthew J. Bruccoli, ed. *New Essays on The Great Gatsby.* Cambridge: Cambridge University Press, 1985.
- 菲茨杰拉德：《了不起的盖茨比》，巫宁坤等译，上海：上海译文出版社，2009 年。

25. Ernest Hemingway

Ernest Hemingway (1899–1961), American novelist and short-story writer, was awarded the Nobel Prize for Literature in 1954. He is noted both for the intense masculinity of his writing and for his adventurous and widely publicized life. His succinct and lucid prose style exerts a powerful influence on American and British fiction in the 20th century.

The first son of Clarence Edmonds Hemingway, a doctor, and Grace Hall Hemingway, Ernest Miller Hemingway was born in the suburb of Chicago. He was educated in the public schools and began to write in high school, where he was active and outstanding. But the parts of his boyhood that mattered most were the summers spent with his family on Walloon Lake in upper Michigan. On graduation from high school in 1917, impatient for a less-sheltered environment, he did not enter college but went to Kansas City, where he was employed as a reporter for *The Kansas City Star*. He was repeatedly rejected for military service because of a defective eye, but he managed to become an ambulance driver for the American Red Cross in World War I. On July 8, 1918, not yet 19 years old, he was injured on the Austro-Italian front at Fossalta di Piave. Decorated for heroism and hospitalized in Milan, he fell in love with a Red Cross nurse, Agnes von Kurowsky, who declined to marry him. These were experiences he was never to forget. After recuperating at home, Hemingway renewed his efforts at writing, worked at odd jobs for a while in Chicago, and sailed for France as a foreign correspondent for the *Toronto Star*. Advised and encouraged by other American writers in Paris — F. Scott Fitzgerald, Gertrude Stein, Ezra Pound — he began to see his nonjournalistic works appeared in print there. In 1925 his first important book, a collection of stories called *In Our Time*, was published in New York City; it was originally released in Paris in 1924.

In 1926 he published *The Sun Also Rises*, a novel with which he scored his first solid success. A pessimistic but sparkling book, it deals with a group of aimless expatriates in France and Spain — members of the postwar Lost Generation, a phrase that Hemingway scorned while making it famous. This work also introduced him to the limelight, which he both craved and resented for the rest of his life. Hemingway's *The Torrents of Spring*, a parody of the American writer Sherwood Anderson's book *Dark Laughter*, also appeared in 1926.

The writing of books occupied Hemingway for most of the postwar years. He lived in Paris, but traveled widely for skiing, bullfighting, fishing, and hunting that by then had become part of his life and formed the background for much of his writing. His position as a master of short fiction had been advanced by *Men Without Women* in 1927 and thoroughly established with the stories in *Winner Take Nothing* in 1933. Among his finest stories are "The Killers", "The Short Happy Life of Francis Macomber", and "The Snows of Kilimanjaro". At least in the public view, however, the novel *A Farewell to Arms* overshadowed such works. Reaching back to his experience as a young soldier in Italy, Hemingway developed a grim but lyrical novel of great power, fusing love story with war story. In the novel, while serving the Italian ambulance service during World War I, the American lieutenant Frederic Henry falls in love with the English nurse Catherine Barkley, who tends him during his recuperation after he was wounded. She becomes pregnant by him, but he must return to his post. Henry deserts during the Italians' disastrous retreat after the Battle of Caporetto, and the reunited couple flee Italy by crossing the border into Switzerland. There, however, Catherine and her baby die during childbirth, and Henry is left desolate at the loss of the great love of his life.

Hemingway's style, the particular type of hero in his novels, and his life attitudes have been widely recognized and imitated, not only in English-speaking countries, but all over the world.

Cat in the Rain[1]

There were only two Americans stopping at the hotel. They did not know any of the people they passed on the stairs on their way to and from their room. Their room was on the second floor facing the sea. It also faced the public garden and war monument[2]. There were big palms[3] and green benches in the public garden. In the good weather there was always an artist with his easel[4]. Artists liked the way the palms grew and the bright colors of the hotels facing the sea. Italians came from a long way off to look up at the war monument. It was made of bronze and glistened[5] in the rain. It was raining. The rain dripped[6] from the palm trees. Water stood in pools on the gravel paths. The sea broke in a long line in the rain. The motor cars were gone from the square by the war monument. Across the square in the doorway of the cafe a waiter stood looking out at the empty square.

The American wife stood at the window looking out. Outside right under their window a cat was crouched under one of the dripping green tables. The cat was trying to make herself so compact that she would not be dripped on.

"I'm going down and get that kitty," the American wife said.

"I'll do it," her husband offered from the bed.

"No, I'll get it. The poor kitty is out trying to keep dry under the table."

The husband went on reading, lying propped up with the two pillows at the foot of the bed.

"Don't get wet," he said.

The wife went downstairs and the hotel owner stood up and bowed to her as she passed the office. His desk was at the far end of the office. He was an old man and very tall.

"Il piove[7]," the wife said. She liked the hotelkeeper.

"Si, si, Signora, brutto tempo[8]. It is very bad weather."

He stood behind his desk in the far end of the dim[9] room. The wife liked him.

She liked the way he wanted to serve her. She liked the way he felt about being a hotel-keeper. She liked his old, heavy face and big hands.

Liking him she opened the door and looked out. It was raining harder. A man in a rubber cape was crossing the empty square to the cafe. The cat would be around to the right. Perhaps she could go along to the eaves. As she stood in the doorway an umbrella opened behind her. It was the maid who looked after their room.

"You must not get wet," she smiled, speaking Italian. Of course, the hotel-keeper had sent her.[10]

With the maid holding the umbrella over her, she walked along the gravel path until she was under their window. The table was there, washed bright green in the rain, but the cat was gone. She was suddenly disappointed. The maid looked up at her.

"Ha perduto qualque cosa, Signora?[11]"

"There was a cat," said the American girl.

"A cat?"

"Si, il gatto.[12]"

"A cat?" the maid laughed. "A cat in the rain?"

"Yes," she said, "under the table." Then, "Oh, I wanted it so much. I wanted a kitty."

When she talked English the maid's face tightened.

"Come, Signora," she said. "We must get back inside. You will be wet."

"I suppose so," said the American girl.

They went back along the gravel path and passed in the door. The maid stayed outside to close the umbrella.[13] As the American girl passed the office, the padrone bowed from his desk. Something felt very small and tight inside the girl. The padrone made her feel very small and at the same time really important. She had a momentary feeling of being of supreme importance. She went on up the stairs. She opened the door of the room. George was on the bed reading.

"Did you get the cat?" he asked, putting the book down.

"It was gone."

"Wonder where it went to," he said, resting his eyes from reading. She sat down on the bed.[14]

"I wanted it so much," she said. "I don't know why I wanted it so much. I wanted that poor kitty. It isn't any fun to be a poor kitty out in the rain."

George was reading again.

She went over and sat in front of the mirror of the dressing table looking at herself with the hand glass. She studied her profile, first one side and then the other. Then she studied the back of her head and her neck.[15]

"Don't you think it would be a good idea if I let my hair grow out?" she asked, looking at her profile again.

George looked up and saw the back of her neck, clipped close like a boy's.

"I like it the way it is."

"I get so tired of it," she said. "I get so tired of looking like a boy."

George shifted his position in the bed. He hadn't looked away from her since she started to speak.[16]

"You look pretty darn nice," he said.

She laid the mirror down on the dresser and went over to the window and looked out. It was getting dark.

"I want to pull my hair back tight and smooth and make a big knot at the back that I can feel," she said. "I want to have a kitty to sit on my lap and purr when I stroke her."

"Yeah?" George said from the bed.

"And I want to eat at a table with my own silver and I want candles. And I want it to be spring and I want to brush my hair out in front of a mirror and I want a kitty and I want some new clothes."

"Oh, shut up and get something to read," George said. He was reading again.[17]

His wife was looking out of the window. It was quite dark now and still raining in the palm trees.

"Anyway, I want a cat," she said, "I want a cat. I want a cat now. If I can't have long hair or any fun, I can have a cat."

George was not listening. He was reading his book. His wife looked out of the window where the light had come on in the square.

Someone knocked at the door.

"Avanti[18]," George said. He looked up from his book. In the doorway stood the maid. She held a big tortoise-shell cat pressed tight against her and swung down against her body.

"Excuse me," she said, "the padrone asked me to bring this for the Signora."

Notes

1. "Cat in the Rain": a very short story by Ernest Hemingway, published in his collection *In Our Time*. Hemingway wrote "Cat in the Rain" for his wife Hadley while they were living in Paris. She wanted to get a cat, but he said they were too poor. This story is about an American couple staying at a hotel in Italy. It is raining heavily one day, and the wife, looking out of their hotel room window, spies a cat under one of the tables outside, trying to shelter from the rain.

2. monument: a building that has special historical importance.

3. palm: a straight tree with a mass of long leaves at the top, growing in tropical countries. There are several types of palm tree, some of which produce fruit.

4. easel: a wooden frame to hold a picture while it is being painted.

5. glisten: to shine.

6. drip: to fall in small drops.

7. Il piove: (Italian) It is raining.

8. Si, si, Signora, brutto tempo: (Italian) Yes, yes, madam, nasty weather.

9. dim: not bright.

10. "You must not get wet,"... had sent her: Needless to say, the boss must have sent her here.

11. Ha perduto qualque cosa, Signora?: (Italian) You lost something here, madam?

12. Si, il gatto: (Italian) Yes, a cat.

13. They went... close the umbrella: They walked back down the gravel road and entered the door, then the waitress closed her umbrella.

14. "Wonder where it went to,"... on the bed: "Where did you go?" he said, looking away from the book. She is sitting on the bed.

15. She went over... and her neck: She walked over, sat in front of the dresser, looked at herself in the mirror with her hand, and looked at her profile. She looked at one side, then the other, and then took a closer look at the back of the head and neck.

16. He hadn't looked... started to speak: From the moment she started speaking, his eyes were inseparable.

17. "Oh, shut up... reading again: "Oh, stop it! Read the book," said George, reading again.

18. Avanti: (Italian) Come in.

Questions for Discussion

(1) The "cat", as a clue running through the whole story, has many meanings. It does not exist and is an image. What does the cat symbolize? Where can you get the clue? How do you interpret the ending of the story?

(2) The main features of Hemingway's "Iceberg Principle" are concise words, vivid images, rich emotions and profound thoughts. What profound thoughts are revealed in this story by using the "Iceberg Principle"?

(3) Why does the American girl like the hotel padrone so much? What can you infer about the relationship among the American girl and the hotel padrone, and the maid?

Suggested Reading

- Gregory Clark. *The Son also Rises: Surnames and the History of Social Mobility.* Princeton, NJ: Princeton University Press, 2014.
- Harold Bloom. *Modern Critical Views: Ernest Hemingway.* High Point, NC: Chelsea House Publishers, 1985.
- 海明威：《老人与海》，吴劳译，上海：上海译文出版社，2004年。

26. William Faulkner

William Faulkner (1897–1962), in full William Cuthbert Faulkner, is an American novelist and short-story writer. He was awarded the 1949 Nobel Prize for

Literature.

Faulkner was born into a prominent family, whose fortune was built by his great-grandfather William Cracow Faulkner but was not inherited by his father. Faulkner was well aware of his family background and adored his great-grandfather so much that he had repeatedly promised to himself that one day he would be a writer like his great-grandfather. He spent his childhood and youth in the town of Oxford. Because he is small in stature, he gradually developed the habit of staying away from the crowd and reading quietly by himself. He left high school without graduating but devoted himself to undirected and massive reading with books and magazines from his friends. His first attempt on poems got few responses. He then tried his hand on writing novels and in 1929 published his first novel *The Sound and the Fury*, which marked him as a professional writer. In the same year, he married Estelle Oldham and started to lead a simple life in his hometown of Oxford. During this period of time, he specialized in writing and rarely participated in activities in the literary and artistic circles. Before he was awarded the 1949 Nobel Prize for Literature, he had already successively published his best works *As I Lay Dying*, *Light in August*, *Absalom, Absalom!*, *The Unvanquished* and *Go Down, Moses*. In addition to these well-known novels, he also created many classic short stories, including "A Rose for Emily", "Red Leaves", "That Evening Sun", and "Dry September".

Faulkner writes a total of nineteen novels and about eighty short stories, most of which are set in Yoknapatawpha County, a fictional name in the American South. The several families who have lived in Jefferson and Yoknapatawpha County for generations belong to different social classes. The stories about these families with more than six hundred characters, span almost two hundred years from the War of Independence to the time after World War II. Following the experimental tradition of European writers such as James Joyce, Virginia Woolf, Marcel Proust, Faulkner perfects the "stream-of-consciousness" technique in his Yoknapatawpha novels and short stories. Employing the long, winding sentences and complex allusions, the character's personality, mental abilities and different levels of consciousness are blended with his flexible use of literary devices of modernism such as stream-of-consciousness, multiple unreliable narrators and non-chronological plot construction. His modernism is presented in his works by his doubly ironic stance towards both the present and the past. The glories of the past are invariably empty or decaying, while his critique of the modern era can always be found in his ironic commentary of the past.

A Rose for Emily

I

When Miss Emily Grierson[1] died, our whole town went to her funeral: the men through a sort of respectful affection for a fallen monument[2], the women mostly out of curiosity to see the inside of her house, which no one save an old man-servant — a combined gardener and cook — had seen in at least ten years.

It was a big, squarish frame house that had once been white, decorated with cupolas and spires and scrolled balconies in the heavily lightsome style of the seventies, set on what had once been our most select street. But garages and cotton gins had encroached and obliterated even the august names of that neighborhood; only Miss Emily's house was left, lifting its stubborn and coquettish decay above the cotton wagons and the gasoline pumps — an eyesore among eyesores. And now Miss Emily had gone to join the representatives of those august names where they lay in the cedar-bemused cemetery among the ranked and anonymous graves of Union and Confederate[3] soldiers who fell at the battle of Jefferson[4].

Alive, Miss Emily had been a tradition[5], a duty, and a care; a sort of hereditary obligation upon the town, dating from that day in 1894 when Colonel Sartoris, the mayor — he who fathered the edict that no Negro woman should appear on the streets without an apron — remitted her taxes, the dispensation dating from the death of her father on into perpetuity. Not that Miss Emily would have accepted charity. Colonel Sartoris invented an involved tale to the effect that Miss Emily's father had loaned money to the town, which the town, as a matter of business, preferred this way of repaying. Only a man of Colonel Sartoris' generation and thought could have invented it, and only a woman could have believed it.

When the next generation, with its more modern ideas, became mayors and aldermen, this arrangement created some little dissatisfaction. On the first of the year they mailed her a tax notice. February came, and there was no reply. They wrote her a formal letter, asking her to call at the sheriff's office at her convenience. A week later the mayor wrote her himself, offering to call or to send his car for her, and received in reply a note on paper of an archaic shape, in a thin, flowing calligraphy in faded ink, to the effect that she no longer went out at all. The tax notice was also enclosed, without comment.

They called a special meeting of the Board of Aldermen. A deputation waited upon her, knocked at the door through which no visitor had passed since she ceased giving china-painting lessons eight or ten years earlier. They were admitted by the old Negro[6] into a dim hall from which a stairway mounted into still more shadow. It smelled of dust and disuse — a close, dank smell. The Negro led them into the parlor. It was furnished in heavy, leather-covered furniture. When the Negro opened the blinds of one window, they could see that the leather was cracked; and when they sat down, a faint dust rose sluggishly about their thighs, spinning with slow motes in the single sun-ray. On a tarnished gilt easel before the fireplace stood a crayon portrait of Miss Emily's father.

They rose when she entered — a small, fat woman in black, with a thin gold chain descending to her waist and vanishing into her belt, leaning on an ebony cane with a tarnished gold head. Her skeleton was small and spare; perhaps that was why what would have been merely plumpness in another was obesity in her. She looked bloated, like a body long submerged in motionless water, and of that pallid hue.[7] Her eyes, lost in the fatty ridges of her face, looked like two small pieces of coal pressed into a lump of dough as they moved from one face to another while the visitors stated their errand.

She did not ask them to sit. She just stood in the door and listened quietly until the spokesman came to a stumbling halt. Then they could hear the invisible watch ticking at the end of the gold chain.

Her voice was dry and cold. "I have no taxes in Jefferson. Colonel Sartoris explained it to me. Perhaps one of you can gain access to the city records and satisfy yourselves."

"But we have. We are the city authorities, Miss Emily. Didn't you get a notice from the sheriff, signed by him?"

"I received a paper, yes," Miss Emily said. "Perhaps he considers himself the sheriff... I have no taxes in Jefferson."

"But there is nothing on the books to show that, you see. We must go by the —"

"See Colonel Sartoris. I have no taxes in Jefferson."

"But, Miss Emily —"

"See Colonel Sartoris." (Colonel Sartoris had been dead almost ten years.) "I have no taxes in Jefferson. Tobe!" The Negro appeared. "Show these gentlemen out."

II

So she vanquished them, horse and foot, just as she had vanquished their fathers thirty years before about the smell. That was two years after her father's death and a short time after her sweetheart — the one we believed would marry her — had deserted her.[8] After her father's death she went out very little; after her sweetheart went away, people hardly saw her at all. A few of the ladies had the temerity to call, but were not received, and the only sign of life about the place was the Negro man — a young man then — going in and out with a market basket.

"Just as if a man — any man — could keep a kitchen properly," the ladies said; so they were not surprised when the smell developed. It was another link between the gross, teeming world[9] and the high and mighty Griersons.

A neighbor, a woman, complained to the mayor, Judge Stevens, eighty years old.

"But what will you have me do about it, madam?" he said.

"Why, send her word to stop it," the woman said. "Isn't there a law?"

"I'm sure that won't be necessary," Judge Stevens said. "It's probably just a snake or a rat that nigger of hers killed in the yard. I'll speak to him about it."

The next day he received two more complaints, one from a man who came in diffident deprecation. "We really must do something about it, Judge. I'd be the last one in the world to bother Miss Emily, but we've got to do something." That night the Board of Aldermen met — three graybeards and one younger man, a member of the rising generation.

"It's simple enough," he said. "Send her word to have her place cleaned up. Give her a certain time to do it in, and if she don't ..."

"Dammit[10], sir," Judge Stevens said, "will you accuse a lady to her face of smelling bad?"

So the next night, after midnight, four men crossed Miss Emily's lawn and slunk about the house like burglars, sniffing along the base of the brickwork and at the cellar openings while one of them performed a regular sowing motion with his hand out of a sack slung from his shoulder. They broke open the cellar door and sprinkled lime there, and in all the outbuildings. As they recrossed the lawn, a window that had been dark was lighted and Miss Emily sat in it, the light behind her, and her upright torso motionless as that of an idol. They crept quietly across the lawn and into the shadow of the locusts that lined the street. After a week or two the smell went away.

That was when people had begun to feel really sorry for her. People in our town, remembering how old lady Wyatt[11], her great-aunt, had gone completely crazy at last, believed that the Griersons held themselves a little too high for what they really were. None of the young men were quite good enough for Miss Emily and such. We had long thought of them as a tableau[12]; Miss Emily a slender figure in white in the background, her father a spraddled silhouette in the foreground, his back to her and clutching a horsewhip, the two of them framed by the back-flung front door.[13] So when she got to be thirty and was still single, we were not pleased exactly, but vindicated; even with insanity in the family she wouldn't have turned down all of her chances if they had really materialized.

When her father died, it got about that the house was all that was left to her; and in a way, people were glad. At last they could pity Miss Emily. Being left alone, and a pauper, she had become humanized. Now she too would know the old thrill and the old despair of a penny more or less.

The day after his death all the ladies prepared to call at the house and offer condolence and aid, as is our custom. Miss Emily met them at the door, dressed as usual and with no trace of grief on her face. She told them that her father was not dead. She did that for three days, with the ministers calling on her, and the doctors, trying to persuade her to let them dispose of the body. Just as they were about to resort to law and force, she broke down, and they buried her father quickly.

We did not say she was crazy then. We believed she had to do that. We remembered all the young men her father had driven away, and we knew that with nothing left, she would have to cling to that which had robbed her[14], as people will.

III

She was sick for a long time. When we saw her again, her hair was cut short, making her look like a girl, with a vague resemblance to those angels in colored church windows — sort of tragic and serene.

The town had just let the contracts for paving the sidewalks, and in the summer after her father's death they began the work. The construction company came with niggers and mules and machinery, and a foreman named Homer Barron, a Yankee — a big, dark, ready man, with a big voice and eyes lighter than his face. The little boys would follow in groups to hear him cuss the niggers, and the niggers singing in time to the rise and fall of picks. Pretty soon he knew everybody in town. Whenever you heard a lot of laughing anywhere about the square, Homer Barron would be in the center of the group. Presently we began to see him and Miss Emily on Sunday afternoons driving in the yellow-wheeled buggy and the matched team of bays from the livery stable.

At first we were glad that Miss Emily would have an interest, because the ladies all said, "Of course a Grierson would not think seriously of a Northerner, a day laborer." But there were still others, older people, who said that even grief could not cause a real lady to forget *noblesse oblige*[15] — without calling it *noblesse oblige*. They just said, "Poor Emily. Her kinsfolk should come to her." She had some kin in Alabama[16]; but years ago her father had fallen out with them over the estate of old lady Wyatt, the crazy woman, and there was no communication between the two families. They had not even been represented at the funeral.

And as soon as the old people said, "Poor Emily," the whispering began. "Do you suppose it's really so?" they said to one another. "Of course it is. What else could..." This behind their hands; rustling of craned silk and satin behind jalousies closed upon the sun of Sunday afternoon as the thin, swift clop-clop-clop of the matched team passed: "Poor Emily."

She carried her head high enough — even when we believed that she was fallen. It was as if she demanded more than ever the recognition of her dignity as the last Grierson; as if it had wanted that touch of earthiness to reaffirm her imperviousness. Like when she bought the rat poison, the arsenic. That was over a year after they had begun to say "Poor Emily," and while the two female cousins were visiting her.

"I want some poison," she said to the druggist. She was over thirty then, still a slight woman, though thinner than usual, with cold, haughty black eyes in a face the flesh of which was strained across the temples and about the eyesockets as you imagine a lighthouse-keeper's face ought to look. "I want some poison," she said.

"Yes, Miss Emily. What kind? For rats and such? I'd recom — "

"I want the best you have. I don't care what kind."

The druggist named several. "They'll kill anything up to an elephant. But what you want is — "

"Arsenic," Miss Emily said. "Is that a good one?"

"Is... arsenic? Yes, ma'am. But what you want — "

"I want arsenic."

The druggist looked down at her. She looked back at him, erect, her face like a strained flag. "Why, of course," the druggist said. "If that's what you want. But the law requires you to tell what you are going to use it for."

Miss Emily just stared at him, her head tilted back in order to look him eye for eye, until he looked away and went and got the arsenic and wrapped it up. The Negro delivery boy brought her the package; the druggist didn't come back. When she opened the package at home there was written on the box, under the skull and bones: "For rats."

IV

So the next day we all said, "She will kill herself"; and we said it would be the best thing. When she had first begun to be seen with Homer Barron, we had said, "She will marry him." Then we said, "She will persuade him yet," because Homer himself had remarked — he liked men, and it was known that he drank with the younger men in the Elks' Club — that he was not a marrying man. Later we said, "Poor Emily" behind the jalousies as they passed on Sunday afternoon in the glittering buggy, Miss Emily with her head high and Homer Barron with his hat cocked and a cigar in his teeth, reins and whip in a yellow glove.

Then some of the ladies began to say that it was a disgrace to the town and a bad example to the young people. The men did not want to interfere, but at last the ladies forced the Baptist minister — Miss Emily's people were Episcopal[17] — to call upon her. He would never divulge what happened during that interview, but he refused to go back again. The next Sunday they again drove about the streets, and the following day the minister's wife wrote to Miss Emily's relations in Alabama.

So she had blood-kin under her roof again and we sat back to watch developments. At first nothing happened. Then we were sure that they were to be married. We learned that Miss Emily had been to the jeweler's and ordered a man's toilet set in silver, with the letters H. B. on each piece. Two days later we learned that she had bought a complete outfit of men's clothing, including a nightshirt, and we said, "They are married." We were really glad. We were glad because the two female cousins were even more Grierson than Miss Emily had ever been.

So we were not surprised when Homer Barron — the streets had been finished some time since — was gone. We were a little disappointed that there was not a public blowing-off, but we believed that he had gone on to prepare for Miss Emily's coming, or to give her a chance to get rid of the cousins. (By that time it was a cabal, and we were all Miss Emily's allies to help circumvent[18] the cousins.) Sure enough, after another week they departed. And, as we had expected all along, within three days Homer Barron was back in town. A neighbor saw the Negro man admit him at the kitchen door at dusk one evening.

And that was the last we saw of Homer Barron. And of Miss Emily for some time. The Negro man went in and out with the market basket, but the front door remained closed. Now and then we would see her at a window for a moment, as the men did that night when they sprinkled the lime, but for almost six months she did not appear on the streets. Then we knew that this was to be expected too; as if that quality of her father which had thwarted her woman's life so many times had been too virulent and too furious to die.

When we next saw Miss Emily, she had grown fat and her hair was turning gray. During the next few years it grew grayer and grayer until it attained an even pepper-and-salt iron-gray, when it ceased turning. Up to the day of her death at seventy-four it was still that vigorous iron-gray, like the hair of an active man.

From that time on her front door remained closed, save for a period of six or seven years, when she was about forty, during which she gave lessons in china-painting. She fitted up a studio in one of the downstairs rooms, where the daughters and grand-daughters of Colonel Sartoris' contemporaries were sent to her with the same regularity and in the same spirit that they were sent to church on Sundays with a twenty-five-cent piece for the collection plate. Meanwhile her taxes had been remitted.

Then the newer generation became the backbone and the spirit of the town, and the painting pupils grew up and fell away and did not send their children to her with boxes of color and tedious brushes and pictures cut from the ladies' magazines. The front door closed upon the last one and remained closed for good. When the town got free postal delivery Miss Emily alone refused to let them fasten the metal numbers above her door and attach a mailbox to it. She would not listen to them.

Daily, monthly, yearly we watched the Negro grow grayer and more stooped, going in and out with the market basket. Each December we sent her a tax notice, which would be returned by the post office a week later, unclaimed. Now and then we would see her in one of the downstairs windows — she had evidently shut up the top floor of the house — like the carven torso of an idol in a niche[19], looking or not looking at us, we could never tell which. Thus she passed from generation to generation — dear, inescapable, impervious, tranquil, and perverse.

And so she died. Fell ill in the house filled with dust and shadows, with only a doddering Negro man to wait on her. We did not even know she was sick; we had long since given up trying to get any information from the Negro. He talked to no one, probably not even to her, for his voice had grown harsh and rusty, as if from disuse.

She died in one of the downstairs rooms, in a heavy walnut bed with a curtain, her gray head propped on a pillow yellow and moldy with age and lack of sunlight.

V

The negro met the first of the ladies at the front door and let them in, with their hushed, sibilant voices and their quick, curious glances, and then he disappeared. He walked right through the house and out the back and was not seen again.[20]

The two female cousins came at once. They held the funeral on the second day, with the town coming to look at Miss Emily beneath a mass of bought flowers, with the crayon face of her father musing profoundly above the bier and the ladies sibilant and macabre[21]; and the very old men — some in their brushed Confederate uniforms — on the porch and the lawn, talking of Miss Emily as if she had been a contemporary of theirs, believing that they had danced with her and courted her perhaps, confusing time with its mathematical progression, as the old do, to whom all the past is not a diminishing road, but, instead, a huge meadow which no winter ever quite touches, divided from them now by the narrow bottleneck of the most recent decade of years.

Already we knew that there was one room in that region above stairs which no one had seen in forty years, and which would have to be forced. They waited until Miss Emily was decently in the ground before they opened it.

The violence of breaking down the door seemed to fill this room with pervading dust. A thin, acrid pall as of the tomb seemed to lie everywhere upon this room decked and furnished as for a bridal: upon the valance curtains of faded rose color, upon the rose-shaded lights[22], upon the dressing table, upon the delicate array of crystal and the man's toilet things backed with tarnished silver, silver so tarnished that the monogram[23] was obscured. Among them lay a collar and tie, as if they had just been removed, which, lifted, left upon the surface a pale crescent in the dust. Upon a chair hung the suit, carefully folded; beneath it the two mute shoes and the discarded socks.

The man himself lay in the bed.

For a long while we just stood there, looking down at the profound and fleshless grin. The body had apparently once lain in the attitude of an embrace, but now the long sleep that outlasts love, that conquers even the grimace of love, had cuckolded him. What was left of him, rotted beneath what was left of the nightshirt, had become inextricable from the bed in which he lay; and upon him and upon the pillow beside him lay that even coating of the patient and biding dust.

Then we noticed that in the second pillow was the indentation[24] of a head. One of us lifted something from it, and leaning forward, that faint and invisible dust dry and acrid in the nostrils, we saw a long strand of iron-gray hair.

Notes

1. Miss Emily Grierson: She is the last survivor of the Grierson family, a descending aristocrat in the South, in Jefferson Town, and the only heir of the family.

2. monument: When a person is compared to a monument, that means he/she remains a reminder of something fine or distinguished, with a kind of importance to be memorized.

3. Union and Confederate: During the American Civil War, the "Union" or the "North" refers to the United States of America, and the "Confederacy" or the "South" refers to the Confederate States of America.

4. the battle of Jefferson: a battle which took place in Port Jefferson, Texas, during the Civil War.

5. Miss Emily had been a tradition: Miss Emily had been representing the American Southern tradition.

6. negro: a term for a black person. It is now considered offensive but was an accepted word for black person until the second half of the 20th century.

7. The description of Miss Emily's dress and appearance highlights her decay in keeping to the old customs. She looks lifeless without any vitality.

8. According to the narrative of the story from "their" visit in the first chapter and the smell issue at the beginning of chapter two and other chapters, we can find that the sequence of time in the story is completely disrupted and the technique of stream-of-consciousness is employed in the development of the whole story.

9. teeming world: another world outside of the Griersons' which consists of an extremely large number of people, animals or objects that are all forever on the go.

10. dammit: damn it.

11. old lady Wyatt: As one of the representatives of family women, lady Wyatt's fate and love tragedy under the shackles and constraints of family traditions also foretells that Miss Emily should also bear the family weight in a way.

12. tableau: a form of silent theater in which a group of actors stand or sit in certain positions to create a picture of a historical scene.

13. In this tableau, from the perspective of "we", the writer hopes to tell the readers that after her father's death, although Miss Emily can become the protagonist of her own life, she still cannot get rid of her father's patriarchal influence in the family.

14. she would have to cling to that which had robbed her: Does "that" in this sentence refer to Miss Emily's father or the tradition she must comply with in her father's concept?

15. *noblesse oblige*: the idea that people born into the nobility or upper social classes must behave in a honorable and generous way toward those less privileged.

16. Alabama: a state in the southeastern United States. It is one of the Confederate states during the American Civil War.

17. Episcopal: relating to the Episcopal Church of North America or Scotland.

18. circumvent: to go around something or to find a way of avoiding something.

19. like the carven torso of an idol in a niche: Emily is compared to a carven idol in a niche — several understanding can be traced here: Emily has gradually become a mysterious existence; Emily has become the incarnation of family glory; Emily has become the funerary of the martyr.

20. The negro met... and was not seen again: the original version of "A Rose for Emily" included a two-page deathbed scene revealing that Tobe, Emily's servant, has shared her terrible secret all these years, and that Emily has left her house to him. Faulkner deleted this scene, and made a decision to use this shorten paragraph.

21. macabre: frightening or unpleasant, and usually involves death, decay, or violence.

22. Here, the "rose" appears twice: one is "rose-colored" and another is "rose-shaded", but a real rose does not appear in the story.

23. monogram: refers to H. B. as the initials of Homer Barron was decorated or designed there on toilet things.

24. indentation: a mark or hole on the surface of something.

Questions for Discussion

(1) Some critics have suggested that Miss Emily is a kind of symbol of the Old South, the last defender of its outdated ideas of chivalry, formal manners, and tradition. Do you think this interpretation is justified? Would you characterize Miss Emily as a champion or a victim of the values her town tries to preserve?

(2) What is the meaning of the title "A Rose for Emily"? Please offer possible interpretations of the title's significance with your understanding of this short story.

(3) Arrange these events in the sequence in which they actually occur: Homer Barron' arrival in the town, the aldermen's visit, Emily's purchase of poison, Colonel Sartoris' decision to remit Emily's taxes, the development of the odor around Emily's house, Emily's father's death, the arrival of Emily's relatives, Homer Barron's disappearance. Then, list the events in the sequence in which they are presented in the story. Why doesn't Faulkner present these events in their actual chronological order?

(4) In a series of novels, Faulkner sets most of the stories in Yoknapatawpha

County and Jefferson Town. The time span is large and the characters are complex, but the location of the story remains unchanged. In "A Rose for Emily", the story of Miss Emily takes place in that wooden house she has hardly left. What is the relationship between the wooden house and the theme of the story? As the place where the story takes place, what role does the wooden house play in the time narrative and space narrative?

(5) Faulkner is fascinated by the *Bible* and mythology. The titles of his two novels *Absalom, Absalom!* and *Go Down, Moses* are all taken from the *Bible*. Do you think Faulkner introduces a certain mythological archetype in this short story? Explain the characters in this short story from the perspective of mythological archetypes.

Suggested Reading

- Philip M. Weinstein 编：《剑桥文学指南：威廉·福克纳》，上海：上海外语教育出版社，2000年。
- William Faulkner. *Absalom, Absalom!*, New York, NY: Vintage Books, 1991.
- William Faulkner. *The Sound and the Fury.* New York, NY: W. W. Norton & Company, 2021.
- 威廉·福克纳，《福克纳短篇小说精选》（英文版），天津：天津人民出版社，2018年。
- 威廉·福克纳，《我弥留之际》，李文俊译，上海：上海译文出版社，2010年。

27. Langston Hughes

Langston Hughes, one of the greatest American poets, is the first African American who successfully brings African-American culture and traditions into American literature. He is also a playwright, novelist, anthologist and newspaper columnist.

Hughes was born in 1902, in Joplin, Missouri to an African American couple.

His parents separated after Hughes was born, and he spent most of his childhood with his grandmother. In childhood, he was nurtured with the stories about African American heroes and heroines that filled him with pride in himself and his own people. At the age of 13, after his mother remarried, Hughes moved to live with them in Illinois where he attended school and became class poet. Following his graduation in 1920, he went to visit his father in Mexico and spent a year at Columbia University in his father's funding. In 1921, Hughes published one of his best-known poems "The Negro Speaks of Rivers" in the most important African American journal, *The Crisis*. After that, with the purpose of visiting Harlem, Hughes left for New York City and joined the groups of black artists, musicians, actors, dancers and writers who gathered there; he became the central figure among them. He continued to write and publish poetry and gave up his studies after one year. He then held odd jobs and traveled to Africa and Europe working as seaman and dishwasher. While his poetry became more political and militant, some experimental elements, like the rhythm of jazz and blue were creatively added in his poetry. Hughes's first book of verse, *The Weary Blues*, was published when he was only 23 years old. In 1927, his second volume of poems, *Fine Clothes to the Jew* was published. He finished his college education at Lincoln University in Pennsylvania in 1929. In 1930 his first novel, *Not Without Laughter*, won the Harmon Gold Medal for Literature. In addition to a large body of poetic work, Hughes published works in a diverse number of genres. He wrote 11 plays and countless works of prose, including *The Dream Keeper and Other Poems*, *The Big Sea, Shakespeare in Harlem, Montage of a Dream Deferred, I Wonder as I Wander: An Autobiographical Journal*, the well-known "Simple" books and "The First" books. Hughes died of cancer in May 22, 1967, in New York.

Under the primary influences of Paul Lawrence Dunbar, Carl Sandburg and Walt Whitman, Hughes began his creations in the era of the "Harlem Renaissance" and was then influenced by the "New Negro Movement". His early creations had a tendency of nationalism and aestheticism. Hughes refused to portray only noble, respectable black characters, but their individual dark-skinned selves, the black masses. His aesthetic was not dominated by the values of the whites, and he desired to write not only about the black masses, but for the black masses. After the Second World War, the spirit of struggle was once weakened in his creations, but he soon turned to reality, and continued to praise the labor movement and oppose racial discrimination in his works. After the 1950s, Hughes tended to create art for art's sake, and some of his poems were considered avant-garde. In short, his poems and other creations always tried hard to show the living conditions of African Americans struggling at the bottom of society. The humor, wisdom, perseverance and belief are notably featured in his free verse poetry, some of which have become popular songs with rhythm and blues and jazz blended in.

The Negro Speaks of Rivers

I've known rivers:
I've known rivers ancient as the world and older than the
flow of human blood in human veins.[1]

My soul has grown deep like the rivers.

I bathed in the Euphrates when dawns were young.
I built my hut near the Congo and it lulled me to sleep.
I looked upon the Nile and raised the pyramids above it.
I heard the singing of the Mississippi[2] when Abe Lincoln[3]
went down to New Orleans[4], and I've seen its muddy
bosom[5] turn all golden in the sunset.

I've known rivers
Ancient, dusky rivers.

My soul has grown deep like the rivers.[6]

Notes

1. I: the implied meaning given to the word "I" shows the influence of both Sandburg and Whitman in its attempt to link the "I" of the poem to a larger, collective self that spans time and space.

2. I bathed in the Euphrates... Mississippi: from Euphrates to Congo, Nile, then to Mississippi. In the poem, the image of rivers is considered as the one that nurtured world civilization, witnessed the glories and humiliations of black people. And it is just as important that by listing these most significant rivers, Hughes identifies the linkage between African and African American.

3. Abe Lincoln: Abraham Lincoln, the sixteenth president of the United States, led the abolition of the Afro-American slavery during his tenure.

4. New Orleans: New Orleans is located in southeastern Louisiana on the Mississippi River in the United States. It was originally a place of residence for Native Americans. In the first half of the 19th century, it became an important cotton export port and a slave trade center.

5. muddy bosom: the open river surface of Mississippi is anthropomorphized into woman's bosom.

6. My soul has grown deep like the rivers: Hughes identifies a self deepened by the past, especially its African past.

As I Grew Older

It was a long time ago.[1]
I have almost forgotten my dream.
But it was there then,
In front of me,
Bright like a sun —
My dream.

And then the wall rose,
Rose slowly,
Slowly,
Between me and my dream[2].
Rose until it touched the sky —
The wall[3].

Shadow.

I am black.

I lie down in the shadow.

No longer the light of my dream before me,

Above me.

Only the thick wall.

Only the shadow.[4]

My hands!

My dark hands!

Break through the wall!

Find my dream!

Help me to shatter this darkness,

To smash this night,

To break this shadow

Into a thousand lights of sun,

Into a thousand whirling dreams

Of sun![5]

Notes

1. It was a long time ago: "Time" here not only denotes the lifespan of several generations of the black people, but also the duration of Black civilization in the world.

2. Between me and my dream: the wall has completely separated me from my dreams. Although they are very close, they are two incommunicable spaces.

3. The wall: the wall in this poem is a metaphor for racial discrimination.

4. In this verse, the "I" becomes painfully aware of the fact as he grows older that he is black and he sees no light of any dream but the remains of pain and torment.

5. The poet's dream for light, freedom and happiness is so strong and dazzling that it can break through "the wall", "this darkness" and "this shadow".

I, Too, Sing America

I, too,[1] sing America.

I am the darker brother.
They send me to eat in the kitchen
When company comes,
But I laugh,
And eat well,
And grow strong.

Tomorrow,
I'll be at the table
When company comes.
Nobody'll dare
Say to me,
"Eat in the kitchen,"
Then.

Besides,
They'll see how beautiful I am
And be ashamed —

I, too, am America.

Note

1. I, too: Echoing Whitman, Langston Hughes affirms black people as Americans with dignity and optimism.

Ballad[1] of the Landlord

Landlord, Landlord,

My roof has sprung a leak,
Don't you 'member I told you about it
Way last week²?

Landlord, Landlord
These steps is broken down.
When you come up yourself
It's a wonder you don't fall down.

Ten Bucks you say I owe you?
Ten Bucks you say is due?
Well, that's Ten Bucks more'n I'll pay you
Till you fix this house up new.

What? You gonna get eviction³ orders?
You gonna cut off my heat?
You gonna take my furniture and
Throw it in the street?

Um-huh! You talking high and mighty.
Talk on — till you get through.
You ain't gonna be able to say a word
If I land my fist on you.

Police! Police!
Come and get this man!
He's trying to ruin the government
*And overturn the land!*⁴

Copper's whistle!
Patrol bell!
Arrest.

Precinct Station.

Iron cell.

Headlines in press:

MAN THREATENS LANDLORD

∴

TENANT HELD NO BAIL

∴

JUDGE GIVES NEGRO 90 DAYS IN COUNTY JAIL.[5]

Notes

1. ballad: a poem that tells a story.

2. way last week: last week.

3. eviction: the process of forcing someone to leave the house they are living in, usually because they have not paid their rent.

4. This verse is typically exhibited in an alternative stroke to highlight the landlord's superiority. In contrast, the African American tenant's appeal and demands get no response from the landlord; they functionally degraded and weakened on the rhythm.

5. This poem by Langston Hughes grew out of conditions in New York City's Harlem in the 1930s. It describes in graphic terms the escalation of anger and frustration that the tenant experiences when trying to get the landlord to make basic repairs. It is structured like an old time blues song until the final verse where the rhythm changes.

Questions for Discussion

(1) Generally speaking, the repetition of words is avoided as much as possible in poetry. In Hughes' "The Negro Speaks of Rivers", besides the mentioning of Euphrates and Congo, the word "river" appears several times. What role does it play in expressing the theme of poetry?

(2) Relate the history of Black civilization with the four rivers listed in the poem "The Negro Speaks of Rivers".

(3) Compare the similarities and differences in the connotation of dreams in Hughes's two poems "Dreams" and "As I Grew Older".

(4) What symbols are used in these poems, and what poetic themes do these symbols imply? What roles do these symbols play in the expression of the connotation of the poem?

(5) Hughes' poems are written in free style since no end rhyme is abided by. The words used in Hughes' poems are also simple and easy to understand. How do you understand Hughes' way of writing "to explain and illuminate the Negro condition in America"?

(6) In terms of performance characteristics, what are the similarities between Hughes' poetry and Black jazz or blues? Please compare and explain.

(7) Some critics believe that when Hughes reveals the social conditions of African Americans through his poetry, various spaces with ideological expression are constructed visibly and also invisibly. Struggle and resistance, torment and pain are all produced in the corresponding cultural space and lead to certain cultural connotations. In these selected poems, consider what images Hughes uses to construct the cultural space of poetry, and how does he realize his political expression in these spaces?

Suggested Reading

- Langston Hughes. *Selected Poems of Langston Hughes.* New York, NY: Vintage Books, of Random House, Inc., 1990.

- Manning Marable and Leith Mullings, eds. *Let Nobody Turn Us Around: An African American Anthology* (Second Edition). New York, NY: Rowman & Littlefield Publishers, Inc., 2009.

28. Sherwood Anderson

Sherwood Anderson is an American novelist and short story writer, known for his subjective and self-revealing works. He is the first writer since Mark Twain to write in the colloquial style that exerts influence on Hemingway, Faulkner, Steinbeck and other big names of American literature. So Anderson has been called "a writer's writer".

Sherwood Anderson was born in Camden, Ohio on September 13, 1876. He was the third child of the family. The family was always struggling financially because his father's small business was not very successful. They were forced to move frequently after Sherwood was born. They finally settled in Clyde, Ohio, but the family's financial condition was still bad. So Anderson chose to skip school and took on odd jobs to support the family. In 1896, Anderson left for Chicago to join his brother. He worked as a manual laborer until he was enlisted in the army for service in Cuba during the Spanish-American War. After that, he returned to Ohio for a final year of schooling at Wittenberg Academy. In September 1900, Anderson got a job as a chore boy in the Wittenberg Academy, where the highly cultured environment ironically helped him to advance in the business world. The Crowell advertising manager secured him a job in Chicago as a copywriter. He was highly successful in this position. In 1904, he married Cornelia Lane, the daughter of a wealthy Ohio wholesaler. For about 6 years, before 1912, Anderson increasingly spent his free time writing while managing a mail-order business. The breaking point came on November 27, 1912, when Anderson suffered a mental breakdown and ended his business. In 1913, he joined Theodore Dreiser and Carl Sandburg, and the group of writers led the Chicago literary renaissance. In 1914, he divorced Cornelia and married Tennessee Mitchell. In 1916, he published his first novel *Windy McPherson's Son*. In 1919, he received much acclaim for his classic collection of tales, *Winesburg, Ohio*, which established him as a talented modern American writer. He took up themes similar to the later works of T. S. Eliot and other modernists. The other works which he published at the height of his repute included short story collections *The Triumph of the Egg* in 1921, *Horses and Men* in 1923, and a memoir *A Story Teller's Story* in 1924. After another failed marriage, Anderson finally got happiness in his fourth marriage with Eleanor Copenhaver. They traveled a lot and studied social conditions; the works concerning these matters are *Death in the Woods, Other Stories of 1933, Puzzled America* and *Kit Brandon*. He died of peritonitis in March, 1941 and was buried at Round Hill Cemetery in Marion, Virginia.

In Anderson's first two novels *Windy McPherson's Son* and *Marching Men*, the psychological themes of inner lives and the pursuit of success and disillusionment are trailed. He is best known for his classic collection of tales, *Winesburg, Ohio*, which adopts the modern novel approach to convey the thematically related sketches and stories. His short story collections, such as *The Triumph of the Egg* and *Horses and Men* direct the concern of American short story from neatly designed plot to causal development of plot, complexity of motivation, and exhibition of psychological process. His colloquial style of writing, with features of clarity, directness, and simplicity influences so many big names of American Literature.

The Egg

My father was, I am sure, intended by nature to be a cheerful, kindly man. Until he was thirty-four years old he worked as a farmhand for a man named Thomas Butterworth whose place lay near the town of Bidwell, Ohio. He had then a horse of his own and on Saturday evenings drove into town to spend a few hours in social intercourse with other farmhands. In town he drank several glasses of beer and stood about in Ben Head's saloon — crowded on Saturday evenings with visiting farmhands. Songs were sung and glasses thumped on the bar. At ten o'clock father drove home along a lonely country road, made his horse comfortable for the night and himself went to bed, quite happy in his position in life. He had at that time no notion of trying to rise in the world[1].

It was in the spring of his thirty-fifth year that father married my mother, then a country schoolteacher, and in the following spring I came wriggling and crying into the world. Something happened to the two people. They became ambitious. The American passion for getting up in the world took possession of them.

It may have been that mother was responsible. Being a school teacher, she had no doubt read books and magazines. She had, I presume, read of how Garfield[2], Lincoln, and other Americans rose from poverty to fame and greatness and as I lay beside her — in the days of her lying-in[3] — she may have dreamed that I would someday rule men and cities. At any rate she induced father to give up his place as a farmhand, sell his horse and embark on an independent enterprise of his own. She was a tall silent woman with a long nose and troubled grey eyes. For herself she wanted nothing. For father and myself she was incurably ambitious.

The first venture into which the two people went turned out badly. They rented ten acres of poor stony land on Griggs's Road, eight miles from Bidwell, and launched into chicken raising. I grew into boyhood on the place and got my first impressions of life there. From the beginning they were impressions of disaster and if, in my turn, I am a gloomy man inclined to see the darker side of life, I attribute it to the fact that what should have been for me the happy joyous days of childhood were spent on a chicken farm.

One unversed in such matters can have no notion of the many and tragic things that can happen to a chicken. It is born out of an egg, lives for a few weeks as a tiny fluffy thing such as you will see pictured on Easter cards, then becomes hideously naked, eats quantities of corn and meal bought by the sweat of your father's brow, gets diseases called pip, cholera, and other names, stands looking with stupid eyes at the sun, becomes sick and dies. A few hens and now and then a rooster, intended to serve God's mysterious ends, struggle through to maturity. The hens lay eggs out of which come other chickens and the dreadful cycle is thus made complete. It is all unbelievably complex. Most philosophers must have been raised on chicken farms. One hopes for so much from a chicken and is so dreadfully disillusioned. Small chickens, just setting out on the journey of life, look so bright and alert and they are in fact so dreadfully stupid. They are so much like people they mix one up in one's judgments of life. If disease does not kill them they wait until your expectations are thoroughly aroused and then walk under the wheels of a wagon — to go squashed and dead back to their maker. Vermin infest their youth, and fortunes must be spent for curative powders. In later life I have seen how a literature has been built up on the subject of fortunes to be made out of the raising of chickens. It is intended to be read by the gods who have just eaten of the tree of the knowledge of good and evil[4]. It is a hopeful literature and declares that much may be done by simple ambitious people who own a few hens. Do not be led astray by it. It was not written for you. Go hunt for gold on the frozen hills of Alaska, put your faith in the honesty of a politician, believe if you will that the world is daily growing better and that good will triumph over evil, but do not read and believe the literature that is written concerning the hen. It was not written for you.

I, however, digress. My tale does not primarily concern itself with the hen. If correctly told it will center on the egg. For ten years my father and mother struggled to make our chicken farm pay and then they gave up that struggle and began another. They moved into the town of Bidwell, Ohio and embarked in the restaurant business. After ten years of worry with incubators that did not hatch, and with tiny — and in their own way lovely — balls of fluff that passed on into semi-naked pullerhood and from that into dead henhood, we threw all aside and packing our belongings on a wagon drove down Griggs's Road toward Bidwell, a tiny caravan of hope looking for a new place from which to start on our upward journey through life.

We must have been a sad looking lot, not, I fancy, unlike refugees fleeing from a battlefield. Mother and I walked in the road. The wagon that contained our goods had been borrowed for the day from Mr. Albert Griggs, a neighbor. Out of its sides stuck the legs of cheap chairs and at the back of the pile of beds, tables, and boxes filled with kitchen utensils was a crate of live chickens, and on top of that the baby carriage in which I had been wheeled about in my infancy. Why we stuck to the baby carriage I don't know. It was unlikely other children would be born and the wheels were broken. People who have few possessions cling tightly to those they have. That is one of the facts that make life so discouraging.

Father rode on top of the wagon. He was then a bald-headed man of forty-five, a little fat and from long association with mother and the chickens he had become habitually silent and discouraged. All during our ten years on the chicken farm he had worked as a laborer on neighboring farms and most of the money he had earned had been spent for remedies to cure chicken diseases, on Wilmer's White Wonder Cholera Cure or Professor Bidlow's Egg Producer or some other preparations that mother found advertised in the poultry papers. There were two little patches of hair on father's head just above his ears. I remember that as a child I used to sit looking at him when he had gone to sleep in a chair before the stove on Sunday afternoons in the winter. I had at that rime already begun to read books and have notions of my own and the bald path that led over the top of his head was, I fancied, something like a broad road, such a road as Caesar might have made on which to lead his legions out of Rome and into the wonders of an unknown world. The tufts of hair that grew above father's ears were, I thought, like forests. I fell into a half-sleeping, half-waking state and dreamed I was a tiny thing going along the road into a far beautiful place where there were no chicken farms and where life was a happy eggless affair.

One might write a book concerning our flight from the chicken farm into town. Mother and I walked the entire eight miles — she to be sure that nothing fell from the wagon and I to see the wonders of the world. On the seat of the wagon beside father was his greatest treasure. I will tell you of that.

On a chicken farm where hundreds and even thousands of chickens come out of eggs, surprising things sometimes happen. Grotesques are born out of eggs as out of people. The accident does not often occur — perhaps once in a thousand births. A chicken is, you see, born that has four legs, two pairs of wings, two heads or what not. The things do not live. They go quickly back to the hand of their maker[5] that has for a moment trembled. The fact that the poor little things could not live was one of the tragedies of life to father. He had some sort of notion that if he could but bring into henhood or roosterhood[6] a five-legged hen or a two-headed rooster his fortune would be made. He dreamed of taking the wonder about to county fairs and of growing rich by exhibiting it to other farmhands.

At any rate he saved all the little monstrous things that had been born on our chicken farm. They were preserved in alcohol and put each in its own glass bottle. These he had carefully put into a box and on our journey into town it was carried on the wagon seat beside him. He drove the horses with one hand and with the other clung to the box. When we got to our destination the box was taken down at once and the bottles removed. All during our days as keepers of a restaurant in the town of Bidwell, Ohio, the grotesques in their little glass bottles sat on a shelf back of the counter. Mother sometimes protested but father was a rock on the subject of his treasure. The grotesques were, he declared, valuable. People, he said, liked to look at strange and wonderful things.

Did I say that we embarked in the restaurant business in the town of Bidwell, Ohio? I exaggerated a little. The town itself lay at the foot of a low hill and on the shore of a small river. The railroad did not run through the town and the station was a mile away to the north at a place called Pickleville. There had been a cider mill and pickle factory at the station, but before the time of our coming they had both gone out of business⁷. In the morning and in the evening busses came down to the station along a road called Turner's Pike from the hotel on the main street of Bidwell. Our going to the out-of-the-way place to embark in the restaurant business was mother's idea. She talked of it for a year and then one day went off and rented an empty store building opposite the railroad station. It was her idea that the restaurant would be profitable. Travelling men, she said, would be always waiting around to take trains out of town and town people would come to the station to await incoming trains. They would come to the restaurant to buy pieces of pie and drink coffee. Now that I am older I know that she had another motive in going. She was ambitious for me. She wanted me to rise in the world, to get into a town school and become a man of the towns.

At Pickleville father and mother worked hard as they always had done. At first there was the necessity of putting our place into shape to be a restaurant. That took a month. Father built a shelf on which he put tins of vegetables. He painted a sign on which he put his name in large red letters. Below his name was the sharp command — "EAT HERE" — that was so seldom obeyed. A showcase was bought and filled with cigars and tobacco. Mother scrubbed the floor and the walls of the room. I went to school in the town and was glad to be away from the farm and from the presence of the discouraged, sad-looking chickens. Still I was not very joyous. In the evening I walked home from school along Turner's Pike and remembered the children I had seen playing in the town school yard. A troop of little girls had gone hopping about and singing. I tried that. Down along the frozen road I went hopping solemnly on one leg. "Hippity hop to the barber shop," I sang shrilly. Then I stopped and looked doubtfully about. I was afraid of being seen in my gay mood. It must have seemed to me that I was doing a thing that should not be done by one who, like myself, had been raised on a chicken farm where death was a daily visitor.

Mother decided that our restaurant should remain open at night. At ten in the evening a passenger train went north past our door followed by a local freight. The freight crew had switching to do in Pickleville and when the work was done they came to our restaurant for hot coffee and food. Sometimes one of them ordered a fried egg. In the morning at four they returned northbound and again visited us. A little trade began to grow up. Mother slept at night and during the day tended the restaurant and fed our boarders while father slept. He slept in the same bed mother had occupied during the night and I went off to the town of Bidwell and to school. During the long nights, while mother and I slept, father cooked meats that were to go into sandwiches for the lunch baskets of our boarders. Then an idea in regard to getting up in the world came into his head. The American spirit took hold of him. He also became ambitious.

In the long nights when there was little to do father had time to think. That was his undoing. He decided that he had in the past been an unsuccessful man because he had not been cheerful enough and that in the future he would adopt a cheerful outlook on life. In the early morning he came upstairs and got into bed with mother. She woke and the two talked. From my bed in the corner I listened.

It was father's idea that both he and mother should try to entertain the people who came to eat at our restaurant. I cannot now remember his words, but he gave the impression of one about to become in some obscure way a kind of public entertainer. When people, particularly young people from the town of Bidwell, came into our place, as on very rare occasions they did, bright entertaining conversation was to be made. From father's words I gathered that something of the jolly innkeeper effect was to be sought. Mother must have been doubtful from the first, but she said nothing discouraging. It was father's notion that a passion for the company of himself and mother would spring up in the breasts of the younger people of the town of Bidwell. In the evening bright happy groups would come singing down Turner's Pike. They would troop shouting with joy and laughter into our place. There would be song and festivity. I do not mean to give the impression that father spoke so elaborately of the matter. He was as I have said an uncommunicative man. "They want some place to go. I tell you they want some place to go," he said over and over. That was as far as he got. My own imagination has filled in the blanks.

For two or three weeks this notion of father's invaded our house. We did not talk much but in our daily lives tried earnestly to make smiles take the place of glum looks. Mother smiled at the boarders and I, catching the infection, smiled at our cat. Father became a little feverish in his anxiety to please. There was no doubt lurking somewhere in him a touch of the spirit of the showman. He did not waste much of his ammunition on the railroad men he served at night but seemed to be waiting for a young man or woman from Bidwell to come in to show what he could do. On the counter in the restaurant there was a wire basket kept always filled with eggs, and it must have been before his eyes when the idea of being entertaining was born in his brain. There was something pre-natal about the way eggs kept themselves connected with the development of his idea. At any rate an egg ruined his new impulse in life. Late one night I was awakened by a roar of anger coming from father's throat. Both mother and I sat upright in our beds. With trembling hands she lighted a lamp that stood on a table by her head. Downstairs the front door of our restaurant went shut with a bang and in a few minutes father tramped up the stairs. He held an egg in his hand and his hand trembled as though he were having a chill. There was a half insane light in his eyes. As he stood glaring at us I was sure he intended throwing the egg at either mother or me. Then he laid it gently on the table beside the lamp and dropped on his knees beside mother's bed. He began to cry like a boy and I, carried away by his grief, cried with him. The two of us filled the little upstairs room with our wailing voices. It is ridiculous, but of the picture we made I can remember only the fact that mother's hand continually stroked the bald path that ran across the top of his head. I have forgotten what mother said to him and how she induced him to tell her of what had happened downstairs. His explanation also has gone out of my mind. I remember only my own grief and fright and the shiny path over father's head glowing in the lamplight as he knelt by the bed.

As to what happened downstairs. For some unexplainable reason I know the story as well as though I had been a witness to my father's discomfiture. One in time gets to know many unexplainable things. On that evening young Joe Kane, son of a merchant of Bidwell, came to Pickleville to meet his father, who was expected on the ten o'clock evening train from the south. The train was three hours late and Joe came into our place to loaf about and to wait for its arrival. The local freight train came in and the freight crew were fed. Joe was left alone in the restaurant with father.

From the moment he came into our place the Bidwell young man must have been puzzled by my father's actions. It was his notion that father was angry at him for hanging around. He noticed that the restaurant keeper was apparently disturbed by his presence and he thought of going out. However, it began to rain and he did not fancy the long walk to town and back. He bought a five-cent cigar and ordered a cup of coffee. He had a newspaper in his pocket and took it out and began to read. "I'm waiting for the evening train. It's late," he said apologetically.

For a long time father, whom Joe Kane had never seen before, remained silently gazing at his visitor. He was no doubt suffering from an attack of stage fright. As so often happens in life he had thought so much and so often of the situation that now confronted him that he was somewhat nervous in its presence.

For one thing, he did not know what to do with his hands. He thrust one of them nervously over the counter and shook hands with Joe Kane. "How-de-do," he said. Joe Kane put his newspaper down and stared at him. Father's eye lighted on the basket of eggs that sat on the counter and he began to talk. "Well," he began hesitatingly, "well, you have heard of Christopher Columbus[8], eh?" He seemed to be angry. "That Christopher Columbus was a cheat," he declared emphatically. "He talked of making an egg stand on its end. He talked, he did, and then he went and broke the end of the egg."

My father seemed to his visitor to be beside himself at the duplicity of Christopher Columbus. He muttered and swore. He declared it was wrong to teach children that Christopher Columbus was a great man when, after all, he cheated at the critical moment. He had declared he would make an egg stand on end and then when his bluff had been called he had done a trick. Still grumbling at Columbus, father took an egg from the basket on the counter and began to walk up and down. He rolled the egg between the palms of his hands. He smiled genially. He began to mumble words regarding the effect to be produced on an egg by the electricity that comes out of the human body. He declared that without breaking its shell and by virtue of rolling it back and forth in his hands he could stand the egg on its end. He explained that the warmth of his hands and the gentle rolling movement he gave the egg created a new center of gravity, and Joe Kane was mildly interested. "I have handled thousands of eggs," father said. "No one knows more about eggs than I do."

He stood the egg on the counter and it fell on its side. He tried the trick again and again, each time rolling the egg between the palms of his hands and saying the words regarding the wonders of electricity and the laws of gravity. When after a half hour's effort he did succeed in making the egg stand for a moment, he looked up to find that his visitor was no longer watching. By the time he had succeeded in calling Joe Kane's attention to the success of his effort, the egg had again rolled over and lay on its side.

Afire with the showman's passion and at the same time a good deal disconcerted by the failure of his first effort, father now took the bottles containing the poultry monstrosities down from their place on the shelf and began to show them to his visitor. "How would you like to have seven legs and two heads like this fellow?" he asked, exhibiting the most remarkable of his treasures. A cheerful smile played over his face. He reached over the counter and tried to slap Joe Kane on the shoulder as he had seen men do in Ben Head's saloon when he was a young farmhand and drove to town on Saturday evenings. His visitor was made a little ill by the sight of the body of the terribly deformed bird floating in the alcohol in the bottle and got up to go. Coming from behind the counter, father took hold of the young man's arm and led him back to his seat. He grew a little angry and for a moment had to turn his face away and force himself to smile. Then he put the bottles back on the shelf. In an outburst of generosity he fairly compelled Joe Kane to have a fresh cup of coffee and another cigar at his expense. Then he took a pan and filling it with vinegar, taken from a jug that sat beneath the counter, he declared himself about to do a new trick. "I will heat this egg in this pan of vinegar," he said. "Then I will put it through the neck of a bottle without breaking the shell. When the egg is inside the bottle it will resume its normal shape and the shell will become hard again. Then I will give the bottle with the egg in it to you. You can take it about with you wherever you go. People will want to know how you got the egg in the bottle. Don't tell them. Keep them guessing. That is the way to have fun with this trick."

Father grinned and winked at his visitor. Joe Kane decided that the man who confronted him was mildly insane but harmless. He drank the cup of coffee that had been given him and began to read his paper again. When the egg had been heated in vinegar, father carried it on a spoon to the counter and going into a back room got an empty bottle. He was angry because his visitor did not watch him as he began to do his trick, but nevertheless went cheerfully to work. For a long time he struggled, trying to get the egg to go through the neck of the bottle. He put the pan of vinegar back on the stove, intending to reheat the egg, then picked it up and burned his fingers. After a second bath in the hot vinegar, the shell of the egg had been softened a little but not enough for his purpose. He worked and worked and a spirit of desperate determination took possession of him. When he thought that at last the trick was about to be consummated, the delayed train came in at the station and Joe Kane started to go nonchalantly out at the door. Father made a last desperate effort to conquer the egg and make it do the thing that would establish his reputation as one who knew how to entertain guests who came into his restaurant. He worried the egg. He attempted to be somewhat rough with it. He swore and the sweat stood out on his forehead. The egg broke under his hand. When the contents spurted over his clothes, Joe Kane, who had stopped at the door, turned and laughed.

A roar of anger rose from my father's throat. He danced and shouted a string of inarticulate words. Grabbing another egg from the basket on the counter, he threw it, just missing the head of the young man as he dodged through the door and escaped.

Father came upstairs to mother and me with an egg in his hand. I do not know what he intended to do. I imagine he had some idea of destroying it, of destroying all eggs, and that he intended to let mother and me see him begin. When, however, he got into the presence of mother something happened to him. He laid the egg gently on the table and dropped on his knees by the bed as I have already explained. He later decided to close the restaurant for the night and to come upstairs and get into bed. When he did so he blew out the light and after much muttered conversation both he and mother went to sleep. I suppose I went to sleep also, but my sleep was troubled. I awoke at dawn and for a long time looked at the egg that lay on the table. I wondered why eggs had to be and why from the egg came the hen who again laid the egg. The question got into my blood. It has stayed there, I imagine, because I am the son of my father. At any rate, the problem remains unsolved in my mind. And that, I conclude, is but another evidence of the complete and final triumph of the egg — at least as far as my family is concerned.

Notes

1. rise in the world: (of a poor man) gain fame and fortune.

2. Garfield: James A. Garfield, 20th president of the United States. He had the second shortest tenure in U.S. presidential history, because he was assassinated by a frustrated office-seeker.

3. lying-in: the period of time during which a woman in the past stayed in bed before and after giving birth to a child.

4. the tree of the knowledge of good and evil: the most significant subject in the Garden of Eden, from which God directly forbade Adam to eat the fruit, but a serpent later tempted Eve to eat the forbidden fruit from the tree and Adam also ate. Then they attempted to cover themselves with its leaves. After their fall, they were driven out of the Garden and forced to survive on the earth and produce heirs by living on agriculture.

5. maker: refers to God.

6. henhood or roosterhood: the condition or quality of being a hen or a rooster, especially as opposed to a chick.

7. had gone out of business: had stopped or closed the business.

8. Christopher Columbus: navigator and admiral whose four transatlantic voyages opened the way for European exploration of the Americas. He has long been called the "discoverer" of the New World.

Questions for Discussion

(1) In this story, "the egg" can be taken as something with symbolic meaning. What does it symbolize in western culture? What role does the egg play in the narrative of this short story? Explain why.

(2) Can the American dream of this family be realized in the context of the industrialization of the United States at that time? Why or why not?

(3) Analyze the character of "mother" in the story. What role does she play in the pursuit of the American dream for the whole family, and for each family member?

(4) There are several references in the story about the "chicken and egg situation". For example, in the fifth paragraph: "[the] hens lay eggs out of which come other chickens and the dreadful cycle is thus made complete." What is implied in these references in the story?

Suggested Reading

- Sherwood Anderson. *Selected Stories.* New York, NY: Dover Publications,

Inc., 2020.

● 浦立昕：《身份建构与男性气质：舍伍德·安德森小说研究》，南京：南京大学出版社，2015 年。

● 舍伍德·安德森：《安德森短篇小说集》，方智敏译，北京：中国书籍出版社，2017 年。